Beverly
March, 1988
Laurel, Md

SEAVER

A Biography by Gene Schoor

CONTEMPORARY
BOOKS, INC.
CHICAGO ■ NEW YORK

Library of Congress Cataloging-in-Publication Data

Schoor, Gene.
    Seaver: a biography.

    1. Seaver, Tom, 1944–   2. Baseball players—
United States—Biography.   I. Title.
GV865.S4S35   1986   796.357′092′4 [B]   86-4605
ISBN 0-8092-5027-6

Photos courtesy of the New York Mets and the Chicago White Sox.

Published by Contemporary Books, Inc.
180 North Michigan Avenue, Chicago, Illinois 60601
Manufactured in the United States of America
Library of Congress Catalog Card Number: 86-4605
International Standard Book Number: 0-8092-5027-6

Published simultaneously in Canada by Beaverbooks, Ltd.
195 Allstate Parkway, Valleywood Business Park
Markham, Ontario L3R 4T8 Canada

For Terry Shore,
the most dedicated Seaver fan
in the nation

CONTENTS

ACKNOWLEDGMENTS

In addition to the numerous baseball people, sports broadcasters, and public relations people at Fresno State College, U.S.C., I have drawn on the works of numerous sportswriters who have written about Tom Seaver during the past three decades of his baseball life:

My sincere thanks to the following: Ed Linn; Dick Schaap; *Sport* magazine; Red Smith, Dave Anderson, George Vecsey, Ira Berkow, and Arthur Daly of *The New York Times*; the late Milt Gross, Jerry Mitchell, Maury Allen, Al Buck, Dick Young, and Jim Cannon of the *New York Post*; Jack Lang; Dave van Dyke, Joe Goddard, and Mike Kiley of the *Chicago Sun-Times*; Sara Davidson of *McCall's*; Robert Markus, Steve Daley, John Husar, Jerome Holtzman, and Skip Myslenski of the *Chicago Tribune*; John Devaney for his book, *Tom Seaver*; Joe Durso; The Amazing Mets; Jim Jensen, WCBS-TV, N.Y.; Pat Fettinger, Hudson Guild; Mets' public relations director Jay Horwitz; and Sox public relations director Paul Jensen.

Special thanks to Eddie Einhorn, president of the Chicago White Sox, Roland Hemond, Carlton Fisk, Jerry Koosman, Ed Kranepool, Ralph Kiner, Rusty Staub, and Bud Harrelson.

And a very special salute to my great editor at Contemporary Books, Shari Lesser.

I
NUMBER 300

He had labored nearly two decades to reach this elusive, magical moment. Yet in his mind's eye, this dream goal had always been just an arm's length away—a goal every young pitcher sets for himself the first time he steps onto a major-league mound.

Now, on a lovely, warm, sunny afternoon—August 4, 1985—Tom Seaver, number 41 of the Chicago White Sox, was on the threshold of baseball immortality, facing the New York Yankees at Yankee Stadium. Just three more outs and he would possess those cherished 300 victories to add to a remarkable career, and his name would be placed among a select group of the most fabled Hall of Fame pitchers in baseball. A group that includes Cy Young, Walter Johnson, Christy Mathewson, Grover Cleveland Alexander, Kid Nichols, Hoss Radbourne, Lefty Grove, Warren Spahn, and ten other hurlers who achieved that almost impossible goal.

Seaver stepped back off the mound, took off his cap, wiped the perspiration from his face, hitched up his pants, and turned to check on the positioning of his teammates in the field. Harold Baines, Luis Salazar, and Rudy Law were set in the outfield. Big Greg Walker at first base, Scott Fletcher covering second, Ozzie Guillen the acrobatic shortstop, Tim Hulett at third base, and Carlton "Pudge" Fisk, his All-Star catcher, were all ready and waiting.

Now Tom could hear, for the first time, the roar of the 54,000 fans who had jammed every inch of this historic ballpark. They were standing and screaming: "Sea-ver, Sea-ver, Sea-ver." The continuous roar pounded in his ears—"Sea-ver, Sea-ver, Sea-ver."

Suddenly, for a fleeting moment, his thoughts turned to the events of this day, and he chuckled to himself as he remembered how he and Nancy had flopped out of their bed at 5:30 A.M. to chase a bat; not a Louisville Slugger but a huge flying mammal that somehow had found its way into their bedroom. He almost laughed aloud as he recalled the startling beginning of a day he would never forget. "What a helluva thing to think about now, chasing a bat with a broomstick at 5:30."

That morning, looking well-rested despite his bout with the bat, Tom Seaver was in the White Sox clubhouse at Yankee Stadium, answering questions from omnipresent reporters. He accepted congratulations from White Sox owners Jerry Reinsdorf and Eddie Einhorn, then autographed a couple dozen balls before going over the Yankee batters with Fisk.

At 2:09, with fans cheering his every move, Tom came out of the dugout, walked across the field, and

2

headed for the bullpen to warm up. And although he wore the White Sox uniform, the fans were cheering for a man who for 11½ years had been one of the most popular baseball heroes that New York had ever known.

As a pitcher for the New York Mets, the strong right-hander was instrumental in leading an inept franchise to two pennants and a World Series victory, and, on the way, he won three Cy Young awards. Now at age 40, in his 19th season and second with the Chicago White Sox, he was the ace of the pitching staff.

The White Sox picked up Seaver in 1984 after the Mets had failed to include the veteran's name on a list of protected players. During the year, which Reinsdorf described as "one of the biggest flops in baseball history," Seaver was the winningest pitcher on the team with a 15–11 record.

But on this day and in this place he was on the verge of pitching immortality.

Tom threw his first pitch to New York's Rickey Henderson at 3:11 P.M., after a ceremony honoring Yankee broadcaster Phil Rizzuto who was celebrating his 25th year on the air for the tradition-rich Bronx Bombers.

And for the next three hours, this was a ball game like so many others Seaver had pitched throughout his splendid career. He was the experienced fighter throwing his best pitches inning after inning, picking his spots, and constantly outsmarting the hitters before giving up a run in the third inning, then patiently waiting for his team to get him some runs.

Over the years, there had been a lot of scuffling, a lot of waiting, a lot of days when Seaver was on the wrong end of a 2–1 score.

3

But this day, the day of the 300, would be different.

The huge Stadium crowd had been on its feet, cheering every pitch, since the sixth inning, when the Sox rallied for four runs to claim a 4–1 lead.

With Yankee pitcher Joe Cowley on the mound, Carlton Fisk opened the inning by walking on four straight pitches. Oscar Gamble rifled a single to center field with Fisk scampering to third base.

Yankee manager Billy Martin walked to the mound, took the ball from Cowley's hand, and brought in Brian Fisher in relief. But the relief was Chicago's as Tim Hulett promptly sent a fastball screaming to left center field and Fisk came across with the tying run.

In the White Sox dugout, shortstop Ozzie Guillen kidded with Seaver: "I'm gonna get the game-winning RBI for you, Tom." Then Ozzie walked up to the plate and promptly singled, scoring Gamble. The White Sox were out in front by a 2–1 score until Rudy Law walked, and then Bryan Little scorched a single to center field, sending Hulett and Law home to give the Sox two more runs and a 4–1 lead.

Now it was strictly up to Tom Seaver.

He breezed through the sixth and seventh innings, pitching brilliantly. He had retired 12 of the last 13 batters he faced and had the heavy-hitting Yankees at his mercy, allowing them but three base hits on his way to the magic Number 300.

In the eighth inning, breathing hard and laboring with each pitch, Seaver walked the first Yankee hitter, Ken Griffey. Don Mattingly singled, sending Griffey to third. Dave Winfield was the next batter, and now the White Sox pitching coach Dave Duncan walked out to the mound to talk with Seaver.

They conferred for a moment, and Duncan trotted back to the White Sox dugout. "He's tired, but he says he can get 'em out," Duncan shared with manager Tony LaRussa. "I'm not taking him out."

On the mound, Seaver stared across at big Dave Winfield, got the signal for the pitch from Fisk, toed the rubber, brought his arm back, and kicked his left leg high in the air, as if he was putting every bit of speed into the pitch. Instead, Tom threw Winfield a tantalizing, half-speed pitch and Winfield, eager to slug the ball, missed it by a foot. Another pitch to Dave and another strike.

Now it was 3–2 on Winfield.

In his youth Seaver would have reached back for a 95 mph fastball. But a 40-year-old pitcher knows better.

"You just know that Winfield is going to be aggressive and you try to take advantage of that aggressiveness and feed it if you can," said Tom.

That's what Seaver calls the grey area of pitching, the difference between pitching and throwing.

"I've never considered myself a thrower," said Tom. "Even as a young kid starting out I tried to pitch with my head."

Once more he faced Winfield and once more he came in with the big body motion and a change-up, knee high to the hitter.

"I used Fisk's feet as my target," said Tom.

Winfield coiled his big bat as the pitch floated in. Expecting a fastball, Dave took a terrific swing and missed the ball for the third strike to end the inning.

As Seaver trudged wearily off the mound, Winfield looked at him, grinned and said softly, "You son of a gun. Fooled me again."

Tom was too weary to reply. He just grinned back.

Between innings, Seaver looked over at his family and said to his restless younger daughter, Anne, "Only three more outs." "Then can we all go swimming?" she asked, to her father's delight.

As Tom walked out to start the ninth inning the crowd rose and applauded. Now each pitch carried with it the kind of tension and emotion normally reserved for a World Series.

Don Pasqua, the Yankees hard-hitting rookie outfielder, smashed Seaver's first pitch off the left-field wall. Only stupendous fielding by Harold Baines held Pasqua to a single.

Willie Randolph sent Tom's next pitch deep to right field. The ball was hit so hard it sounded like something shot out of an air rifle. Once more Baines, running like an antelope, leaped high into the air to make a breathtaking catch up against the wall.

One out later, Yankee Stadium sounded like old Shea Stadium when the planes were taking off and banking over the field. The crowd roar was deafening. Everybody was up screaming.

So was manager Tony LaRussa, who was ejected in the sixth inning after disputing a close play at the plate in which outfielder Rudy Law was called out.

"The rules plainly state that I've got to be in the clubhouse," said Tony, "but I wasn't going to miss this game. I watched Tom's every move from the runway. This is my pitcher Seaver, going for No. 300 for history. I had to be there."

Seaver, now in a hurry to end things, walked the Yankees light-hitting Mike Pagliarulo on four straight pitches.

Acting manager Dave Duncan came out to the mound along with Fisk.

They had made a similar visit in the eighth inning.

Both trips were characterized by Seaver as, "a kick-the-pitcher-in-the-rear" pep talk. Looking at Fisk and Duncan, Seaver said, "Nobody is taking me out of this game."

Later in the clubhouse Tom said, "If you can't get up for the one out that's going to get you that 300, then you ain't never gonna get up."

Seaver once more brought that strong right arm—baseball treasure for all times now—forward with the "top to bottom" motion that has been his glorious trademark. One last time he tried "to keep the ball active in the hitting zone." He did, and Don Baylor lofted a high drive to left field.

Halfway between the pitching mound and the first-base line, Seaver watched, hands on knees. Reid Nichols in left field easily gloved the ball. Shortstop Ozzie Guillen did a Mary Lou Retton somersault in short center and it was all over.

And Tom Seaver bent over at the waist, waiting, watching, jumping into the air. Carlton Fisk ran to the mound to grab Tom and lift him high; they were hugging and laughing, enjoying the cheers of the crowd.

Then Seaver was kissing his wife, Nancy, and his daughters, all of them crying and laughing at the same time.

He embraced his seventy-four-year-old father, Charles Seaver.

"I couldn't have Dad flying all over the country at his age waiting for me to get Number 300."

In the clubhouse bedlam reigned.

His teammates doused him with champagne and he was congratulated by White Sox owners Reinsdorf and Einhorn and besieged by reporters and television cameras.

The Yankees presented Seaver with a silver bowl to honor him on this historic day.

With the final out, Seaver became the 17th pitcher to reach the 300-win plateau, the 13th right-hander, and the fourth oldest, having pitched in both the National and American leagues. He is the only 300-game winner to have written three books on pitching mechanics and the only moundsman able to cite Bernouilli's law to explain why a fastball rises.

Tom Seaver should have a free ride one day soon into Baseball's Hall of Fame. But he says that the 300 victories is not what he wants to be remembered for; consistency is his choice, the fact that he has 112 more career victories than defeats, (304–192). The fact that "every time they put the ball in my hand I went to the mound."

He will wait until the off-season to reflect more on the incredible accomplishment.

"Perhaps, sometime in April or May, when I'm out dining with Nancy, I'll be able to really savor and appreciate it," he said. "Then I'll really pour my heart out.

"It was really a day I'll remember for the rest of my life."

2
EARLY DAYS
AND EARLY GOALS

George Thomas Seaver was born in Fresno, California, on the seventeenth of November, 1944, the youngest of four children in a fairly well-to-do and comfortable family. Charley Seaver, the paterfamilias, was a young up-and-coming executive with the Bonner Packing Company, a growing firm that packed the rich fruits of the country and sent them off to all points north, south, and west.

He was also a great amateur athlete and an outstanding competitor. At age fifteen he was a two-handicap golfer at Stanford University, where he won letters in football and basketball. He also won the University Golf Championship, beating Lawson Little, who was to become one of the country's greatest professional golfers.

Charley Seaver was good enough to play championship golf for the American team in its clash with the British for the coveted amateur Walker Cup. He

9

also came within a hole of making the final round in the U.S. amateur championship in 1930 and a chance to play the great Bobby Jones in his last match as an amateur.

Charley, along with Pro Mike Fetchik, won the Bing Crosby Pro-Am in 1964. "He and Fetchik play together every year at the Crosby," said a local sportswriter. "Charley is a great competitor, one of the few amateurs who can handle Pebble Beach."

Charley never gave up his amateur standing, but golf was his game, and six times from 1945 to 1954 he won the Fresno City Golf Tournament. He also married a good golfer, the young woman who would beat him for nickels and dimes at the Sunnyside Country Club in Fresno.

No one questioned the importance of sports in the Seaver household. Aunt Katie had no trouble lugging a 75-pound surfboard around the beaches of Hawaii, while Katie, Tom's oldest sister, was a fine swimmer and volleyball player at Stanford, and was known all over campus as the girl who flattened a guy with one punch after he had gotten fresh with her at a nearby pub. Brother Charles Jr. was a skilled swimmer and a fine sculptor; he later became a social worker in Brooklyn and brought a batch of underprivileged youngsters to every home game that Tom pitched.

One day Charles walked into a poor tenement to visit a welfare client and immediately spotted a picture of his famous brother on a bureau in one of the rooms.

"That's my brother, Tom," Charles said, surprised.

"Wow! Your brother. Hey! He's some pitcher," the man said. "Last year at Jacksonville he won 12 games and was talked about as the best young pitcher the Mets had ever signed."

10

Charley listened, amazed. This fellow knew more about his brother than he did.

Sister Carol was a physical education major at U.C.L.A. and spent two years in Nigeria with her husband, a Peace Corps official. Thus it was no great surprise when Tom, the youngest member of the family, turned out to be a great athlete. Little George Thomas, six years younger than Charley Jr., had a tough job competing with his big brother and sisters, but competition was practically a way of life for the Seavers. Young Tom, like the runt in every family, was forced to be the most competitive of all.

Betty Seaver helped. Her favorite book for the children, and little Tom's favorite story too, was *The Little Engine That Could.* It's the story so many of us have heard from our parents, or read to our own children—all about the little engine that struggled to climb the mountain, saying to itself, "I think I can. I think I can. I *know* I can," until it made it.

Betty believed that if you tried hard enough, and persevered long enough, you could achieve any goal. And Tom never had any trouble understanding the story, or its deeper meaning. "I think I can. I *know* I can." Even as a toddler, Tom Seaver set himself a goal; he knew that he would achieve that goal and, as the baseball world knows, he succeeded.

If drive and optimism were the characteristics Betty Seaver contributed to the shaping and building of Tom Seaver, both as boy and man, his father bequeathed to Tom something more: the insistence on perfection.

At work or at home, nothing less than flawlessness would satisfy Charley Seaver. He tended the cherry trees, the orange trees, and the fig trees in his own backyard. The soil had to be perfect, the tree food perfect, and the pruning perfect, and only the perfect fruit was brought into the house. If he painted the cupboards in his kitchen, there were to be no smudges, no streaks, and the painting had to be even and uniform. On the golf course his swing had to be perfect, his grip on the clubs perfect, and there had to be the perfect club for the perfect shot.

Charley Seaver demanded perfection of himself. He also demanded it from his children. And we're all witnesses over these so many years of how that drive for perfection became an integral part of his most famous son, Tom Seaver.

Tom didn't do so well on the golf course. He could hit well enough with a baseball bat, but he could do nothing with a golf club and was unable to compete with family members. He kept shanking the ball, which never traveled more than 50 feet.

One day, following a particularly pathetic shot, he threw his club at the ball in disgust.

"If you're going to throw your clubs around," said his mother, highly annoyed with Tom's temper tantrum, "you'll not be playing golf with me anymore."

"I'm not playing golf anymore with anyone," snapped back the angry youngster. "I'm not playing golf with anybody!"

And he didn't. At least not until age 18.

Baseball was his game, and he was still too little to look over the hedges in his backyard when he recognized the fact and began to pursue his own personal perfection in the sport.

When he was only five years old, he would play a wholly imaginary game of baseball with imaginary players, bases, and umpires in his backyard, among the cherry, orange, and fig trees.

"You, George, play here," he would say, pointing to

a George who wasn't there, his mother later reported. She would sometimes watch him at play, from a window.

"You play here, Charley," he said, pointing to another invisible youngster.

"He would run toward a tree, turn, and slide into one of the imaginary bases he had designated, just like he saw the big leaguers do on TV," his mother said.

"Someone, somewhere must have shouted, 'Out,'" she continued, "and Tom would jump up screaming, 'I'm safe! I'm safe!'

"It was all in his head, of course. But he certainly had a great time of it."

It was in the spring of 1953, when Tom was eight and a half, that he tried to join a Little League club, the North Rotary team of the Fresno Spartan League.

A lot of kids in Fresno wanted to play Little League ball, and there was quite a turnout for the scheduled tryouts. Hal Bicknell, a high school teacher and the manager of the North Rotary team, looked over the huge crowd that had assembled on the sandlot where the tryouts were to be judged and knew there were far too many kids for the club. He wasn't too happy about the situation, and knew he would have to do some quick eliminating before he could begin to give the youngsters a fair shake at bat and in the field.

It was easy enough to eliminate young Tom Seaver. He was slight and small. He just about reached the shoulders of the other kids on the sandlot.

"How old are you?" he asked Tom.

"I'm eight and a half," said the youngster.

"Sorry," said the manager-coach Hal Bicknell. "You've got to be at least nine before you can play on this club."

Tom could all but keep the tears from his eyes, and Bicknell felt bad about it. He had to keep a manageable number on the field.

"Sorry, kid," he said. "That's a league rule, and we have to keep the league rules, you know. But try again next year."

Tom said nothing. He just turned and slowly walked off the sandlot. He walked home slowly, too. But once he got into the house, he rushed into his room and let the tears flow.

His mother walked into the room, sat down beside him. She didn't have to ask any questions; she knew what had happened.

She tried to comfort him, but nothing would ease the pain young Tom Seaver felt that afternoon. He cried and cried and cried. The disappointment was too much for the youngster to take.

But one bad experience wasn't going to deter Tom from the pursuit of his goal.

Next year, in the spring of 1954, Tom was back on that sandlot, again trying out for the North Rotary ball club of the Fresno Spartan League. And this time there was no rebuff and no tears. He made the team. He was going to pitch for the Little League nine.

Hal Bicknell would talk about young Tom many years later. "He had this tremendous desire to succeed. He had this tremendous need to win.

"There was one time when some grown-up tried to rattle the kid. He was rooting for the opposing team and he kept shouting insults at the young pitcher, trying to unnerve him.

"Tom's face got red as a beet. He could hear the

man all right and the man should have known better but he kept shouting insult after insult at the kid.

"Tom looked down at the ground. He did his best to keep those tears back, but he was only a young-ster and the tears kept rolling down his cheek. But give up? Never!

"He kept right on pitching. He kept firing that ball to his catcher as if nothing at all were happening. He didn't complain. He didn't quit. He just kept pouring that ball across the plate.

"I never saw anything like it!"

That was Tom Seaver at nine and a half, with a gallant display of concentration and that indomita-ble will that was to set him apart from the rest of his Little League teammates.

The will to win, the will to achieve perfection—these were the drives that came early to Tom Seaver, and were to stay with him throughout his career.

Perfection in pitching is that no-hit, no-run game that very few pitchers ever achieve on the diamond in an entire career. But it came early for Tom Seaver—very early. It was to be a long time coming in professional ball, but it came soon in his career as a Little Leaguer.

His mother was in attendance that day, sitting near the bench, and she watched admiringly as Tom mowed down batter after batter. Inning after in-ning, it was three up and three down. Perhaps inspired by his gutsy performance, Tom's team-mates played flawlessly behind him, and no one on the opposing team had gotten as far as first base.

It was the last inning. Just three more outs to go and Tom would have his perfect game.

The first batter of the opposing club stepped to

the plate and Tom took care of him with a curveball for strike three. The second batter walked, but was out on a routine ground ball from second to first. One out to go. How often does that third out come hard? How often does that coveted third out never materialize? How often does that last man up in the last inning hit the one blast beyond the reach of the outfield, that one slice through the tense infield, that one lucky blooper to kill the no-hitter, to ruin perfection?

Tom took his windup, threw another curveball, and the batter connected. But it was not hit solidly, and the ball went up, high into the air.

Tom ran off the mound toward the bench. He couldn't bear to look. But his mother looked, her heart momentarily in her mouth, as she watched the shortstop circle around and around under the tall pop fly.

And then the shortstop had the ball in his glove.

"He caught it!" shrieked the mother of the young hero. "He caught it!"

And Tom stopped his journey back to the bench, looked at the shortstop, then at his mother. The tears were streaming from his eyes.

He had pitched a no-hit, no-run game. A perfect game. Such games are never forgotten. It is a lifetime ambition of every player who has ever pitched a baseball to achieve that perfection.

Tom Seaver got it early, in Little League ball. It would be a long, long time before he would pitch that perfect game, that no-hit, no-run game, in his long professional career.

3
WELL-LAID PLANS DON'T ALWAYS WORK

Tom Seaver, at the age of 12, was one of the best Little League players Fresno had ever produced. He was the leading hitter in the league, batting at a .540 clip, and he was the Fresno North Rotary Club's ace pitcher. When he wasn't pitching, he hit the ball too hard and was not often left out of the lineup. Since he was a power hitter, the leading home run hitter in the league, he was used in the outfield when not on the mound. But by the time he was 13 he had become a has-been in Little League.

No, Tom didn't lose his fastball overnight, nor did he suddenly lose his eye at the plate. It was just that young Seaver didn't grow as fast as the boys who played with him, didn't put on the weight or add the muscle. While Tom stayed stagnant, his peers suddenly put on several inches in height, their shoulders and backs broadening. Not Tom. Three years later, when he got to high school, he didn't weigh more than 130 pounds and wasn't more than five feet four inches tall.

Of course he didn't feel good, losing all that hero status in the Little Leagues. No matter how hard he tried to throw, the bigger guys would hammer the ball. He couldn't have realized it at the time, but this revolting development would benefit Tom in the long run. To compensate, he spent all of his practice time pitching to spots. He would mark off a target on a wall in back of his house and spend hours trying to hit the target. His father helped out, offering tips and suggestions, and often would pitch to Tom so he could practice his batting, too. The Little Engine could, Tom would never forget, and so could he.

In high school Tom went out for the Fresno High varsity baseball team his sophomore year. He was five foot six and weighed all of 140 pounds. There was another youngster, a good friend of Tom's, who went out for the team that year named Dick Selma. Dick Selma had suddenly grown a head taller than Tom, and with his "live" fastball easily made the team. Young Tom Seaver just barely made the junior varsity, and he was far from first-string. There were a couple of pitchers on that JV squad who were bigger and stronger than Tom and threw the ball a lot faster.

To make up for his lack of strength and speed, Tom carefully scrutinized the good pitchers, studying and probing every move they made on the mound. He analyzed the pitching stance, the wind-up, the release of the ball, and the follow-through, and thought deeply about pitching strategy, applying everything he learned to the perfection of his own performance. Then he practiced, and practiced, and practiced some more.

He didn't possess the physical prowess the other pitchers on the junior varsity squad had; he knew that well enough. He also knew that he would have to compensate for that lack of strength if he was going to pitch at all. So he learned to throw a slow, tantalizing curve, and had those heavy batters lunging for the ball, popping it up or just blasting at the air. He began to experiment with the change-up pitch, a half-speed pitch, and, with the excellent control he was now exhibiting, could easily strike out many of the bigger players because he mixed his pitches well and could throw strikes. He could throw a knuckleball, too, as a sophomore in high school, and he knew how and when to use it for maximum effect.

"As a teenager," said Tom, "I had the widest assortment of pitches imaginable. And I needed all the off-speed pitches I could find, because I just wasn't big enough to throw hard. When I was 13 I started throwing a slider, a pitch that dipped sharply down and away from a right-handed hitter. At 14 I started throwing an exaggerated change-up, and by the time I was 15 I was throwing every kind of curve, sidearm, overhand, and three-quarters overhand. I was very lucky that all those freaky pitches I threw before I really was physically mature didn't strain or hurt my arm. I guess I was lucky."

"Tom was a hell of a pitcher," Dick Selma would say many years later. "He wasn't just a thrower. Even as a kid pitcher in high school, Tom was a thinking pitcher. He knew how to set up a hitter by working the corners of the plate, and the batter would usually pop the ball into the air or into the ground for an easy out.

"And that was when he was playing ball in high

school," continued Selma, who also made it to the major leagues. "And I'm still trying to learn how he does it."

Tom did finally make the varsity squad at Fresno High, in his senior year. He had grown to five feet ten inches and weighed in at 165 pounds, but was still shorter and lighter than most of the other fellows on the squad, and his fastball was nowhere near what it was to become. He posted a respectable 6–5 record, but that wasn't the type of mark that would attract the big league scouts who regularly observed the Fresno High School players. Jim Maloney had been one of their finds. So had Dick Ellsworth. Dick Selma, too, was to be picked up out of Fresno. In 1963 the New York Mets signed Selma to a contract, and gave him a $20,000 bonus for his signature.

Not Tom. Not yet. But his time was to come, and fairly soon.

At that moment, in his senior year, there were other things, people, and activities that took up Tom Seaver's time and energy.

For one thing, there was the basketball team. His father had been a good basketball player, and had won his letter at Stanford. Tom was going to follow in his father's footsteps. At least when he was in high school that was what he had in mind to do.

Tom wasn't the best outside shot on the team, although he had a fine hook shot off the pivot. His forte was the floor game. He was a marvelous passer and was a master at finding the open man for the sure two-point basket. No, Tom was not the greatest outside shooter on the court, but his team play and passing were enough to make him an All-City selection.

Even on the basketball court, however, Tom never lost sight of his baseball ambitions. Running up and down on that court was strengthening his legs. The stronger his legs, Tom knew, the stronger and faster would be the ball he pitched across the plate.

There were his other studies, too, besides his study of the game. At home, both his mother and father stressed the importance of a good education. His two sisters and brother would be sent through college. He aimed for college too.

Tom was a good student. He had even begun to think of the college he would go to and the profession he would follow, if his dreams of baseball glory became just that: dreams and no more. He thought seriously of going to dental school like old Casey Stengel.

And then, of course, there were the girls.

Tom wasn't the tallest or the biggest fellow in the school, and certainly wasn't the campus football hero, but he had the face and the style that attracted the prettiest girls. He wasn't tall, dark, and handsome, but he had that pleasant, even handsome, round face and that ready smile, and he was never short with that ready phrase, that ready word, that easy manner that the girls liked. The teachers liked it, too, and the fellows as well. No one had more friends in Fresno High than Tom Seaver, and no one resented the fact that it was always the prettiest girls in the school that Tom Seaver dated.

Yes, it may be difficult to believe, but today there are a good number of people who don't like Tom Seaver, and some who even hate him. "He's too absorbed in his own image," one player said. "He's just a snob," said another. But Tom didn't feel any of that, not in his high school days. What he did feel, however, was a keen sense of disappointment. More than anything else, during those school days, he had dreamed and hoped that he would be drafted by a major league team, like Wade Blasingame, Dick Ellsworth, Dick Selma, and Jim Maloney had been before him. But it wasn't in the cards, not just then anyway.

He would drive up to a ball game in San Francisco to watch the Giants play, or drive down to Los Angeles with his Dad to see the Dodgers in action every now and then, and often he would envision himself on the mound, striking out every big hitter that came to the plate. He was especially taken with Sandy Koufax, the great Dodger pitcher. Tom admired the command of the man on the hill, the way he strode to the mound, the way he handled the ball, his cool delivery, and his completely professional manner.

But oddly enough, it wasn't Koufax who was Tom Seaver's idol, not when he was a youngster. It was the great home run hitter Hank Aaron of the Milwaukee Braves who was the center of Tom's attention.

Most of the Fresno kids were Yankee or Dodger fans. Maybe it was because the Yankees and Dodgers were always winners, and maybe that's why Tom didn't root for them. The rest of the kids at school rooted for the Dodgers or the Giants, and that was quite natural, since Fresno was just about halfway between Los Angeles and San Francisco. But Tom, because of his affection for Hank Aaron, latched onto the Braves.

"How come," he would be asked often enough, "you're a pitcher, you've always been a pitcher, and your big hero is a slugger?"

Tom Seaver scratched his head on that one, but he had an answer.

"I guess it was his form that got me," he said. "He's so graceful, at bat and in the field. For me, he's always been the complete professional."

It was that training he had received at home from his father, the urge and the need to be perfect in everything he did that led Tom to admire those qualities in "Hammerin' Hank." It would never leave him.

He had been miserably disillusioned when, at eight and a half, he was turned down by the Little League coach. He was just as downtrodden when he wasn't picked up by a major-league team following his senior year in high school. But his disappointment was better controlled this time, and he wasn't giving up on his hopes, on his dream.

Tom had the plans for his career all set. He would try to get a scholarship to a junior college. That was step one. At junior college, his pitching for the baseball team would be good enough to attract the attention of some major college scout. That was step two. Step three was the was the day some big league scout would watch him masterfully mow down the opposition in a college ball game. Step four, and he was as sure this was going to happen as he was of his name, a major-league team somewhere between New York and San Francisco would offer him a contract.

It didn't happen quite that way. A couple of things, and rather good things at that, happened on the way to that junior college.

The United States was involved in the war in Vietnam, and young men of Tom's age were being drafted. A hitch in the service meant three years out of the mainstream Tom had decided on for himself.

23

He talked the situation over with Russ Scheidt, a friend who lived across the street from the Seavers and who had played ball with him since they were just five years old. Neither of the young fellows was certain about the course of action he ought to follow, but Russ thought it might be a good idea to enlist in the Marine Reserves. There would be a six-month wait before they donned the Marine Reserves uniform, and the hitch in that service was for only six months.

"That ought to give us enough time to make the big decision," said Tom, and Russ agreed with him.

Together, they traveled down to the Marine Reserves enlistment center, and joined up.

"Now what?" asked Tom. "What do we do with the six months before we get into uniform?"

His father had the answer for that; at least, he had the answer as far as Tom was concerned. Charley Seaver was now vice president of the Bonner Packing Company. He suggested that Tom come to work for Bonner.

Actually, Charley Seaver had wanted Tom to get a degree in business administration at the Fresno City College, then join the company. Tom, of course, had other plans.

Nevertheless, Tom took the job his father offered. There was nothing better to do. Besides, it was one way of building up the cash reserve he figured he would need once he enrolled in the local college.

However, if Tom had figured on a snap job in the Bonner Packing Company office, he was in for a rude surprise. It was as tough a job in the plant as Charley Seaver could find.

For his first day on the Bonner job, Tom was hustled up and awake before the sun came up. It was still pitch-dark when he arrived at the plant.

"See those sweat boxes there?" asked the foreman on the job.

He pointed to a pile of boxes six feet high and about four feet square.

"Get them up on this platform," said the foreman. "They need to be washed."

It was easier said than done.

The boxes were heavy, very heavy; almost too much for one man to lift. Tom hauled one to the platform and began to sweat. He hauled another and the sweat began to pour down his face. The foreman knew what he was saying when he referred to those boxes as sweat boxes.

Tom picked up a fifth box and suddenly there was a pair of eyes looking straight at him.

"Hey!" he yelled, almost dropping the box. "There's a snake in this box!"

"Sure," said the other men working the platform, and they got a kick out of the kid just standing there, petrified. "That's nothing," they said. "Wait till you see the rats jumping out of them!"

Tom didn't want to wait, but he didn't want to quit, either. He stuck it out, but hated every minute of the time he spent in the Bonner plant and began to count the days before he could get into the Marines.

He played American Legion baseball at night, during that stint with Bonner, and managed to get to Dodger Stadium every now and then, particularly when Koufax was scheduled to pitch.

"The man has style," said Tom of the great southpaw. "He has the smoothest, most fluid delivery of any pitcher I've ever seen, and the best curveball I've ever seen."

The mechanics of the great pitcher intrigued Tom Seaver. He watched every move that Koufax made

on the mound, analyzed the mechanics, and remembered them; and in due time he would put to
good use the lessons he learned while watching
Sandy Koufax perform.

The Marines proved to be another unexpected
ordeal. Tom's first three months in the service were
spent in Marine boot camp, training at the Marine
Corps Recruit Depot in San Diego, and Tom didn't
take to the drills and the discipline too well. And he
hated the often vicious punishment he would receive for what seemed to him petty infractions. He
had to laugh at the absurdity when a drill instructor
standing on top of his mess table repeatedly kicked
Tom in the side after he dared to talk to his friend
Russ Scheidt during dinner, but the punishment he
took when another drill inspector discovered some
specks of dirt in his rifle was almost too much.

For three and a half hours a relay of instructors
kept barking orders at him as, following commands,
he pushed his rifle straight out from his chest, then
lifted it high over his head repeatedly, without even
a split second to rest his arms. His arms and chest
ached, and the rifle felt like it weighed a ton. He
didn't complain; there was no one to complain to.
But again he began to count the days of torture he
would still have to endure before he could take off
his military uniform for good.

The boot session finally over, Tom spent the next
three months in Pendleton and then at the Marine
base in the Mojave Desert. The Marines and the
fruit packing job were just about the worst 12
months in Tom Seaver's life. But as with most things
evil, some good came out of all the mental and
physical pain he suffered.

Tom was five foot ten and weighed 165 pounds
when he was graduated from Fresno High. After six

months at the Bonner Packing Company, lifting all those bulky sweat boxes, and after the six more months of rigorous training with the Marines, Tom weighed 195 pounds and, toe to crown, measured a good six foot one. Back home in Fresno he was walking down a street one day when he passed someone who had been a friend of the Seaver family since Tom was in grade school. The man looked at Tom and walked right on by him.

"Hey," Tom said. "Don't you remember me?"

The man turned and looked at him carefully.

"My God," he said. "Is that you, is that little Tom Seaver?"

Now back home—stronger, more powerful, and perhaps more confident—Tom was ready to go to work on that plan he had figured out for himself, the plan that would land him just exactly where he intended to be, as a major-league pitcher.

4
FRESNO CITY TO ALASKA

Out of the Marines, Tom Seaver enrolled at Fresno City College in the fall of 1963, and the first thing he did after enrolling at the college was to try out for the Fresno City College baseball squad. Tom had no great hopes about being drafted by the big leagues out of the City College baseball team, though he knew that Dick Selma and Jim Maloney, both pitchers, had been signed by major-league scouts out of Fresno. He didn't think he was that good, not yet, anyway. But he did feel that he could pitch well enough to be noticed by one of the big college or university coaches and be offered a baseball college scholarship. If he got that far, he figured (and he had the University of Southern California in mind), he'd be getting greater exposure, would more likely attract a bid from some major-league scout.

He hadn't forgotten about dental school. All else failing, if he got that scholarship, he believed that the University of Southern California would be a good place to study for the dental profession.

Tom's tryout for the Fresno City baseball squad provided something of a surprise for everyone concerned. It was certainly a shock for Len Bourdet, coach for the Fresno City ball club.

Len Bourdet had heard a good deal about Tom from his friend Fred Bartels, the Fresno High School coach.

"Let's see how you throw that ball," Bourdet said to Tom, getting him up on the mound.

Tom took the ball and stepped up on the mound. He had to be nervous. So much depended on this man, Len Bourdet, and so much more depended on himself.

He knew that he would be stronger and faster, for he had gained three inches in height and some 30 pounds. He also knew that his pitches would be faster because of the newly developed muscles in his arms, his chest, and his legs. Plus, he had worked and studied to improve his technique. His legs were much stronger and sturdier. "That's where a pitcher needs most of his support, the legs," Tom would say.

But what about his control? Could he get the ball over the plate, could he pinpoint his control?

Tom took a deep breath, and carefully toed the rubber.

He took his windup and then, putting his whole body behind the pitch, he whipped the ball to the catcher behind the plate.

The ball moved fast, faster than any pitch Tom Seaver had ever thrown.

"Good pitch!" Len Bourdet exclaimed.

Tom knew it was a good pitch. He had seen it rise up and in. He could not only throw a fastball, he could pitch a fastball that hopped, was alive. Again and again he hurled the ball across the plate, and each time the ball crashed into the catcher's mitt with a thud.

His old high school coach, Fred Bartels, was there to see Tom try out for the Fresno City team. He watched Tom throw another, and another, and another fastball across the plate. He couldn't quite believe what he saw.

"That's a new Tom Seaver you have there," he said to the Fresno City coach. "Just used to throw junk balls for me," he continued. "You've got a good one there."

He was good enough to win 11 games in a row for Fresno City. His fastball rose up on the right-handed hitters. Sometimes Tom broke the pitch off, and it dipped, in and down from the batter.

But Tom wasn't just a fastball pitcher.

"I stopped being a thrower a while ago," he said. "That's when I took the first step towards being a pitcher in grade school. I learned then that the difference between good pitchers and bad pitchers was that the good ones got the ball over the plate; they threw strikes.

"The better pitchers," said Tom, "threw low strikes, and so I began to practice, practice, throwing low strikes. Then I had to decide and study which batters had the most trouble with certain pitches. Once I was able to pitch low inside strikes to hitters who couldn't hit that pitch, and low outside pitches to hitters who had trouble with it, then I began to concentrate on spots. On inside pitches, I threw to an inside spot, like the hitter's belt buckle, or to his hands, depending on where I wanted the ball to go and, of course, where he stood in the batter's box. On outside pitches, I learned to throw to a spot on the catcher's knee—his right knee for right-handed hitters, his left knee to left-handed batters."

Tom had also studied the controlled pitching form of the stars like Sandy Koufax, Don Drysdale, and Bob Gibson, and now he began to perfect his own technique.

He talked with his father about his father's compact, effortless golf swing and tried to incorporate some of that in his pitching motion, and he discussed pitching style and form with his coaches at school and worked on his rhythm and delivery, breaking down each movement, over and over and over.

Now on the mound, he would hold his arm as tightly to his body as possible before delivering the pitch, thereby reducing the margin of error much as a golfer pulls his elbows tight into his body. The high kick with the left foot allowed him to get all of his 195 pounds into each pitch. Then, as the leg reaches its highest peak, the pitch is hurled toward the batter with the right arm, utilized as the extension of the entire body, and then the follow-through so that the entire body is behind each and every pitch. At the finish of each pitch, the fingers of the right hand all but scrape the ground, in a natural extension like a golfer's follow-through.

And as Tom worked over his delivery, the pitches were getting faster and faster, and his control was improving each day.

Now the big college and university scouts began to take notice of this young pitcher who was setting records for Fresno City College by winning 11 games in a row and striking out a record number of batters.

As he had hoped, Tom Seaver wasn't wasting any time taking step two in his ambitions for the big leagues.

Rod Dedeaux, baseball coach at the University of Southern California, got in touch with Tom.

"How would you feel about switching to U.S.C.?" he asked.

"I'd like that very much," said Tom, struggling to hide his emotions.

"That would be on a full scholarship," said Dedeaux. "I think we might work it out."

"I hope we can," said Tom.

"There's a real problem though," said Dedeaux. "I've only five scholarships available and I'd like to be sure I'm doing the right thing as far as you're concerned."

Tom waited, anxiously. What was the "right thing" Dedeaux had in mind?

"Would you be willing to really test yourself in first-class competition, a top-notch amateur league?" the coach asked.

"If that's what you had in mind, of course," said Tom.

"In Alaska?" asked Dedeaux.

"Sure, why not?"

And within a few days, during the summer of 1964, Tom was on his way to Alaska with a chance to play for an outstanding, recognized Alaskan team known as the Goldpanners.

Red Boucher, mayor of Fairbanks and a great sports fan, had organized the Fairbanks Goldpanners. Every summer he invited 18 of the finest college players to compete for the Goldpanners, who played against the best military, college, and university teams in the country. Each of the Fairbanks players was promised a job in that city,

33

earning about $700 a month. For sure, the jobs didn't take any of the young fellows away from the game, and they weren't strenuous jobs either; but Boucher made certain to keep the amateur status of his players intact. Most of the boys would be going back to school in the fall, to continue their studies and to develop their talents on the diamond.

Rod Dedeaux's reputation was outstanding. He had developed a number of big league players at U.S.C. He recommended Tom to Boucher, and Boucher was quick to ask the young pitcher to come up to Alaska.

With the spring session at Fresco City College over, Tom took the plane to Fairbanks.

He arrived alone, not knowing quite what to expect when the plane taxied to a stop in the airport. Who was going to meet him, or would he have to find his own way to the ballpark or wherever it was that he was supposed to meet up with Red Boucher? He didn't have any idea about where he would live or where to go.

The answers came fast, so fast he didn't have time to think or to evaluate them.

Mrs. Boucher met him at the airport.

"Are you Tom Seaver?" And then, hurriedly and clipped, "We're playing a game right now. I brought a uniform with me. I hope it's the right size. You can put it on when we get to the field. We may need you for the game. It's a very important game."

There wasn't even time to think.

They were at the ball field in no time flat.

"That's where you get into your uniform," said Mrs. Boucher, pointing to a shack outside the ballpark.

Tom dressed as fast as he could, then walked to the dugout.

"Good to see you," said Red Boucher.

A quick shake of the hands and Boucher said, "You'd better get right down to the bullpen."

Running down to the bullpen as Red Boucher had ordered, Tom glanced up at the scoreboard and noted the 2–2 score. The Washington State Bellingham Bells were at bat in the bottom of the fifth inning.

Tom said hello to the other pitchers in the bullpen and immediately began to throw to his catcher.

In the bottom of the sixth, Boucher waved Tom in from the bullpen to the mound. He had just about gotten off his plane and here he was expected to pitch to a bunch of college stars. He was still groggy from the plane ride. It had been a bumpy trip.

But the adrenaline had started to flow the moment he began his walk to the pitching mound, and despite the bumpy flight and the flutters of excitement in his stomach, he immediately calmed down. Once he was on the pitching mound, he was cool and deliberate. He struck out the first batter on three whizzing fastballs, got the next batter to pop up, and then went on to pitch the rest of the game and win it for the Goldpanners.

"The kid's got confidence," said Red Boucher. "He's got to build on it, build it up. But he looks like a winner."

Boucher and his wife, Heidi, took young Tom into their spacious home and in a few minutes made Tom feel at home, almost a part of the family.

Red Boucher talked baseball and baseball and more baseball to the young pitcher. He seemingly never stopped talking.

"You have to have control," said Red. "You have to learn to pitch with your head, not your arm. Keep ahead of every hitter. Outsmart him. Keep those

35

hitters off balance and think, think, think all the time.

"To be successful, you must think you're successful. The first thing you say to yourself every morning is, 'I'm a major leaguer, a winner!' "

When Tom wasn't playing ball, he worked in Boucher's sporting goods store behind the counter, and also was the groundskeeper for the baseball field.

Tom recalls his first happy experience in Alaska: "All the Goldpanner games were played at night, but because the summer sun didn't set in those northern latitudes until 10 or 11 o'clock, most of the games were played in the twilight. The big game of the season was the game played on the night in June when the sun never set. The game started at 11 P.M. and ended about 2 A.M. with the sun still setting on the horizon. And then after the game, the fun began. There would be a great party right on the playing field—Eskimo dances, square dances, and finally the selection of a baseball queen.

"Alaska was something else," said Tom Seaver. "You simply can't realize what a magnificent place it is unless you've been there. And it's a lot different than most people picture it.

"I can remember my first trip there," he recalled. "I expected it to be so cold. I wore a heavy sweater and a topcoat as I got off the plane. But Mrs. Boucher, who met me at the airport, was just wearing a sleeveless dress.

"The weather in July and August is ideal. It's in the high sixties and seventies every day and no humidity. It's the time of year when they have 24 hours of sunlight and it's pretty weird.

"I can remember waking up one night at three

o'clock. I saw the sun coming in through the windows, and my first thought was that I'd overslept and I would be late for my day's work. I was a groundskeeper," said Tom, laughing. "I'd cut the grass and water the infield."

At the end of the regular summer season, the Goldpanners were invited to Wichita, Kansas, to play in the National Baseball Congress Tournament. Thirty-two teams, each a state champion, participated in the tournament. The rules limited each team to 18 players. The Goldpanners had 20 on the squad. Red Boucher had a problem. Who was he going to cut?

Cutting one man off the team was comparatively easy. But then it became a question of whether to cut Tom Seaver of Fresno City College or Ken Holtzman of the University of Illinois. Ken Holtzman would one day become a 21-game winner and a two-time no-hit pitcher for the Chicago Cubs and the Oakland Athletics, and play a couple of seasons with the Yankees.

On the way to Wichita, the Goldpanners stopped at Grand Junction in Colorado, and Tom Seaver was hammered out of the box in a game with the local team. It looked sure that Tom would be cut and Holtzman would stay on the club.

"How do you feel about it?" Red Boucher asked Tom. "Have you lost your confidence?"

"Try me," said Tom. "Just try me."

Boucher cut Holtzman, and it was no mistake. He was not to regret it; at least he was not to regret keeping Tom Seaver on his roster.

In his most dramatic appearance in the Wichita tournament, Tom was called in from the bullpen with the Goldpanners leading by 2–0 but with the opposing team, the Wichita Glassmen, threatening. Wichita had three men on base and nobody out.

Tom was understandably nervous; he kept rolling the ball in his hands. Boucher tried to calm him down, reviewing the situation in the game, the kind of pitch he'd like Tom to throw, how to keep the runners close to their bases.

"OK," said Tom. The talk wasn't making him feel less edgy. He wanted to get down to his job, and all Red Boucher was doing was making him that much more tense.

"OK," he said. "I heard you. I listened to everything you said. I've been listening to you all summer. It's up to me now. Let me get in there and pitch."

Red was a bit stunned by this sudden outburst. This was the first time he'd had anything like back-talk from the youngster. But he wasn't unhappy about it.

"The kid is going to make it," he said to himself, marching back to the dugout. "With that kind of confidence, he can't miss."

But Tom did miss. Two walks and a hit and the Wichita Glassmen had a 3–2 lead.

If this rattled Tom, nobody noticed. In the bottom of the eighth, the Goldpanners rallied to load the bases and Tom Seaver was in the on-deck circle.

Everyone in the ballpark was sure Boucher would lift Tom for a pinch hitter. Not Tom. He grabbed his batting helmet and, in measured strides, walked to the plate. Later, Red Boucher said, "He was so full of confidence, I just had to let him hit for himself."

It was one time a manager's instinct paid off.

Tom let the first pitch go by. It was a ball. The second pitch was a fastball and Tom laced into it. The ball shot off Seaver's bat like a cannonball, rising high, some 450 feet, finally clearing the center-field wall for a grand slam home run. The Goldpanners walked off the field with the win, 6–3.

Tom won two games for the Goldpanners at Wichita and was named to the All-Tournament team. There was no question about his getting that baseball scholarship to the University of Southern California.

"He's going to be your best pitcher," said Red Boucher to U.S.C. baseball coach Rod Dedeaux.

To a professional baseball scout, Red Boucher said after the tournaments, "We had a lot of young fellows who could throw the ball harder than Seaver. He has a fastball that moves, and is tough to hit. His curve and slider are just about average for a college pitcher. But he has a tremendous will to win. That's his greatest asset. And his concentration is super. That kid believes he can put the ball right through the bat if he wants to."

Tom enrolled at the University of Southern California in the fall of 1964. He went heavily for courses in pre-dentistry.

Tom roomed with Justin Dedeaux, the baseball coach's son, and they became great friends. They hunted pheasant together and Tom cooked the birds they had bagged. He had his own special recipe and even Justin enjoyed his cooking.

"One of the things about Tom that most players and coaches didn't realize," says Dedeaux, "is that he was very agile and he really was fast on his feet. Dad would have the U.S.C. baseball squad run wind sprints, and Tom could almost run nose to nose with Mike Garrett, one of our 10-second sprinters. Mike would win by a stride, but the next day Tom would run even with him."

One day a friend of Tom's, Jerry Merz, a physical

education major and weight lifter, discussed his theories about body building with Tom.

"It would add muscle to your shoulders, build up those big trapezius muscles of the back, and the deltoid muscles. A steady program," said Merz, "would do wonders for your pitching, and would reduce a lot of those sore arm problems a lot of pitchers get."

Tom thought about the idea and decided to adapt a modified weight lifting program, and through the years it has helped him reduce arm fatigue and even added speed to his fastball.

Busy as he was at U.S.C., Tom still had some ties in Fresno. There was his family, to which he was much attached. But there was one other person for Tom in Fresno, a beautiful young lady who would rival his love for baseball.

Nancy Lynn McIntyre had been in his English class at Fresno. They sat just a few feet apart and Tom often glanced at her. She was a cheerleader, and easily the prettiest girl in the school, but Tom, for all his dating, never had the courage to say more than a couple of words to her all year.

It was the last day of school, a time for celebrating.

Tom and several friends had a couple of beers and worked up a softball game just a couple of blocks from school. For some reason Tom doesn't remember, during the game he hopped into his car and drove back to the college. It was then that he spotted Nancy walking alone.

He stopped his car, jumped out, ran up to Nancy and, because he couldn't think of doing anything else, he tackled her—not hard, but a real tackle and strong enough to sweep her off her feet.

40

He laughed, that odd, high-pitched, boyish laugh that has become so familiar through the years, picked her up and hoisted her into her car.

"Want to go to a softball game?" he asked.

She must have thought he was mad; at best, she must have thought he was drunk.

"No," she said. "I don't want to see a silly softball game."

Now that he had finally brought himself to speak to this girl who had him tongue-tied all year, he wasn't taking no for an answer. He drove her to the game. The ride, the fun, and the excitement of the game cooled Nancy's annoyance and she finally agreed to another date.

"After a couple of dates and a lot of fun Nancy told me her hopes of becoming an airline stewardess," said Tom.

In his book *The Perfect Game*, Tom said, "Nancy and I seemed to realize that we could be serious about ourselves and about other things without being pretentious or somber. Nancy enjoyed people and caring about them; what they were actually like, not just on the surface. She wanted to live in a real world and so did I."

When Tom went back to U.S.C. in the fall of 1965, he and Nancy agreed that he wouldn't date anyone at U.S.C. and she wouldn't date anyone at Fresno. But one night at U.S.C. a friend came into Tom's room and told him about a party he was going to.

"And I have a date for you," the friend said.

Tom went to the party with the girl. The next weekend back in Fresno, he dated Nancy. She asked him if he had gone out with someone else; perhaps she sensed a bit of guilt or uneasiness in his manner.

"Yeah, some guy arranged this blind date."

There were angry words and then, after a scene, there was a mutual agreement and finally peace.

"I decided right then and there," said Tom, "that I didn't want to lead my life that way, hurting the one person most important to me."

Tom and Nancy began to talk seriously about the future, marriage and their life together, and a career for Tom as a solid, prosperous dentist. And somewhere in the back of his mind, perhaps there was another, more exciting career in the major leagues.

5
A VOID CONTRACT AND A LOTTERY

Tom Seaver came through even better than expected in his first year on the diamond for the University of Southern California. He won ten games for U.S.C., while losing only two, and struck out 100 batters in 100 innings. He wasn't yet attracting too much attention from the big league scouts, but Tommy Lasorda, a former Dodger pitcher, then a scout for the Los Angeles Dodgers and, of course, later their manager, did approach Tom with an offer to sign with the Dodgers.

"There's a $2,000 bonus for you, Tom, if you'll sign the contract," said Lasorda. "That's $1,500 more than I got to sign," he laughed.

Two thousand dollars? The New York Mets had handed his pal Dick Selma twenty thousand dollars as a bonus. And Tom knew it.

"How about fifty thousand dollars?" countered Seaver.

Tommy Lasorda stepped back, looked the kid over. He couldn't help admiring him. "Kid, I'll say one thing. You have a hell of a lot of guts. That's what great pitchers need. But you're much too rich for my Dodger blood. Not today."

Tom Seaver had coolly and calmly turned down the first bid from a major-league club.

"In the summer of 1965," recalled Tom, "I rejoined the Goldpanners instead of playing pro ball. We entered the National Baseball Congress tournament once again. Our pitching staff included Andy Messersmith, Al Schmelz, Danny Frisella, and myself—I had a chance to pitch and we won one game before we reached the semi-finals. Then I started against the Wichita Dreamliners. They had a strong lineup that included four major leaguers: Bob Boyd, Jim Pendleton, Charlie Neal, and Rod Kanehl. Charlie Neal had played for the Mets two years earlier, Rod Kanehl a year earlier.

"The Dreamliners hit me hard, beat me 6–3, and then went on to win the NBC tournament," Seaver said. "Charlie Neal hit my first pitch for a triple, Boyd got three hits, and Rod Kanehl stole home on me.

"When the game ended, Boyd, who had been a solid .300 hitter for the Baltimore Orioles for about six years, came over to me. 'Kid,' he said, 'you got a helluva pitch. You've got a great future ahead of you. You're going to be a great big league pitcher.'

"I just stared at him. I didn't believe a word he said. Here's this guy—this really good ex-major-leaguer. He's just gotten three hits off me. I don't believe him. He's crazy. Me a big league pitcher? A great one?

"That night I met Rod Kanehl, the first time I actually met someone who'd played for the Mets, and Rod told me, too, that I would be a big league pitcher. Two ex-major-leaguers had told me in the same day that I could make it in pro baseball, and that day I really began to believe it. Perhaps for the first time, I really actually began to believe that I could be a major-league pitcher. The thought had me walking on air for a couple of weeks."

As soon as the tournament was over, Al Schmelz signed with the Mets, as did Dan Frisella, and Messersmith signed with the California Angels.

Baseball practice begins early at the University of Southern California, and the baseball scouts come out early to size up the college ballplayers. It was early in the year, after U.S.C. had played a pre-season game against a team from the Marine base, that Tom got a bit of unexpected but exciting news.

"Did you see this morning's papers?" Tom was asked.

"What papers?"

"Don't tell me you don't know what's happening?"

"Know what? What the hell are you talking about?"

"Tom, the Braves, the Atlanta Braves, have picked you in the draft!"

Tom just couldn't believe it. Sure, he expected to be picked up sometime, but heck, he'd pitched only one year for U.S.C.

"Where is it? Show me the story."

It was there all right, in black and white on all the sports pages. And in several papers. He still couldn't believe it. Tom Seaver drafted by a major-league ball club. It was a dream . . . a dream come true. He couldn't believe it.

The Atlanta Braves front office brought him back to the reality of the situation, but not all the way back.

45

Chief scout Johnny Moore called to say he was driving up to see him.

Moore drove up to the Seaver home on East El Rancho Drive in a shiny new Cadillac. That meant big money to Tom and he began to get excited. Easy now, don't panic. He needed to be calm, not too anxious, when talking about money.

Moore and Tom talked and talked and, finally, they came to an agreement. It was one fantastic agreement for a 21-year-old youngster without any professional experience back in 1965.

It was an incredible, unbelievable contract.

First, there was to be a $40,000 cash bonus, just for signing the contract with the Braves. There would be an additional $4,000 to pay for his tuition for his final year and a half at U.S.C. There was to be another bonus of $1,000 for playing at least 90 days of double-A ball and another $1,500 for playing at least 90 days of triple-A ball. There was also a clause for another $5,000 bonus for playing at least 90 days of major-league ball. All in all, the bonuses came to $11,500.

The entire contractual package amounted to $51,500.

Not a bad deal for an untried 21-year-old.

Not bad at all.

But there was one hitch. There is a major-league rule that prohibits the signing of a college player to a professional contract after the college baseball season has started.

"The college season hasn't started," said Moore.

"But, we've played a couple of pre-season games," said Tom.

"Let me check it with the front office," said Moore.

The Atlanta Braves front office checked out the

deal and ruled that it was OK for Seaver to sign the contract. The regular season had not begun.

Tom signed on the dotted line, but that wasn't to be the end. As a matter of fact, Tom would never wear the uniform of the Atlanta Braves.

Rod Dedeaux, the U.S.C. baseball coach, did not agree with the interpretation of the rules as the Atlanta front office read them. Neither did Baseball Commissioner William Eckert.

It was only a matter of a few days after he had signed the contract with the Atlanta Braves that Tom received a devastating call from John McHale, the general manager of the Atlanta club.

"Sorry, Tom, but the baseball commissioner's office has ruled against us. They've voided our contract."

"How can they do that?" asked Tom, the bottom dropping out of all his hopes, his plans, his dreams.

"They make the final decisions, Tom. Sorry. There's nothing I can do about it," said McHale.

Tom couldn't hide his keen disappointment. He fretted and fumed and cursed out the baseball commissioner's office.

"To heck with them!" he said, finally. "I'll go back to school, pitch another year. Maybe I'll be getting a sweeter offer from the Braves, or maybe some other club in June. Maybe it's all for the best."

But nothing was going to be for the best, or even better, for some time yet. On the contrary, he was going to be in for some more bad news before his luck in the baseball wars would turn at all.

It was Dedeaux, the U.S.C. coach, who would call next with the bad news.

"You know, Tom, you won't be able to pitch for us this year," he said. "No. You've signed a contract with the intention of becoming a professional.

47

You're no longer considered an amateur. You cannot play for the school."

"But the contract with the Braves has been voided," Tom protested.

"It doesn't matter," said Dedeaux. "The intention was there. You're no longer an amateur. That's the way the National Collegiate Athletic Association sees it."

"That's a helluva thing!" said Tom. "Can't you do anything about it?"

"Sorry, Tom. There's just nothing I can do about it. They've made the decision and their decision is final. Sorry, Tom."

Everybody was sorry about it, but it was Tom who was paying for all the rules that threatened to end the baseball career that had just begun to get off the ground. Tom knew well enough that his chances of getting a big league contract were just about nil if he couldn't play for U.S.C. where the scouts could see him.

"It's unfair," said Tom, and all his friends agreed with him; but, like everyone else, all they could do was to feel sorry for him.

March came along, with all the news about the big leaguers traveling to the warmer spots in Florida and Arizona for spring training, and Tom couldn't take his frustration any longer. He got on the phone and called William Eckert, a retired Air Force general who was baseball's commissioner at the time. He was going right to the top to plead his case.

He couldn't get the commissioner in New York, but after a short delay he was connected with Lee MacPhail, the commissioner's assistant at the time, and later president of the American League.

As briefly as he could, but without missing any of the details, Tom explained the entire procedure: the contract with Atlanta, the baseball commissioner's decison, and his being declared ineligible to play ball for U.S.C.

"Isn't there something you can do about it?" he asked MacPhail. "I want to play ball. I want to be able to pitch again."

Lee MacPhail listened patiently and attentively to the young fellow, said he would look into the situation, and promised to call him back. And MacPhail was as good as his word. Evidently he was taken aback by the seemingly unfair decision, and Lee was impressed with Seaver's earnestness, and it wasn't long before MacPhail was on the phone with him again.

"I think I have a solution for you," said MacPhail.

"Great!" said Tom, though he was a bit wary of what that solution would be.

He needn't have worried. MacPhail had a solution that would prove to be something more than Tom expected, and would make history for at least one club in the major leagues.

"Your contract with Atlanta is null and void," began MacPhail. "They will not be able to sign you, not this year anyway."

"Oh, damn," said Tom, like someone waiting for the other shoe to drop.

"No, they can't sign you. But Commissioner Eckert will notify all the other clubs in the majors that you are available and eligible for an immediate contract.

"And," said MacPhail, "If more than one team agrees to the same $51,500 package deal, then those teams would participate in a drawing to determine which club would have the rights to you."

"Sounds great to me," said Tom, cheering up for the first time in months.

"I want to repeat the formula," MacPhail went on: "any major-league team that's willing to match the $51,500 contract the Braves promised you will be free to negotiate their own contract with you. OK?"

All that had been cloudy and dark, all the disappointment was suddenly gone for Tom. The sun was shining brightly and his joy could scarcely be restrained. He was going to get another chance to sign with a big league club. And maybe, with a bit of luck, he would be able to pitch in the big leagues!

But one day went by, then another, and then another, and there was no news from the commissioner's office, no word from any of the clubs. Tom began to worry once more—$51,500 was a great deal of money; was there even one club, just one club that would spend that kind of bonus money for a young, untried pitcher, and a college pitcher at that?

Finally, the word from the commissioner's office came just two weeks after that talk with MacPhail. There were three clubs that were willing to match the Atlanta offer: the Philadelphia Phillies, the Cleveland Indians, and the New York Mets.

And once again Tom Seaver was climbing the skies.

"There'll be a lottery in General Eckert's office," said Lee MacPhail, on the phone to Seaver. The lottery would be held the afternoon of April second. The names of the three clubs would be written on three pieces of paper, the pieces of paper put into a hat, one piece of paper drawn. The lucky club, and only that one club, could talk contract with Tom Seaver

There was a great deal of talk in the Seaver household, a lot of happy talk and happy speculation, during the days that followed. Suppose the

Phillies won the lottery, suppose the Indians had their name plucked out of the hat, suppose the New York Mets. Suppose, suppose, suppose. It was like a game, an expensive game.

"The Mets," said Tom. "That's the team I want. That's what I'd like. The Mets are the best team for me."

The Mets were a cellar team and that wasn't particularly attractive to Tom. There was, however, a very good reason for Tom's preference. He was always good at analyzing the game, and his analysis was generally sharp and right on target.

"The Indians have Sam McDowell and Sonny Siebert, that's darn good pitching. The Phillies have good pitching and a good team. It's the Mets that can use me most. And I can get up to the majors faster in the Mets farm system," said Tom.

He had it all figured out.

"The Mets have been losers too long. They'll have to do something about turning things around. They have to become winners. And the only way they can do that is to bring up young players from their farm system."

The reasoning was sound and, for once anyway, the luck was good, too.

The afternoon of April 2 the phone rang in the Seaver home, and Tom picked it up in the kitchen.

"Hello."

"Tom Seaver?"

Tom recognized the voice of Lee MacPhail.

"It's Tom Seaver, Mr. MacPhail."

"Good," said MacPhail.

He spoke very quietly.

"The three teams have their names in the hat. Are you there?"

"I'm here, Mr. MacPhail."

51

There wasn't need for it, but Tom was speaking as quietly as the commissioner's assistant.

"The commissioner is putting his hand into the hat. He's drawn a name and—the team—is—the New York Mets!"

It was almost too much for Tom Seaver to take. There were lots of questions he wanted to ask. Who do I talk to? Who's going to get in touch with me? Where do I go, or when is whoever's supposed to going to come to see me? Do I go down to Florida? Do they come out to California?

But he asked none of those questions, or any other questions. His chest, his legs, his arms, his mouth were too full of joy.

"Thank you very much, Mr. MacPhail. Thanks for everything you've done for me. You're not going to be sorry. You're not going to be sorry."

Then to his family, leaping clear out of himself, "I'm going to be a Met! I'm going to be a Met!"

6
A STAR IN TRIPLE A

April 3, the day after the drawing in the commissioner's office, Nelson Burbrink, a scout for the New
York Mets, pulled up to the Seaver house in a
Chevrolet. Tom remembered that Johnny Moore,
the Atlanta scout, had arrived in a Cadillac. Young
Tom had had ideas about raising the ante on his
bonus; he had second thoughts about those ideas,
but he gave them a try anyway.

"Cleveland was ready to offer me $70,000," he
said to Burbrink, and Burbrink made no comment.

"Don't you think I'm worth more than $51,500?"
asked Tom.

"Maybe," came back Burbrink, "but you can take
what we agreed to, or wait till the next draft."

Tom wasn't waiting. He'd waited long enough. He
signed the contract and he knew exactly what to do
with his bonus.

A few days later Tom bought Nancy McIntyre a

diamond engagement ring, he bought himself a brand-new car, and he deposited the rest in an investment plan operated by his father's company. He then flew down to the Mets minor-league training camp in the small town of Homestead, Florida, a bit to the south of Miami.

The training camp reminded him of the Marines boot camp. The players lived in dormitories, ate in large mess halls, and worked out in groups of fifty and a hundred. But this wasn't the Marines, and Tom took to the training with his customary zeal and enthusiasm. He met and became friendly with a young shortstop by the name of Bud Harrelson, and a couple of kid pitchers named Jerry Koosman and Nolan Ryan. All four of the youngsters were destined to make good in the big leagues.

Nolan Ryan and Jerry Koosman were sent to a double-A team at the end of the spring training session. Buddy Harrelson and Seaver were sent to Jacksonville, a triple-A team. For Tom this was being moved to a league just one step below the major leagues and he was ecstatic. It was most unusual for a youngster with no minor-league experience to start his career in the top minor leagues, but Solly Hemus, a fine infielder and former manager of the St. Louis Cardinals, was now manager of Jacksonville and he was sure the youngster could make the grade. He wasn't mistaken. Bob Scheffing, the director of the Mets farm system, was in complete agreement with Hemus.

"He learns fast," said Scheffing of young Seaver. "All you have to do is show him something once. He never makes the same mistake twice. I showed him a pickoff play and in a couple of hours he had it down pat."

Once the International League season started, Hemus kept Tom on the bench for several weeks. Finally, on April 25, 1966, Hemus told Tom he would pitch that day. It was a day Tom would never forget.

The opposition that night was the Rochester Red Wings, and Tom had everybody in the ball park wondering about him. He pitched eight and one-third innings and gave up just six hits and two runs, while striking out nine batters, to earn a 4–2 win.

"Fun is fun," said a Rochester sportswriter after the seventh inning, "but where the hell has this kid been? Who is he? Where'd he come from?"

"This kid," said manager Hemus, "is the best pitching prospect the Mets have ever signed."

In the ninth inning of that first game, Hemus took Tom out with a man on base and one out. He knew Tom was tired, dead tired. The Jacksonville relief pitcher came in and saved the game.

Five days later, against Buffalo, a team loaded with former major leaguers, Seaver limited the heavy hitting Bison to only two hits, while scoring a 6–0 victory. He struck out 11 Buffalo hitters with a fastball that was clocked at 90 miles per hour. It was the finest pitching of the young season.

"We may be watching the development of one of the great ones of our time," said Red Davis, manager of the Buffalo team. "This kid didn't pitch and beat a bunch of rookies. He beat a veteran team. From what I saw, Seaver could be one of the great ones."

Five days later he beat Buffalo once again, allowing them four hits and one unearned run while striking out seven as Jacksonville walloped the Bison 12–1.

"We're not apt to see him again," said Buffalo

manager Clay Dennis with a sigh of relief. "He'll be pitching for the Mets before the end of June."

In his first three starts, Tom Seaver completed two games, one a shutout, and struck out 27 in 26 and one-third innings, while compiling a fantastic 0.68 earned run average.

And to add to this bit of glory, Seaver collected three hits and batted in three runs in ten trips to the plate. He hammered home the winning runs in his first game with a two-run double.

But all of a sudden there was a complete let-down.

He lost his fourth start. Then he lost his fifth game when he was hammered out of the box in five innings. There was surely something wrong with the young phenom. The skeptics now had a field day, for they had seen and had reported on numerous "spring sensations" and had seen them fade away in May and June, never to be heard or seen again, never to return to their former glory.

Tom was terribly lonely. He missed Nancy. That was what was wrong. His mind and his heart were back in Fresno.

Yes, his fastball was sailing—not hitting a corner of the plate. His curveball was hanging, his sliders were missing and he was aiming the ball and getting behind the batters. And when he did come in with his fastball, the pitch was over the heart of the plate and opposing batters were cranking the ball out of the park; but it was all because he was lonesome and homesick for Nancy and he simply could not concentrate on his pitching.

He wrote to Nancy, telling her of his unhappiness and how much he missed her. He asked her to come down to Jacksonville on the next plane . . . and marry him. He enclosed a one-way plane ticket to Jacksonville in the envelope.

The original plans called for Tom and Nancy to be married right after the baseball season, but it didn't take Nancy long to board the next flight to Florida and on June 6, Tom and Nancy were married in a very quiet and private ceremony in Arlington, a suburb of Jacksonville. The marriage was going to be a good one and Tom, happy once again, quickly got back his winning form. By the end of the season Tom Seaver was the talk of the entire International League.

"He has so much poise," said manager Solly Hemus. "Tom reminds me of Bob Gibson out on the mound. He's in command all the time," said Hemus, "and the kid is only 21 years old."

Despite Tom's success, the Jacksonville Suns finished their disappointing season in seventh place, 15 games behind Rochester. They won 68 games, but lost 79.

But Tom did well enough, well enough considering the circumstances in which he worked. He won 12 and lost 12, but 4 of his victories were shutouts and he struck out a total of 188 men, a record for the International League. He struck out 10 in the last game of the 1966 season, beating Toledo by the score of 5–1.

There could be no doubt about where young Tom Seaver was headed.

The sportswriters were calling him "the Jacksonville wonder boy."

They called him "the super-rookie!" and his teammates began to call him "Supe."

Solly Hemus couldn't find enough words to praise his young pitching star.

"Tom Seaver," he said, "has a 35-year-old head on top of a 21-year-old body."

He shook his head.

"Usually we get a 35-year-old arm attached to a 21-year-old head."

As the season ended, Tom and Nancy said their good-byes to their friends Bud Harrelson and his wife, Yvonne. Nancy and Yvonne had become great friends and made plans to be together at St. Petersburg, where the Mets trained, in February. Tom said his farewells to Tug McGraw and Ken Boswell and thanked his manager Solly Hemus for all his help and good advice. "It's my pleasure, Tom," said Hemus. "I'll see you in the 'biggies' next season."

Driving back to California in their new convertible, Tom wanted to talk to Nancy about his first marvelous year in professional baseball and about their plans for the future, which conceivably might mean living in New York if he made the grade with the Mets. But Nancy sat stiffly, constrained, reading a magazine. She seemed angry and disturbed. He asked her what was wrong, and she told him she was concerned about their hasty marriage. She didn't like being a ballplayer's wife. While Tom traveled with the team, she was alone for ten days, perhaps two weeks at a time. Besides the loneliness, she had been talking to other ballplayers' wives and they told her about the drinking and carousing and infidelity that were prevalent.

Tom blanched at the tears in her eyes. "Look," he said firmly, "as much as we're going to be separated, you're going to have to trust me. When you married me, I think you knew that I could be trusted. Besides, I'll take you with me whenever it's possible."

Nancy nodded, but both knew that the separations would strain their marriage. Discussing this later with a reporter, Nancy said:

"You know something? When I first married Tom, I guess I didn't know him very well. During our dating period he was gone an awful lot of the time. He was either away at school or he went to play winter ball in Alaska or to summer camp with the Marines. You know, I knew he was an awfully nice guy. I mean, I loved him but I knew that he was just a nice guy. And I think that when you feel secure with somebody there must be a reason why. And I'll be frank, I really never thought we would ever, ever be where we are today. I never, well, for one thing, I didn't quite realize what professional baseball had to offer. And then when you do get to understand a little more about baseball, you consider the superstars the ultimate. They're not of the same kind. They're rare gems. And you never consider yourself married to one.

"I guess I just didn't know that much about it to be able to see what Tom had. And the more I see him play, every year, I feel like I don't know him as well as I thought I did. I just learn something new about him every year. It's just situation after situation. To go to New York and do what he did, win 16 games with the Mets, a tenth-place team, in his very first year—that amazed me. I thought he was the most wonderful miracle worker I'd ever encountered. Just incredible. It was like I didn't even know him.

"In that first All-Star game, I prayed and prayed: 'Please, don't put Tom in, don't put him in. He's too little. He's just a little young guy, don't put him in the game.' And then he walked out on the mound and I couldn't believe it was Tom. I thought: I don't even know him. It was the strongest experience.

"In the World Series game, God, it was just like he was a total stranger. He's my own husband and I don't even know him. He's my own husband and I don't know what he can do. He amazes me."

After the International League's season was over, Tom and Nancy settled, temporarily at least, in a small apartment in Manhattan Beach, not too far from the University of Southern California's campus. Tom was going back to school.

"College has helped me," he said. "College develops the mind, gets you to think, and more than ever, I know how important the mind is to a pitcher."

It was while Tom was at the college, taking a class in public relations, that Nancy got a call at home from the Mets front office.

"They want you to report to St. Petersburg for spring training," she relayed to Tom when he got home from school.

"St. Petersburg?" queried Tom, excitement suddenly building in him.

Nancy didn't know much about the business side of baseball, and what life would be like with a major-league prospect. She learned it all, as the weeks, the months, the years rolled by, and she enjoyed every minute of every day.

"That's what the Mets office said," said Nancy.

"That's where the Mets go for their spring training," said Tom excitedly. "Didn't you know about that?"

60

"No, not at all" said Nancy innocently. "Just never thought about it. It's happened so quickly."

"Don't you know what that means?" pressed Tom.

Nancy shook her head, a little bewildered.

"That means I'm going to get a chance to play for the New York Mets. At any rate, I'm going to spring training. Something I've dreamed about, talked about since I've been a little kid," shouted Tom. "And now its happening to me, to us."

And he hugged the startled Nancy and danced her all around the floor.

"I'm going to pitch for the Mets! We're going to live in New York!" he shouted. "And we'll be making a lot more money, Nancy! A lot of money!"

Money was important to Tom Seaver; not as important as baseball, perhaps, but very important!

It wasn't easy keeping his mind on his studies after that call from St. Petersburg. His mind kept wandering. He kept seeing himself in a Mets uniform, striking out the great stars, zipping the ball by sluggers such as Willie Stargell and Roberto Clemente of the Pirates, Pete Rose of Cincinnati, Willie McCovey of San Francisco, Ernie Banks and Ron Santo of Chicago, and even his boyhood idol, Hank Aaron. He even dreamed of pitching in a World Series.

Tom Seaver had confidence in himself. He wasn't the kind of youngster who went around bragging about his ability, but he just knew that he was good—very good. Sure, he had a great deal to learn. He knew that, too. But not for a moment did he doubt that he was going to be a great major-league pitcher as he and Nancy headed for the Mets spring training camp in St. Petersburg, Florida. He had no idea, however, that within two years he would be the spark that would help ignite a laughing-stock of a team into a World Series winner. Never in his wildest dreams could he have known that one day he would become a great pitcher, so great that he would be nicknamed "the Franchise"!

7
THE METS

In 1966 the New York Mets finally climbed out of the cellar, after languishing there since their 1962 inception as a National League expansion team. They hadn't climbed very far, however; nor was the outlook any brighter for the immediate future.

Under the old master of the double entendre, good old wisecracking Casey Stengel, the Mets were something of a joke in baseball circles. But a lovable joke. Even before they booted the first ground ball and dropped the first throw, those freshman Mets of 1962 were as disaster- and accident-prone as any major-league team in history, and they were demonstrating an uncanny knack for losing ball games.

A day before the inaugural season, pitcher Sherman Jones, aptly nicknamed "Roadblock," was lighting a cigarette when part of the flint flew into his eye. Roadblock had been scheduled to pitch on the second day of the season against St. Louis, but when he appeared on the field with a black patch over his right eye, Joe Durso of the *New York Times* suggested that Stengel ought to nominate Road-block for a Purple Heart. Just three weeks earlier in Florida, a line drive had bounced off Jones's leg and he then spent some ten days hobbling around on crutches.

Then, on the eve of opening day in St. Louis, 16 Mets got stuck in an elevator at the Chase Hotel and the exhibition game was delayed for about one hour until they were rescued. Later, Casey slammed the door of his office, and when he tried to get back in, he discovered he had locked himself out and that nobody had a key. A crew of workmen had to take the door off the hinges so Casey could dress for the game.

The Mets finally were able to start the season at home April 11. Pitcher Roger Craig committed a balk in the first inning, while the Cardinals scored two runs. The Mets made four errors and hit into two double plays as they lost to the Cardinals 11 to 4.

Professor Stengel, commenting on the game, said, "Our infield was weak only in making double plays and our outfield was weak only in that too many fly balls were dropping in.

"Sometimes," he added, "the pitchers throw bullets in the bullpen. But I want them to throw those bullets in a game."

The rest of the season was an exercise in incompetence. Pitchers Roger Craig and Al Jackson, who were better than their records show, lost a record total of 44 games. The pitching staff broke a National League record by yielding 192 home runs. The team itself led the majors in errors, with 210. Of every four games they played, the Mets were able to win only one. Even as they fumbled and bumbled away their first home games played in the old Polo Grounds to the Pirates, a group of teenagers behind the third-base dugout began a chant, "Let's Go Mets!" It sounded so odd, that clarion call of support, that others took up the war cry. Within a few games the banners began to appear, fashioned from old bedsheets: "What, me worry? I'm a Mets fan." And, "All the world loves a loser, especially the Hicksville Fire Department."

A cult was forming, and its teenage members searched for a place to focus their love. They quickly found it in first baseman Marv Throneberry. "Marvelous Marv" was a monument to imperfection. His capacity for blunders verged on the supernatural. What made him especially marvelous was his sense of drama. He saved his snafus for close games when they really hurt the team. Once he drove out a three-base hit with the bases loaded, only to spoil his triumph by failing to touch first or second base.

Marvelous Marv received more fan mail that summer than the rest of the team combined. There was a Marv Losers Club and a Marv-for-President Club, and thousands of kids wore T-shirts with VRAM (Marv spelled backwards) emblazoned on them.

But a few of the Mets did not enjoy the antics of the Merry Mets and Marvelous Marv, such as rookie Ed Kranepool, who found the business of losing every day downright humiliating. "At times," said Eddie, "the crowd would rise and give you a standing ovation if you just caught and held onto the ball."

In 1963, the Mets opened the season once again against the Cardinals, and once again dropped the opener by a 7–0 score. Roger Craig, who had lost 24 games in 1962, committed two balks in this game. He was to lose 22 games in 1963.

In 1964, apparently strengthened by more than a dozen player shifts, the Mets raced off to a 4–0 lead over the Phillies in the opener, but finally dropped the game 5–3. Back in New York for the home opening game of the season, the Mets scored three runs against the Pirates early, but once again dropped the game by a 4–3 score.

During the preseason camp in Florida, Stengel was impressed by four young rookies: Ron Swoboda, who hit 450-foot drives; Dick Selma, a cocky, combative pitcher; a rabbitlike infielder, Buddy Harrelson; and Eddie Kranepool, who had been signed as an 18-year-old out of high school in 1962 and had sat on the bench in 1963, but was now ready to take over at first base.

There wasn't much reason to think that the 1964 team would be better than the previous Mets editions, but at least there were some tangible signs that a Mets farm system did exist and there were some promising players "down on the farm." Within five years Harrelson, Swoboda, and Kranepool would be the nucleus of a Mets team that would capture a World Series.

Opening day, 1965, Ed Kranepool was the starting first baseman as the Mets tried to break their streak of opening day losses. But the Dodgers' Don Drysdale allowed just four hits and added insult to injury by hitting a home run off Mets pitcher Al Jackson.

Howard Taubman, distinguished drama critic of

The New York Times, was watching the game in the hope of favorably reviewing the Mets, but he wrote: "Despite drastic cast changes and a promise of new scripts stressing drama of earnest conflict, the Mets still are enmeshed in the theatre of the absurd."

When the Mets came home from a road trip on July 22, they had a record of 30 wins and 63 losses. They were, however, three games ahead of the 1964 pace.

On July 25, after the Mets had lost to the Pirates 5–1, there was a birthday party for Casey Stengel. Old-timers who had gathered for the annual day at Shea Stadium packed Toots Shor's restaurant that night for Casey's party and it was a gala affair that lasted most of the night.

The next morning, Casey wasn't at the ballpark.

He was in the hospital with a broken hip.

At some point during the festivities, quite late, Casey left the party with a friend, Joe Gregoria, comptroller of the Mets. Getting out of the car, Casey had either stepped heavily or had fallen and suffered a bad muscular spasm that resulted in a fractured hip.

Wes Westrum, who had been Stengel's coach, was nominated by Casey to take over as interim manager for the rest of the season. The next day Casey was operated on and a small steel ball was placed in his hip. He spent more than three weeks in Roosevelt Hospital and then, on August 30, announced his formal retirement.

Westrum, a calm, cool, capable catcher for the New York Giants from 1948 to 1957 and a coach for the Giants when they moved to San Francisco in 1958, was given a two-year contract to manage the Mets.

And despite every strategic move he could employ, the Mets under Westrum lost 17 of their first 20 games. Once again they dropped into the cellar, with a season record showing 50 wins and 112 losses.

Still, the seeds of future success were slowly but surely being planted. The front office had developed a five-club farm system and hired a group of first-rate scouts to prowl about the school stadiums and the sandlots in search of any promising talent.

But the scouting system sometimes fell flat on its face, as in the following instance:

In 1966, the Mets had the first draft choice and selected as their number one player catcher Steve Chilcott, thereby passing up a hard-hitting outfielder from the University of Arizona by the name of Reggie Jackson. Chilcott never did play a game with a major-league club, and all Reggie did was to provide the spark, power, and punch that enabled Oakland, Baltimore, and the Yankees to win one pennant and World Series after another. Twenty years later, in 1986, Jackson is still driving out those towering home runs for the California Angels.

The Mets were somewhat better in 1966, aided by such players as Ron Hunt, the All-Star second baseman, Cleon Jones, Ken Boyer, catcher Jerry Grote, Ron Swoboda, and pitchers Dick Selma, Tug McGraw, Dennis Ribant, Bob Shaw, and Jack Fisher.

So the blueprint was quite clear: the 1966 Mets would have more hitting, but the season would depend on their young pitchers.

But there was a serious flaw—the right young pitchers didn't exist.

The Mets, once again, were in dire straits.

They needed pitching help—a great deal of help.

8
THE ROOKIE, 1967

After no more than 10 days at the Mets' spring training camp in St. Petersburg in 1967, Tom Seaver began to wonder why he had been so eager to join the New York club. Every ballplayer at the camp went through the motions of playing the game, all right, but no one seemed to take a serious view of what he was doing on the diamond. They joked and laughed in the clubhouse after the games about their bad baserunning, their lapses in the field, and their errors. It was one helluva good time for all.

Tom couldn't quite understand it. He was in the game to give it everything he could, and more. Even in the calisthenic drills, when everybody else was doing 25 pushups as ordered, Tom was doing 50. If he was supposed to run one lap around the field, he ran two. On rainy days when everyone was excused from the run, Tom was out there pumping his legs and loosening up his arm. He was throwing every morning and every afternoon to his catcher. He worked on his control, pitching to spots in and up to right-handed batters and low and tight to left-handers. He wasn't about to let up on a single minute of any day. He would take nothing for granted. Nothing and no one could alter his training grind.

Whatever morale the Mets had, it was infinitesimal. The Mets were losers. The Mets were a joke. That was the image that had been built around the club for years, and the sportswriters grew fat on that image. There wasn't a day when the Mets couldn't provide an amusing story for their next day's column.

Tom Seaver didn't fit that image, and never would. Maybe that was why Tom was all but ignored by the sportswriters covering the Mets camp and the games during the preseason in the Grapefruit League. They concentrated their stories on the Mets new centerfielder, Don Bosch.

All winter long, the sportswriters had pointed out his great fielding, his long-distance hitting, his great arm, and his speed on the bases. The front office had released a plethora of publicity about this phenom, whom the Mets brain trust had actually never seen in action. He was likened to Mickey Mantle and Willie Mays. He was going to electrify the entire league with his brilliance.

In appearance, Bosch was a short, chunky fellow, some five feet ten inches tall. He was 25 years old, but his hair was already gray with a spot of baldness here and there. He was jittery and nervous about all the publicity, and when he did appear and begin to play, he could do nothing right.

In fact, he misplayed very ordinary plays in the

field, and Westrum and the Mets front office people were appalled by his ineptness at the plate; once again the press had a field day.

Actually, the front office did very little to change the comedic image of the team. When Tom Seaver got down to St. Petersburg, the team he joined included a group of old-timers, all of whom had seen better days, and a number of young players who would not be major-league players for several years.

One veteran was Tommy Davis, brought over from the Dodgers. Tommy, a native Brooklynite and twice National League batting champ, had enjoyed nine tremendous years with the Dodgers, but had broken an ankle in 1965. Now handicapped by his bad ankle, he no longer had the speed and power he once possessed. Regardless, the Mets outfield consisted of Davis, Bosch, and Cleon Jones. Ron Swoboda and Ed Kranepool would platoon at first base, Jerry Grote was the regular catcher, and Ken Boyer, a Cardinal star for 11 years, was at third base. Bud Harrelson was the shortstop, and the pitching staff included Don Cardwell, Chuck Estrada, Ron Taylor, Ralph Terry, and Jerry Koosman, who had pitched at Auburn and had fanned 174 men in 170 innings.

Koosman's acquisition was truly unbelievable. Who but the Mets would act on a tip from Jack Luchese, one of their ushers at Shea Stadium? The usher's son, John Luchese, who caught for the Army team at Fort Bliss, Texas, wondered whether the Mets might be interested in the team's star pitcher, who had won 20 games, lost only three, and averaged 18 strikeouts a game. The Mets definitely were interested. They looked at Koosman, signed him, and packed him off to the minors in 1965, and in 1966 he won 12 games for the Auburn Mets. In 1968 Jerry registered shutouts in his first two appearances with the Mets and wound up the year with seven blankings of the opposition, winning 19 and posting a 2.08 earned run average.

Another acquisition to report to camp was left-handed outfielder Larry Stahl, who had once hit a home run that had traveled more than 500 feet. It was his one claim to fame. He had done nothing before he hit that homer, and nothing since.

To balance the oldsters, there were some youngsters with the Mets in 1967. And, in fairness to the front office, they included some talented ballplayers, such as Bud Harrelson, Tug McGraw, and Nolan Ryan. But, except for Bud Harrelson, they were still a year or two away from their potential. And they would all be protected from the devastating comic image the Mets had built themselves by the efforts of the rookie Tom Seaver.

The first time Tom went to the mound for the Mets, he demonstrated that he was of a different breed than the general run of the Mets ballplayers. The Mets were playing the Minnesota Twins in a Grapefruit League game in Orlando. He was brought into the game in the fourth inning, with two men out and a couple of men on the base paths. The man at the plate was Harmon Killebrew, one of the greatest sluggers in the game. That year, 1967, he would lead the American League with 44 home runs.

Tom took the ball from Wes Westrum, his manager, like a veteran. He got the catcher's signal, took his windup, and then whipped a fastball over the plate. Strike one! Another fastball and it was strike two! One more fastball. It exploded at the plate and Killebrew couldn't touch it, going down swinging.

He was still a kid, and his stomach must have been jumping, but no one in the ballpark would have known it. Like a veteran, the 21-year-old with the brains of a 35-year-old walked nonchalantly back to the dugout, as if striking out Harmon Killebrew was just an everyday chore.

He allowed the Twins just two hits in the three innings, striking out five batters as his fastball literally crackled on its way to the plate. Westrum had his young pitcher relieve in a few other Grapefruit League games and Seaver continued to impress with his performance.

A few days later, Wes started Seaver against Kansas City and Tom pitched five superb innings, giving up just one run, while striking out five of the Royals. Against the World Series champions, the Baltimore Orioles, Seaver pitched shutout ball for five innings in another impressive display. And suddenly Westrum began to think seriously of starting Tom in the opening game of the season.

He had second thoughts, though, when collared by several sportswriters who had heard rumors that Tom was to pitch the opener. Wes knew he would be criticized in the press for starting a raw rookie. He didn't want that.

"I'm starting Don Cardwell," he told the writers.

Don Cardwell had been a successful major league pitcher for 10 years with the Pirates, Phillies, and Cubs and knew the hitters. "Seaver will go in the second game," he added. "I don't want you sportswriters second-guessing me right off the bat."

"Who starts a rookie for the second game?" asked sportswriter Terry Shore. "Do you think that's smart?"

"Maybe," said Westrum. "I've got to admit he hasn't had much experience, but," he added, "he gets people out."

April 12 was the second day of the 1967 baseball schedule and, as Westrum had announced, Tom Seaver was going to start for the Mets. This was Tom's debut as a big league pitcher. It was a day he had often dreamed of and now it had come true, and he was all nerves as the great day dawned.

It was a cold day, a gray day, nothing to cheer him up. Tom, always on edge the day he was scheduled to pitch, had the jitters, and he had never had them so bad. As he recalls that April 12, he just nibbled away at the bacon and eggs that Nancy had set on the table for his breakfast. And after the skimpy meal, he kept pacing the floor of the small furnished apartment he and Nancy had rented in Bayside, Queens, just a hop, skip, and a jump from Shea Stadium. All he could think of was the tremendous power and speed of the Pittsburgh players he was to face that afternoon: the great Roberto Clemente, Maury Wills, Bill Mazeroski, slugging Willie Stargell, and Matty Alou. Clemente and Stargell were capable of breaking a pitcher's heart with a single swing of their great bats.

He went to the barber shop nearby; he always got his hair cut the day he was to pitch. "My head is cooler when I get a haircut," said Tom. Then it was a short drive to the Mets park.

For a few moments in the clubhouse, the joshing and horseplay of Bud Harrelson and the other Mets calmed him down. But the walk through the tunnel and the sights and sounds of the 20,000 noisy fans in the stands brought back the jitters once more.

Warming up in the bullpen, he was still nervous. The walk to the pitching mound did nothing to calm him. He began his warmup pitches to catcher Jerry Grote. He threw them quickly. Tom Seaver was always quick on the mound. He wasn't one of those pitchers who needed to psyche himself up for every pitch.

The first Pittsburgh Pirate, Donn Clendenon, came to bat. Tom impatiently watched Clendenon swing a couple of big bats, discard one, and amble to the plate. He stared at Don, remembering that Clendenon could hit with power.

It seemed like forever to Tom as the batter stretched his muscles and took a couple of practice swings before he got to the plate. But there he was at last, the first batter Seaver would face in his major-league career, looking right at him, his bat poised, menacing, ready to swing.

Tom bent toward the plate, took the signal from his catcher, wound up, and threw his first pitch in his first appearance as a full-fledged Met in a regulation National League game.

It was a fastball which sailed over the plate and in to Clendenon, a right-handed batter; a good pitch for a beautiful strike. It was the pitch that Tom Seaver needed to shake him out of his jitters. Confident now, no longer nervous about his job, he turned away from the batter, looked out to his outfield, and rubbed up the ball. He knew he had good stuff. All he had to do now was to concentrate, and concentrate he did. Clendenon popped out, Mazeroski struck out on three crackling fastballs, and Alou flied out.

In the second inning, the Mets bunched their hits and gave Tom a two-run lead. Sometimes a pitcher will let up a bit and lose his concentration when his club gives him an early lead, but a two-run advantage didn't count for too much, the way the Mets played ball, and Tom knew he couldn't let up, or lose any of his concentration if he was to bring in a winning game.

The Pirates got to Tom for a run in the third inning, and another in the fourth, tying the game at 2–2.

Tom began to pitch more carefully.

He had already thrown about 60 pitches, and he hadn't pitched more than five innings in any of the preseason games. He was beginning to tire. Still, he walked to the mound in the fifth frame, and got out of the inning without allowing the Pirates a run. But as he walked back to the Mets dugout, he knew he couldn't go on much longer. His arm was dead.

He could feel the strain in every muscle in his body as he started to throw in the sixth inning. His arms, chest, and legs ached with every pitch. He tried to concentrate and forget the soreness. He threw a fastball and Roberto Clemente slammed a sharp two-base hit into center field.

He could hardly breathe now. He'd had it for this day. He knew it, and so did his manager, Wes Westrum, who walked out to talk with him.

"You did fine, Tom," said Westrum, taking the ball. "You pitched a helluva game. Now take a shower."

He certainly had done a marvelous job. In his first outing as a major league pitcher, Tom held the slugging Pirates to but five hits and only two runs, while striking out nine of the hardest hitting sluggers in the league, all in just five innings.

Chuck Estrada came in to relieve Tom in the sixth, as Tom picked up his jacket in the dugout and walked to the clubhouse. In the clubhouse, Tom turned on the radio and listened to the rest of the game—listened as Estrada shut out the Pirates the remainder of the way, as the Mets scored a run in their half of the eighth inning to win the game, 3–2.

For the record, Chuck Estrada was the winning pitcher in that game, and as the players moved back into the clubhouse, Tom pushed through the crowd to grab hold of the veteran Estrada and shake his hand.

In the record books, the win against the Pirates would mean nothing for young Tom Seaver, but it was just like Tom to congratulate a pitcher on a fine performance, and that's what he did; that's what he would always do.

Tom's second game, on April 21, was against the Chicago Cubs, against hitters such as Ernie Banks, Ron Santo, Billy Williams, and Randy Hundley. Before the game Seaver went into conference with his catcher Jerry Grote, playing his second year with the New York Mets. They talked about the strengths and weaknesses of the Cubs roster, particularly those who were in the day's lineup. They decided that the best way to throw against the Chicago powerhouse was to keep the ball low and away, and the strategy worked—at least it worked in the first inning.

A low fastball got Billy Williams in that first inning, as he went down swinging for a strikeout.

Billy Williams threw away his bat in disgust.

"Damn," he said back in the Cubs dugout, "that kid's throwing hard out there. He brings it in. He brings it in."

In the third inning, a wiser Billy Williams waited

77

for his pitch and hammered Tom for a triple, sending home a man from first and giving the Cubs a 1–0 lead.

"It was a good pitch," said pitching coach Harvey Haddix when Tom got back to the dugout at the end of the inning. "He just got hold of it. It's going to happen again, and often enough. You throw a good pitch to a good hitter and he'll hammer it. Nothing you can do about it, kid," added Haddix. "Just keep your mind on the game, and concentrate on the next batter."

Tom listened, and he learned, and learned quickly. Billy Williams' hit had really upset him. He wasn't going to get upset again whatever the batter did at the plate, just so long as he knew he was pitching good ball.

Tommy Davis tied the game for the Mets with a home run in the fourth inning, then he put the Mets ahead in the sixth, sending two men home with a double. The Mets were leading 3–1 when Tom walked out to the mound for the eighth inning.

By that time his legs had become leaden. He was tired. He wasn't pushing off the mound the way he had in the earlier frames. His fastball had lost its hop. Glenn Beckert, not one of the most powerful hitters on the Cubs roster, hit one deep toward the left-field wall. Tom, dashing over to cover a possible relay to third base, saw Tommy Davis run, leap, and glove the line drive.

The crowd cheered the play, but Tom Seaver was just too tired to join in the acclaim for the veteran outfielder. Ken Boyer walked over from his position at third base to the mound to join him.

"How do you feel?" he asked Tom.

"Tired," said Tom, simply.

Ken Boyer did a double take. Most rookie pitchers, veterans too, always said that they felt great, even if they were collapsing on the mound. There were very few pitchers who liked to be taken out of the game, not even when staying in meant a game in the loss column for them.

It was Westrum who now came out to talk to Tom.

"How do you feel?"

"Pooped," said Tom.

That was the truth, and Tom never shied away from telling the truth. And he did want that 3–1 lead the Mets had to hold.

Wes Westrum sent his signal to the bullpen for Don Shaw to come in to relieve, and the Met fans gave Tom a hand as he moved back into the dugout.

"Way to go!" yelled the Met players in the dugout, slapping his back. "Good game, kid! Good game!"

The Mets were swinging that afternoon. They scored three more runs in the eighth and came off the field with an 8–1 victory. It was Tom Seaver's first victory in the major leagues.

Bud Harrelson was the first to congratulate him. He threw his arms around his roommate and gave him a big hug.

"That was a great game, roomie!" he yelled. "A great one!"

The writers came in, too. This was the first time they had taken the young pitcher seriously. Maybe they'd have something besides jokes about the fumbling, bumbling Mets.

"Congratulations," they said.

"Good stuff," they said.

"You certainly had it today," they said.

There would be many more days, countless days, when Tom Seaver would have it, and the sportswriters would be all over him for something to put in their papers.

Tom hurried out of the dressing room. Nancy was in the hall, waiting for him. She was an especially proud lady that afternoon; her Tom was a hero.

She kissed him. He kissed his pretty little wife. Arm in arm, they went out to celebrate with a festive Chinese meal at Tom and Nancy's favorite restaurant, Lum's, out on Northern Boulevard in Flushing, where Tom could also enjoy his favorite drink, a whiskey sour, with dinner. "The whiskey sour just seemed to taste better with a Chinese dinner," said Tom.

9
THE INTANGIBLES: CONCENTRATION AND DEDICATION

The Mets flew down to Atlanta. Tom was on the mound, pitching against the Braves, pitching against Hank Aaron. He turned his back to the plate, looked out into center field. This was one of his boyhood dreams. He couldn't tell how often he had fantasized this moment, Tom Seaver pitching against his boyhood idol. No one in baseball had captured his admiration and adoration as had this all-time great slugger, Hank Aaron.

He didn't have to look at the man who is the greatest home-run hitter in baseball, the man who surpassed the fantastic record held for so many years by the immortal Babe Ruth. Tom knew Aaron's stance by heart. He knew how he swung his bat. He knew every strength of the batter, and every weakness. At least, he thought he did.

"It was a dream world," he said later. "I wasn't sure it was actually happening. Hank Aaron at bat against me. Inside the big ball game was a little game between Henry Aaron and me, a game he knew nothing about."

There was a runner on first base when Hank stepped to the plate. Tom got set on the mound and he looked at the runner edging off the first-base bag.

"I've got to get Aaron to hit into a double play. Got to get the pitch in low and away. Get him to hit on the ground," he was thinking.

Seaver took his windup and whipped a half-speed pitch that was low and away, and Aaron took his big swing. He didn't get much of the ball, just enough to send it hopping down to Bud Harrelson at short. Bud grabbed the ball nicely, winged it to second base, and the second baseman whipped the ball to first. Double play.

Tom Seaver didn't even smile as he walked back to the dugout, but he was thrilled, exultant! He had met a supreme test he had set for himself and come out with flying colors.

Two innings later, Hank Aaron came up to hit for his second at bat.

"Curve him, inside and low," said Tom to himself. "That was the pitch I got him with the first time. I'll get him again."

Tom toed the rubber, looked down at Aaron, kicked his left foot high into the air, and came in with the pitch. It was down low and inside, perfectly thrown to Hank. This time Aaron wasn't fooled. He expected the rookie to come in with the same low curve, and he promptly met the ball with the fat part of his bat. The loud crack of the bat on ball told Tom the story, as the ball took off on a line some 400 feet away, up and over the fence for a home run.

"Hell," said Tom. "I guess I'll have to try to be smarter next time I pitch to Aaron."

The next day Tom was standing by the batting cage before the game started. Aaron walked by. "You've got a nice pitch, kid. Good fastball, nice curve," his boyhood idol said.

Tom grinned. He nodded his head, his tongue suddenly stuck in his mouth. He was, however, elated at the recognition.

He'd remember that pitch he threw to Hank Aaron, a low inside curveball. Tom remembered almost every pitch he ever threw. After a game, he'd spend his time going over all the pitches he had thrown and made notes in the little black book he kept on every hitter. He would study the book, memorize every note.

"I can remember every pitch I ever threw," he said. "Maybe I'll forget one or two, then I'll check the book. But I never forget the pitches that were crucial in the game. I just never forget those big pitches that give me a key strikeout or a double play. It's all down there in my black book. It's a permanent record for me of what I have done to every hitter I've faced—and, of course, what he's done to me."

One week later, Tom took the mound against the Los Angeles Dodgers and pitched the finest game a Mets pitcher had thrown in years, as he sent down the hard-hitting Dodgers with but five base hits and came away with a stunning 3 to 1 victory. It was the first win for the Mets in over a week and did much to bolster the team's sagging confidence.

On April 25, Tom faced the Chicago Cubs and once more performed brilliantly. He held the tough Cubs batters at bay for nine innings. The score was

83

tied 1–1 in the tenth when Tom came up to hit and calmly slugged the first pitch for a clean single. He raced to second on a sacrifice, went to third on a wild pitch, and then scored the winning run on a hit up the middle by the Mets leftfielder, Al Luplow. Tom's all-around play, plus his superb pitching, had aroused everybody on the team.

It didn't take long for the dormant Mets fans to discover their new hero, and to make noise about it. For a while, New York forgot its great idols of the past: DiMaggio, Mantle, Mays. Seaver was the big man in town. Everybody talked about Tom Seaver, in the Brooklyn bars, on the street, and in the playgrounds. Even the fellows down on Wall Street were talking about Tom Seaver.

Was Tom Seaver the man to finally lead the sorry Mets out of the doldrums and into the rarified atmosphere of a pennant contender?

He would do that in time, but 1967 was a little too early for that "impossible dream."

Two more fine pitching performances by Seaver and now the kids on the street were yelling, "Tom Seaver, Tom Seaver." Cab drivers and construction men too, and soon the entire town was beginning to sing the praises of their newest celebrity pitcher.

The Mets themselves were singing praises for the kid pitcher they now called "Soupy," not after the antics of comedian Soupy Sales, but for a super pitcher.

"There was an aura of defeatism about the team," said Tom a few years later, reviewing his earlier experience with the Mets, "a feeling of hell, let's get the game over with, we're not going anyplace anyway.

"But the team seemed to play a helluva lot better

when I pitched, but dammit, that wasn't right and I said so. I probably got a few people mad, but I went around and told the guys that if they played better while I was pitching, and not for somebody else, it was wrong as hell."

It was noticeable on the field. It was noticeable up in the stands. It was noticeable to Seaver, and so he went around the locker room to each and every player and told them all that if they could play that well behind him, they damn well could play the same way behind everybody else on the staff. And that if they didn't, they were cheating the team, the other pitchers, the fans, and themselves.

Talking to a group of the players, Seaver said, "I don't think you owe the world anything, and the world certainly doesn't owe you anything. The only thing the world owes you is the opportunity to use your God-given talents, and the only thing you owe the world, and yourself and your team is your very best effort every day out there. To take what talents you have," said Tom, "and to make the very best effort you can. The difference between the physical abilities of the players in the major leagues is not that great and, something going in hand with that, the difference between teams is not that great. So what it ultimately comes down to is the dividing factor between the player or team that wins and the one that loses—your *personal mental attitude*. The effort you give, the mental alertness that keeps you from making the mental mistakes. The concentration, the dedication, those are the intangibles, those are the deciding factors, I think, between who wins and who loses.

"I firmly believe that. I really do."

Bud Harrelson, Tom's best friend and roommate,

said, "You got to notice his concentration out there on the mound when he's pitching. And playing behind him, you try to match it. It is inspiring."

There was no doubt about it. The presence of Tom Seaver out on the pitching mound made the Mets a different team.

However, they weren't too much better, and by the end of June they were in their customary place in the league: last. Tom, however, continued to pitch and to win.

By the end of June he had collected eight wins against five defeats. There hadn't been a Mets pitcher in all its history who had won more than thirteen games in an entire season. Tom's performance was good enough for Walt Alston, manager of the Los Angeles Dodgers, to name him to the National League All-Star squad to face the American League All-Stars at Anaheim, California.

"I just can't believe it," said Tom Seaver.

He'd be playing on the same team with Clemente, Willie Mays, Orlando Cepeda, Hank Aaron, Johnny Bench, Lou Brock, Pete Rose, and the like; plus pitchers such as Don Drysdale and Ferguson Jenkins.

"I can't believe that just a year and a half ago," said Tom, "I was sitting back in California just dreaming about playing in the major leagues. Now I'm here thinking how I'm going to pitch to guys like Mickey Mantle."

But it was true enough, no dream, and with Nancy he was off to Anaheim for more wonderful experiences.

Tom intentionally arrived at Anaheim Stadium four hours early. He wanted to see and meet some of his heroes.

He walked into the locker room and there was Lou Brock of the St. Louis Cardinals, tying his shoelaces.

Lou Brock looked up at the youngster, a round-faced young fellow who didn't look any older than a teenager.

"Can you get me a Coke, kid?" he asked.

Brock assumed that the "kid" was a clubhouse boy.

"Sure," said Tom. He was too full of awe to let Brock know that he wasn't one of the clubhouse working hands.

He got Brock the Coke, then thrust out his hand, and finally said, "I'm Tom Seaver, a pitcher for the New York Mets."

Brock looked at the kid. It was his turn to be embarrassed. But the embarrassment didn't last too long.

"Hi!" Brock said, shaking Tom's hand, then roared with laughter; they both roared with laughter.

Out on the field, near the batting cage, his boyhood idol Sandy Koufax was standing around observing the scene. Tom moved over, edging toward Sandy. He was eager to get to know Sandy better and to be able to discuss pitching with the great star.

A ball rolled out of the cage near Koufax. Tom ran to retrieve it. Actually, he wanted to get close enough to say hello.

But it was Koufax who said hello.

"Hello, Tom. Nice to see you. Hearing some fine things about you."

Tom was flabbergasted. The great Sandy Koufax actually knew who he was. Knew something about him. Tom stopped short and for the next 15 minutes talked baseball with Sandy. It was a moment that Tom would never forget.

Back in the clubhouse, Sandy came in to say hello to some of the players he knew, then sat down with Tom, and they again talked pitching strategy—just Tom and his hero.

"Being with Koufax was my second-greatest thrill of that unbelievable day," said Seaver. "The greatest thrill would come later, out on the field."

As the game started, Tom walked out to the bullpen along with the other star National League pitchers. With the All-Star quality of pitching that Walt Alston had brought out to Anaheim, Tom wasn't expecting to pitch for the National League All-Stars. It was exciting enough for him just to be in their company. But events would change that, too.

It was a close game. The ninth inning came to an end with the Nationals and the Americans in a 1–1 tie. It continued at 1–1 through the thirteenth inning. In the fourteenth inning, Walter Alston signaled Tom Seaver to start warming up.

Tom took off his jacket, but with Don Drysdale pitching, he continued to doubt that he would get into the game.

Nothing for either squad in the fourteenth. It was still 1–1 when Tony Perez came to bat in the top of the fifteenth inning. But Tony got hold of a fastball and sent it into the seats for a home run. The National League led 2–1.

Don Drysdale had been taken out for a pinch hitter in the fifteenth. Tom had begun to warm up in earnest in the bullpen. And now he was being called in from the bullpen to protect the one-run lead in the bottom of the fifteenth.

He picked up his jacket and began the long walk to the mound. The stands were jammed with thousands of fans. There were millions watching the game on their television screens. Tom knew it, and felt as if he were dreaming as he walked across the field, his knees suddenly weak and quivering. He began to wonder whether he could make it to the mound.

He walked past Roberto Clemente and hoped Clemente wouldn't notice how nervous he was.

"Let's get three and go home," Seaver said, with as much bravado as he could muster.

Clemente grinned. He knew just how nervous the young pitcher was.

"That's right," he yelled back at Tom. "Go get him, keed!"

Pete Rose was standing around second base as Tom approached him.

"How about you pitching and me playing second base?" said Tom.

"No," said Rose, grinning. "I'll stay where I am. You can do it, kid! You can do it!"

Seaver was still nervous as he continued his warm-up pitches to his catcher, Tim McCarver.

The infield tossed the ball around, after Tom had warmed up, and it was third baseman Tony Perez who flipped the ball to him.

Tom looked around. There were Roberto Clemente and Willie Mays and Hank Aaron in the outfield. Cepeda, Rose, Gene Alley, and Perez were his infield. What a drastic difference from what Seaver had become used to with the Mets! How could anyone ask for better support?

"Imagine turning around and seeing all those great players behind you," said Tom. "That was the greatest thrill I got that day, and one of the great thrills in my life."

He looked toward the bench and saw Alston, his arms crossed, as calm as anyone could be.

"If the manager had that much confidence in me," Tom said. "How could I have any less?"

There was a powerhouse of American Leaguers due up at the plate in that fifteenth inning: the Red Sox Tony Conigliaro; the man who would win the Most Valuable Player for the year, Carl Yastrzemski; Bill Freehan; and, if anyone got on, Ken Barry. Tom settled down to his task and, as always once he started to pitch, the butterflies flew out of his stomach and he could and did give all his concentration to the job at hand.

He whipped a low fastball to Tony Conigliaro, and the Red Sox star hit an easy fly ball to Clemente.

Tom pitched carefuly to Carl Yastrzemski, trying for the inside or outside corner. But Yaz waited for a good pitch that never came and he walked to first base after four pitches.

Seaver wasn't troubled. Yaz was a left-hander. Freehan and Berry swung from the right side of the plate. Tom kept his eye on Yaz on first and didn't allow him to get far off the bag, and then got Bill Freehan on a weak pop to Willie Mays in center.

The count on Berry went to two strikes and two balls. Tom whipped in his sailing fastball. Berry swung for the fences but missed the pitch by a wide margin.

"Strike three!" barked the umpire behind the plate and the game was over.

Tim McCarver, Ernie Banks, Gene Alley, and Tony Perez rushed to the mound to shake the hand of the rookie pitcher. At the dugout, Mays, Clemente, Rose, and Aaron all slapped him on the back.

"Great job, kid!"

"Great job, keed!"

Tim McCarver handed the ball to Tom—the game ball. Tom saw Don Drysdale. He was the pitcher of record when Tony Perez had slammed the home run to give the National League All-Stars the leading and eventually winning run in the fifteenth inning.

"Here," said Tom to Drysdale, handing him the ball. "You get the ball. You're the winning pitcher."

"No, you keep it," said Drysdale generously.

"You take it," came back Tom. "You won the game."

It was a proud moment for the ace Los Angeles pitcher. It was a prouder moment for the rookie pitcher of the New York Mets.

When Tom Seaver returned to New York after the All-Star game, full of the excitement that the big game engenders, he was more than ever determined to pull the Mets out of the doldrums and infuse the players with the desire and will to win. He tried in every way he could think of to needle the others on the team, to get them to go all out every minute of every game. He wanted them to despise losing and to think win—win—win.

He did win the next two games he pitched for the Mets, hiking his won-lost record to 12 and 8, but the Mets were still mired in tenth place at the bottom of the league's standings. How can I goad the team into refusing defeat, into hating it? Tom asked himself. He was depressed by defeat. He just couldn't understand how his teammates could go down to defeat day after day and just take it, as if that were the normal thing to do.

"Gentlemen," he announced one afternoon, getting up on a stool in the locker room after the team had fumbled and bumbled still another game away to the Pittsburgh Pirates. "Gentlemen, after watching you perform in the field today, I would like to take this opportunity to announce my retirement from the game of baseball."

That didn't get more than a shrug and a laugh from his teammates.

The Mets kept losing.

After another inept performance and another loss, he grabbed a bunch of spiders that were clustered in the corner of the dugout and threw them at his teammates. He thought that would shake the players, put some spirit into them. There was a lot of jumping and hollering, and a lot of laughing, too. The bench suddenly was alive, but that was all. The Mets kept losing.

But eventually some of his spirit did rub off on the club. When he made an error in the field, Tom could not forgive himself, and his teammates couldn't help but see that.

"Everyone makes mistakes," someone in the clubhouse said.

"That's no excuse," said Tom. "I'm wearing a big league uniform. I've got to play like a big leaguer."

A lot of the players in the Mets uniform weren't playing big league ball. They knew it. They began to think of their own errors, their own lapses on the field, the difference that a win or a loss meant to their own self-image and the image of the ball club.

One night after a game against the Cubs, Tom noticed a change in the attitude of some of the players. It was a tense, exciting game. Any game against the Cubs was tough. Bud Harrelson had allowed a routine ground ball to scoot through his legs in the bottom of the ninth, and the Cubs tied the game 1–1.

In the tenth inning, Tom led off with a single and Cleon Jones sacrificed him to second. A wild pitch allowed Tom to move on to third, and a single by Al Luplow sent him home.

Tom cut down the Cubs in the bottom of the tenth and the Mets had a 2–1 win, but Bud Harrelson, after congratulating Tom on his victory, just sat down on a stool in the clubhouse after the game, covering his face with his hands, and looking terribly disturbed.

"What's up, Buddy?" asked Tom of his pal and roommate. Seaver and Harrelson roomed together for years. "What's got you?"

"I shouldn't have let that ball get away from me. I shouldn't have booted that ball. I cost you a shutout! We might have lost that game!"

This was something new in the Mets clubhouse. Now, for the first time, there was no joking and laughing about an error. Winning the game had suddenly become important to the Mets. The players were serious; they just walked around the clubhouse, dressed quietly, spoke almost in whispers. There were no jokes, no horsing around.

Tom observed the scene thoughtfully. He couldn't quite believe what he was seeing.

"For the first time," he said later, "the boys in the clubhouse realized that we had players who cared deeply whether we achieved, that we even had pitchers who could hit occasionally and who wanted desperately to win. Looking back, I think it was the first time in my experience with the Mets that we believed in each other, the first time I felt I wasn't here to lose."

No, Tom Seaver was not with the Mets to lose.

On September 13, 1967, he won his fourteenth game, a sensational four-hitter against the powerful Atlanta Braves, holding the Braves hitless for five innings. Tom struck out eight batters and came away with a 2–1 triumph, thereby becoming the winningest Mets pitcher in history.

On September 17, Seaver handcuffed the strong Dodgers, allowing the L.A. club but eight base hits, all singles, as he helped the Mets snap a seven-game losing streak, beating the Dodgers 7–2. It was victory number 15 for Tom.

On September 23, Seaver turned in the finest performance of the season as he yielded only three hits, fanned eight, and beat the Houston Astros 1–0 in a thriller of a game.

On September 25, the Mets had a new manager, Salty Parker, a Mets coach who took over for Wes Westrum.

Aside from his handling of Tom Seaver, Westrum had done little that was positive. With the Mets languishing in last place, some 12 games behind the ninth-place Astros and some 40 games behind the league-leading Cardinals, Westrum handed in his resignation.

"Previously and honestly," said Westrum, "I came to the conclusion that the strain of waiting for a new contract, which never came, had become increasingly severe, and that maybe the whole thing had developed into a blessing for me."

Parker handled the Mets in their final eleven games of the season and they finished disastrously, with a 61–101 record, some five and a half games behind their 1966 pace.

As the long, dismal season tailed down, Tom began to work on his curveball. He figured that he had been relying too much on his fastball and his slider. He was trying to blow the ball past the hitters, but there would come a day, soon, when he would have to set up batters with his fastball, then come in with a sharp-breaking hook to keep them off balance. He never let up on himself. He was always busy studying new pitches, new methods, new strategy. He had to become the finest pitcher in baseball.

He set new records for the Mets in four different categories. By the end of the season he had won 16 games while losing 13, and had recorded an ERA of 2.76. He had pitched in eight complete games and recorded 170 strikeouts. In all, Seaver accounted for over one-fourth of all the Mets victories in 1967.

"I feel I've become a better pitcher," he said to reporters, answering the questions they kept peppering him with now. "I'm not trying to throw the ball past the hitter as much as I did in the beginning of the year."

Harvey Haddix, the Mets pitching coach, said, "Yeah, I've helped him a bit. But he's the sort of kid that doesn't need much help. I just watch him, make a suggestion once in a while and he takes it from there. He's easy to work with and very quick to learn. He knows just how to use his pitching strength against a hitter's weakness. He's a helluva kid and is going to be one of the great ones."

Despite the Mets finishing in the cellar again, Tom had established a remarkable record for himself. If he had been pitching for almost any other club in the league, he would easily have been a 20-game winner.

The newspapermen voted Tom the Rookie of the Year for 1967. It is an honor every rookie who has ever played in the big leagues dreams of. Tom Seaver had earned it, and earned it brilliantly.

"I don't want to see you anywhere near the beer cooler after the game," Lou Brock had said to young Tom at the All-Star game, after Tom had told him that he was 22 years old, old enough to drink beer.

There'd been a lot of beer since, and whiskey sours, and now champagne to celebrate that coveted Rookie of the Year Award.

It was Tom Seaver's first award in baseball, outside the letters he had won pitching for Fresno City College and the University of Southern California. It certainly wasn't going to be his last.

10
1968 AND GIL HODGES

In 1968, the Mets had a new manager, Gil Hodges. Hodges was something of a living legend in New York. He had been the star first-baseman for the Brooklyn Dodgers and then had moved west with the Dodgers. He had been one of the original Mets when the New York club became one of the expansion teams in 1962 and played their games in the Polo Grounds, the home of the old New York Giants. He lived in Brooklyn with his wife, Joan, a native New Yorker, and his four children. Even when he was managing the Washington Senators of the American League from 1963 to 1967, his home base was Brooklyn, where he ran a bowling alley and an automobile agency and was a quiet and friendly neighbor.

When a baseball club is a loser, the manager is fired. It isn't a baseball law, but it's the common practice. It doesn't matter what kind of team the front office has put together, if the team continues to lose year after year, the manager is fired. Before the end of the 1967 baseball season, Wes Westrum, the unassuming ex–New York Giant catcher, who was seemingly without an ego and was uncomfortable in the limelight, was out as the Mets manager and Gil Hodges was in.

Hodges had proven that he had a unique ability to handle young and inexperienced ballplayers, and that was exactly what he had in the Mets. He was a man with old-fashioned beliefs but up-to-date mannerisms—a father-figure type. With his broad shoulders, massive arms, and big hands he made a strong physical impression, but he was soft-spoken, clear-cut, and decisive. He communicated, by action much more than by words, that if you didn't execute properly, you didn't play, and it didn't matter who you were or what your past record showed. When a player had to be reprimanded, it was done quietly, without causing the player any embarrassment. Hodges laid down the rules for his players and expected them to be followed to the letter. He was quick to punish for any infraction of these rules, and he was uncompromising about the behavior of his players on or off the field.

Within hours after the Mets arrived at camp in the spring of 1968, and after thoroughly studying and reviewing the roster with his coaches, Hodges had the Mets standing tall: curfews were to be strictly enforced, jackets and ties were to be worn on all road trips. For all his sternness, however, Hodges was a pleasant man who appreciated that life and baseball in general must be fun. And—most important for a young ball club—Gil was a positive

thinker: "You have to think you can win," he said.
And though he was a realist about everything about
him, he was an optimist. The Mets new manager
was not a loser, and he stressed the point at every
clubhouse meeting with his coaches and players.

Mindful of the team's conspicuous weaknesses,
Gil stressed basics by the hour—day after day, hour
after hour—pickoff plays, cutoffs, double plays—
until the player had them down pat. "In prior days,"
said St. Louis manager Red Schoendienst, "you
could always expect the Mets to give you a few runs
in every game by doing dumb things. Suddenly they
were making plays during spring practice, like
professionals."

Said Hodges, "My main goal was to change the
notion that everything the Mets did was wrong. I
wanted them to do things right."

Back in Fresno, California, just before the Mets
assembled for the 1968 spring training season, Tom
Seaver was having the time of his life, reaping in all
the good fortune that had come with his marvelous
rookie year and his selection as Rookie of the Year
in 1967.

Early in January, his hometown honored him by
appointing him "Mayor for the Day." Together with
Nancy, he appeared at the Fresno City Hall and at
the City Council meeting place, and every council-
man in the house rose to his feet and applauded the
hometown hero.

There was the speech of thanks that Tom delivered to the councilmen and more applause, and the
exit with everybody grabbing his hand to shake it,
and congratulating him again on his great year.

"After which," said Tom later, recounting the very

pleasant experience, "I did what every politician does. I double-parked and went out to play golf."

Dave Anderson of *The New York Times* called cross-country that afternoon. He wanted a story from the Rookie of the Year.

"What did you learn most in your rookie year?" asked the newspaperman.

"I learned," said Tom, "that a major-league hitter capitalizes on every mistake a pitcher makes.

"I've got to cut down on my mistakes," he added. "Nineteen of my mistakes went over the fence for 19 home runs."

Anderson, in his column on Tom Seaver, pointed to the fact that Tom had lost four games by one run, and that in two of his other losses the Mets had been shut out.

Still, in January of 1968, Johnny Murphy, general manager of the Mets, flew out to California to talk contract with the young pitcher. He had to cool his heels for some three hours waiting for Tom, who was in his journalism class at the University of Southern California.

There wasn't too much to talk about when Tom and Murphy finally got together. The general manager offered Seaver the then magnificent sum of $24,000 for his services for 1968, and that was just about twice as much as Tom got in his rookie year. It was a good offer, as Tom Seaver saw it, and he signed on the dotted line right then and there.

"I got what I wanted," said Tom. "If I had gotten more, it wouldn't have been fair to the club."

There aren't many ballplayers, or any other people signing any other kind of contract, who would make a statement like that. Tom knew his value to the Mets, and like the rest of us he liked making money, but he always had a rational understanding of fair play, and fair pay.

In February, he was in New York for the New York baseball writers' annual dinner. Buddy Harrelson, his road roommate, was there too, and all they could talk about was Gil Hodges and what he might mean for the Mets. They were both already itching to get down to spring training.

It was going to be a different ball club in 1968. Actually, it was going to be a better ball club, but not as good, unfortunately, as Tom and Harrelson thought while gabbing away at the writers' dinner. The potential would be there, but it would be some time in the future, not in 1968, before that potential was going to mean anything in the league standings.

Ed Charles, the literate, well-traveled, ten-year veteran of several major-league clubs, would be back at third base. Ed Kranepool, the original Mets youngster and now a five-year veteran, would be perched at first base. Ken Boswell and Al Weis would share time at second, and Buddy Harrelson, who according to his best friend, Tom Seaver, was the finest shortstop in the league, would be back at his old post.

In the outfield, the Mets had the moody, muscular Ron Swoboda, Art Shamsky, Cleon Jones, and Mike Jorgensen. The most promising acquisition of 1968, however, was Tommie Agee, the youngster who had been Rookie of the Year in 1966, while playing with the Chicago White Sox. Tommy hit .273 for the Sox, including 22 home runs, and proved his worth on the bases by stealing 44. But in 1967, Agee slumped to a .234 batting average and was promptly traded with Al Weis to the Mets for Tommy Davis and three other players.

Nolan Ryan and Jerry Koosman, two very promising young pitchers, were brought up from the Mets farm team. Koosman, playing for Jacksonville, had struck out 183 batters in 1967. Cocky, brash Dick Selma, after a good season at Jacksonville, was also brought up to the team.

The holdover pitchers included Cal Koonce, Don Cardwell, little Al Jackson, Jim McAndrew, and that amateur barber, dog-lover, and outspoken free spirit, Tug McGraw, who had shown a world of promise, but was as wild as a march hare. Jerry Grote was a fine all-around catcher. A hard-nosed, aggressive, take-charge player, he could fire up and handle the younger pitchers. It was a young squad. Actually, the whole New York club was a young club. Ed Charles, Al Jackson, and Don Cardwell were over 30, but most of the others had yet to celebrate their twenty-fifth birthday. Of course, young players are more prone to make mistakes, especially mental mistakes.

"The team that wins is the team that makes the fewest mental mistakes," said Gil Hodges.

The Mets were going to make a lot of mental mistakes in 1968. For all their potential, they were winners of only 9 games in 27 during spring training. It was a sad omen of things to come.

With Juan Marichal pitching for the Giants in the opening game of the 1968 season against the Mets, at Candlestick Park, Hodges decided that Tom Seaver would oppose the Giants star. He would use Buddy Harrelson as the lead-off hitter, playing shortstop. Ken Boswell, who looked good, would play second base. Tommie Agee, in the number three batting position, would be in center field. Ron Swoboda, the clean-up hitter, would play in right field. Eddie Kranepool would be at first base, Art Shamsky would play left field instead of Cleon Jones, J. C. Martin would catch Seaver, and Ed Charles would bat in the eighth spot and would play third base.

Hodges' judgment was good. In the first inning Swoboda slapped a sharp single to center that scored Tommie Agee, who was on second base. It was the first Mets run of the 1968 season. In the third inning Ken Boswell and Agee singled in rapid succession and Swoboda made Hodges' decision to start him look positively brilliant, as Ron slammed a three-run homer to give the Mets a 4–0 lead.

Seaver pitched an outstanding game for eight and two-thirds innings and had a comfortable 4–2 lead. Tom had allowed the hard-hitting Giants just seven base hits and had struck out three hitters. In the ninth inning Marichal was out of the game for a pinch hitter, and Tom needed just three outs for a brilliant victory. But victory was not to be for the Mets.

Willie Mays lined a sharp single off Ed Charles's glove at third base. Ed dived for the ball and got his gloved hand on it, but by that time fleet-footed Willie Mays was on first base. Dangerous Willie McCovey, who had homered in the fifth, flied out.

But a passed ball moved Willie Mays to second base. A foul tip broke catcher Martin's finger and Jerry Grote replaced him. Jim Hart's single brought in Mays and now the score was 4–3 Mets.

Hodges walked to the mound, asked Tom how he

felt. "I'm dog-tired. My legs are tired," said Tom. Hodges beckoned to the bullpen and waved in Danny Frisella. Danny couldn't hold the Giants. Nate Oliver, a recent acquisition from the Dodgers, was the batter, and Oliver slapped Frisella's first pitch for a clean single. Jay Alou doubled into the left-field corner and the tying run was in. But Oliver saw that Jones was having trouble with Alou's hit and came all the way home from second base for the winning run. The Giants had the game 5–4, and the Mets had lost an opening-day game, for the sixth straight year.

In his next effort Seaver was almost perfect, tossing 10 scoreless innings against the Houston Astros, and allowing the aggressive Houston club but two base hits. Tom gave the Astros one hit during the first 9 innings, struck out four, and did not issue a base on balls. In the 10th inning, tiring badly, Seaver allowed another hit and Gil Hodges then brought in Ron Taylor to end the inning. The Astros and Mets matched scoreless innings for what seemed like an eternity—through 24 innings and some six hours in a game that went down in the record books as the longest night game in history.

The contest was highlighted by Seaver's magnificent pitching. There were moments of humor, drama, and frustration, but most of all it was a nightmare for the Mets' Al Weis. Weis, a utility infielder filling in for the injured Bud Harrelson at shortstop, let a bases-loaded grounder go through his legs, allowing Norm Miller of the Astros to score in the twenty-fourth inning to give the Astros a 1–0 victory.

Tom's first triumph of the season came against the L.A. Dodgers a week later. He sent the doughty

Dodgers down with just seven hits, while striking out 12 to record a spectacular win, 3–2.

In the clubhouse after the game, Tom took a chaw of tobacco to relax. It was Dick Selma who, when they were both at Fresno High School, had introduced him to the delights of chewing tobacco.

"It'll relax you. Make you feel better," said Selma.

Perhaps it did and then perhaps it didn't. Tom didn't take to the habit that is so common among ballplayers.

"The tobacco in my mouth gets in the way of my concentration," said Tom. He chewed gum instead.

Chewing gum was more consistent with the image Tom Seaver had created for himself and the fans. He was the All-American Boy, the youngster with the cherubic face and the ready smile, and Tom liked it that way. He was the wholesome kid who made good. But sometimes Tom tried to let people know there was a real flesh and blood person who ate, drank, and pulled on a pair of pants like everyone else.

Actually, Tom did like to chew tobacco. He liked his beer and his whiskey sour. He could swear and his mouth could be as foul as the next fellow's on occasion, many occasions.

"I was never entirely a choirboy," he said.

But he did wear a St. Christopher medal almost all the time, especially when he pitched. There was a time in Atlanta when, walking to the mound, he clutched for it and it wasn't there, and he just about panicked.

"I can't pitch without that medal!" he yelled, scrambling back into the dugout. "Who's seen my medal?"

Buddy Harrelson saved the day. He was walking

through the tunnel into the dugout, holding up the medal on its chain.

"You left it back in the room," said Harrelson.

"Thanks," said Tom.

He put the medal around his neck, walked back to the mound, and beat the Atlanta braves 2–1.

"I don't know whether it's lucky for Tom or not," said Buddy Harrelson. "But if Tom thinks it is, then it is."

By the All-Star break, Tom had won 10 games for the Mets. Along with Jerry Koosman and Jerry Grote this time, he was selected to play in the All-Star game for the second time in two years.

He pitched two innings in that game in the Houston, Texas, Astrodome, the seventh and eighth, and gave the fans a demonstration of his fastball, his curve, and his slider. He gave them a demonstration of his confidence as well.

The first man to bat against Tom in the sixth inning of the All-Star game was Mickey Mantle.

"Did you ever think you'd pitch against Mickey Mantle in an All-Star game?"

"Never," grinned Tom. "Never."

He knew Mickey had slowed down at the plate, that he couldn't bring his bat around as fast as he used to. There were lots of fans in the stands that day who, sentimentally, wanted to see the great Mantle hit one out of the park just one more time, but Tom would have none of it.

"You've got to know your batter," he said. "You've got to know his weakness; and you've got to pitch to it."

With three fastballs, Tom Seaver struck out the mighty Mickey Mantle. A lot of the fans may not have liked it, but Tom Seaver liked it very much.

He struck out Carl Yastrzemski, too, in his two-inning stint on the mound that afternoon, plus Joe Azcue, Boog Powell, and Rick Monday. In all, Tom Seaver struck out five of the finest hitters in the American League. It was a major achievement that had all of baseball talking about the young phenomenon. It was a marvelous period for Seaver in 1968, but it did not last very long.

When the regular schedule was resumed, Dick Selma beat the Cubs 1-0 in a fine exhibition of pitching. Then there was a 2-0 loss to the Cubs, a win by Koosman 4-0 over Chicago, a 2-1 loss to the Cubbies, and then a harrowing six-game losing streak, the longest of the season.

The Mets were now in eighth place, but only three and a half games out of second in a very tight race. Maybe they could finish above .500, maybe even in the first division?

Throughout the first 69 games, when the Mets were the talk of the league with their fine pitching staff, no one mentioned the hitters, perhaps because there wasn't anything much to talk about. The pitchers—Seaver, Koosman, Selma, and Ryan—were pitching beautifully, but as July lengthened into August the young lions on the pitching staff began to weaken, and the lack of hitting became more pronounced. It was obvious, as the team began to sag, that the pitchers had carried the club this far. If they could not carry it farther, a long, hot, and disappointing summer lay ahead.

Seaver was sensational as he won five straight games in July, then lost a heartbreaker to the Astros. He was pitching a brilliant game, beating them 1-0 in the ninth inning. Then he threw a slider to Jim Wynn. The pitch seemed to hang in midair, right across the heart of the plate, and Wynn slammed the ball over the center-field fence to tie the game 1 to 1. In the twelfth inning, visibly tiring, Tom gave up two straight hits to give the Astros a 3–1 win. It was a tough loss to swallow—for Tom and the team.

That might have turned out to be one of the worst nights of the season for Seaver. He was dog-tired when he went to bed, but try as he might, he couldn't sleep a wink. Over and over, he relived that pitch to Wynn. Now he was on the mound, winding up, and there was the pitch, right there across the plate, and then Wynn was hammering the ball up, up, and out of the park. The pitch kept haunting him, hour after hour, as he tossed and spun in his bed. He felt tired and drawn for three days.

He felt a great deal better when he shut out the Pirates with a great effort, allowing them but seven hits in a 3–2 win. After the game, Hodges told a group of sportswriters, "Seaver is a Whitey Ford; younger, but he has more stuff than Ford."

Tom was thrilled after he saw Hodges' comments in the papers. He idolized his manager and was happy to know Gil thought that much of him, but later he calmly told teammate Bud Harrelson and the reporters who asked him to comment, "I think it's much too early in my career for any such comparisons. Wait until I've been around as long as Whitey, and have been as consistent as someone like Sandy Koufax or Don Drysdale."

By the first week in September the Mets were 26 games behind the first-place Cardinals. The Mets' record was now 63–78, and with only 21 games left to play, the sportswriters were now saying they doubted the team would reach Hodges' goal of 70 victories. Even if they did win 70 games, they would finish in tenth place and that would be no better than Westrum's finish in 1967.

On August 29 the Mets faced the first-place Cardinals in a game that attracted a crowd of more than 35,000 fans. It was a huge turnout for a midweek game. No doubt the fans were anxious to see the Cardinals and their stars: Lou Brock, one of the great base stealers, the slugging Roger Maris, Orlando Cepeda, and Tim McCarver.

Tom Seaver took the mound for the Mets. He was opposed by the Cardinals' ace, Nelson Briles, winner of 18 games. Seaver, with a 13–9 record, started off by quickly retiring Brock, Curt Flood, and Roger Maris in the first inning, and Briles retired the first three Mets, Harrelson, Boswell, and Stahl, in rapid order. The Mets scored in the second inning to take a 1–0 lead as Seaver took care of the next three Cardinal batters, Tim McCarver, Mike Shannon, and Julian Javier, via strikeouts. In the third, Seaver took care of Phil Gagliano, Johnny Edwards, and Briles, and the game settled down to a splendid pitching duel between Briles and Seaver.

Inning after inning, Seaver would kick his left leg high, pivot sharply on his right, and bring in his fastball for a strike. Then the low, tantalizing curveball, then the slider as he cunningly outsmarted one Cardinal hitter after another, and now the crowd was up on its feet, screaming and cheering for Seaver and the Mets as the game continued, inning after inning.

By the fifth inning Seaver had struck out 7 batters and had not allowed a hit, setting down 15 Cards in order. It looked as if Tom Seaver was on his way to a no-hit game, and the fans were cheering like mad. In the Mets' half of the fifth inning, Grote singled, Seaver dropped a perfect bunt down the third-base line, reaching first base safely to fill the bases. Art Shamsky slugged Briles's first pitch for a grand-slam home run, and before the inning ended the Mets had piled up six runs.

Tom took care of the three Cardinal batters in the seventh inning, two via the strikeout route, and now he was striding off the mound just two innings away from a perfect game.

Up in the stands Nancy Seaver sat with the rest of the Mets wives and was as thrilled as any of the fans jumping up and screaming. Nancy wasn't doing much screaming; she just glowed inwardly—it was so exciting to see her husband and watch him pitch with such effortless form. It was so beautiful, it hurt. Several times when Tom came out to the on-deck circle to hit, he'd glanced at her and tipped his cap. She smiled back and waved her Mets hat back at him. She was thrilled for Tom and for the team.

Now Tom was on the mound in the eighth inning. He was just six outs away from a pitcher's dream game. And he knew it. He had retired 21 Cards in a row, and the fans were screaming for more strike-outs as the dangerous Orlando Cepeda stepped in to hit.

"Got to be careful with this guy," Tom said to himself as he set to pitch. A ball—a strike—another ball—another ball.

"I'm getting too careful," thought Tom. "Can't walk him. Got to come in with my slider now." Tom got ready, pumped, threw the slider in low, and saw the ball sink. Cepeda lashed into the pitch with a tremendous *thwock* and Tom, turning, saw the ball heading high out toward the center-field fence between Swoboda and Tommie Agee. As the two players raced for the ball, it hit the fence, bounced back to Agee, and Cepeda was safely on second base for a clean two-base hit, spoiling the perfect game bid.

Tom shrugged his shoulders, took a deep breath, looked around in Nancy's direction, tipped his cap, then set for the next hitter.

"It was a good pitch," he said to himself, "a helluva pitch. But what the hell. I'll get him next time."

An inning later Tom trudged off the field with a three-hit, 8–2 victory over the Cardinals. He had struck out 11 and had not walked anyone. It had been one of the finest pitching performances of the season by any National League pitcher, and Tom was delighted with his performance and the team's.

"I really thought I had that no-hitter," he said to the reporters in the clubhouse. "Someday I'll have that perfect game."

The Mets couldn't do better than win 73 games while losing 89 in 1968. Although it was the best won-lost record they had compiled in all their seven years in the league, they couldn't finish higher than ninth in the league standings, one notch above tenth-place Houston.

As a team, the Mets had hit only .228, the lowest in the National League. They had managed an average of fewer than three runs a game.

"Hell," said Tom in disgust, "you have to pitch a shutout to win."

Tom Seaver had pitched five shutouts during the season and had struck out 205. At one point in the season Tom had collected only two wins in 11 starts:

he had had a remarkable 1.91 earned-run average, but all the Mets could do was produce 19 runs in all those 11 games. At the end of the season, Tom had put together an exceptional record for a ninth-place team. He won 16 games and lost 12, with an earned-run average of 2.20.

"If only we got a little hitting," said Tom.

The hitting would come, along with other great feats, next year, in 1969, with the heroics and the glories of the 1969 Miracle Mets.

II
"YOU GOTTA BELIEVE!"

"During the training camp period in the spring of 1969," said Seaver, "Buddy Harrelson, Grote, Nolan Ryan, and I often went fishing at night. We went fishing for silver trout off one of the causeways in St. Petersburg, Florida. We brought along coffee and beer and doughnuts, and while we fished we talked about everything, of course, baseball too."

" 'You know,' said Harrelson, 'we could win our division if we play up to our potential.'

"None of us disagreed.

"We didn't talk that way too loudly, because we knew that if certain New York sportswriters heard us they'd scoff, and if the average baseball fan heard us he'd ignore us. Because they had already decided that the odds of the Mets winning the division title were one hundred to one.

"But our own fans," said Seaver, "and just about everyone on our ball club didn't care if the writers

113

and the other fans scoffed at us. We really felt we could win.

"Realistically we knew that, man for man, the Cards, the defending champions, had a stronger team. But beyond that we conceded nothing to the teams in our division. We didn't think the Cubs could beat us, or the Pirates. We thought we were better than the Phillies and certainly better than the Montreal Expos.

"Most of the guys had a philosophy similar to mine," said Tom, "Maybe they didn't all articulate it, maybe they didn't all dwell on it, but down deep, they shared my attitude. I wanted to be the very best ballplayer, the best pitcher, Tom Seaver could possibly be. Jerry Grote wanted to be the best catcher Jerry Grote could be, and Cleon Jones wanted to be the best outfielder Cleon Jones could be, and Bud Harrelson wanted to be the best short-stop Bud Harrelson could be.

"Often during spring training, Jerry Grote and I stood on the lawn of my rented home in St. Petersburg and analyzed our chances, and we finally decided that we actually could win, provided Nolan Ryan fulfilled his promise as a pitcher, provided Ron Swoboda and Ed Kranepool fulfilled their promise as hitters, provided Tommie Agee regained his batting eye.

"And most important," said Tom, "we had the right attitude. We weren't the Old Mets, the ones who'd been resigned to the fact that they weren't supposed to win. Koosman, Ryan, Grote, Harrelson, Jones, and me," said Seaver, "none of us had spent more than three full years in the major leagues: we had all been busy learning our trade, not learning to lose. Some people said that I set a winning example for the Mets by winning 16 games in each of my first two seasons, but that was only part of it. I had confidence in my teammates: I knew what they could do. And I always went on to the mound expecting to win, and my teammates expected to win and most of the times I pitched, we did win," said Tom.

A couple of unrelated events, off the playing field, made for a considerable change for the Mets in the season of 1969. First, in April of 1968 the National League had voted to expand to 12 clubs. There were to be two divisions, East and West, of six clubs each.

"That means we can't be lower than sixth in 1969," said one of the Mets.

"We can do better than that," said another.

Tom Seaver and manager Hodges were the only members of the New York organization who believed that the Mets were a potential winner of the newly created Eastern Division of the National League, but both Seaver and Hodges kept their opinions out of the press.

Second, there was a potential strike of all the big league players in 1969. There was a hassle about pensions, and the club owners were dragging their feet in the negotiations. The player representatives were urging the ballplayers to refuse to sign their 1969 contracts.

The delay wasn't doing the pitchers, who generally report the earliest to spring training, any good. It was at this point in time that Tom Seaver, on his own, organized an informal conditioning camp, and the Mets pitchers, unlike other pitchers in the league, reported and lost no time in working into condition for the 1969 season.

Tom Seaver's "conditioning camp" included Jerry

Koosman, Ron Taylor, Al Jackson, and shortstop Buddy Harrelson working out on a schedule that reminded some of the players of a Marine boot camp without, of course, the rigid Marine discipline. Under Seaver, the pitchers and Harrelson, joined by several other players later, worked hard. They wore sneakers and Bermuda shorts and Tom put them through a series of snappy workouts that had them huffing and puffing.

The players were served tasty lunches prepared by Nancy Seaver, and did not seem at all to be hampered by the fact that they were in a voluntary group. They probably worked harder under "Coach" Seaver because Tom made it a fun series of workouts. And he prepared himself thoroughly each day for the sessions.

"I believe baseball remains one of the few things in our nation that rewards individual effort," Seaver said, "and I want it to remain that way. I do not want to become unionized, that's why I don't believe in a strike.

"I feel a certain loyalty to the club, which has treated me royally. . . . I feel a certain loyalty to my family and myself. . . . On the other hand, I certainly believe in a players' association and what they are trying to do, and I do have a certain feeling for my fellow players."

A few players, including representative Ed Kranepool, moved to stay away from any camp until the strike was settled. And finally, on February 24, when the club owners and the players' association finally agreed to terms, the mass of players began to report to their various camps.

Most of the veterans were back in uniform when the Mets opened their 1969 spring training camp, after the pension differences between the owners and hired hands had been settled.

Back in 1968 Donald Grant and his new general manager John Murphy had concluded an astonishing trade with the Chicago White Sox, a trade that was considered by almost everyone in baseball as the biggest deal in the history of the Mets organization.

The Mets sent Tommy Davis, a hard-hitting, fleet-footed outfielder, pitchers Jack Fisher and Billy Wynne, and Buddy Booker to the White Sox in return for a quiet, soft-spoken, smallish infielder, Al Weis. And all Weis did, in his quiet way, was to write history for the Mets with his play in 1969. Another quiet but startling player that the White Sox unloaded in the deal was Tommie Agee.

Agee had been Rookie of the Year in the American League in 1966, when he hit for a .273 average for the White Sox, but Tommie slipped badly to a .234 average in 1967, and Eddie Stanky, who managed the Sox at that time, decided that Agee was just a flash in the pan rookie and got rid of him.

Gil Hodges had seen Agee play and was delighted to get him for the Mets. Cleon Jones, who was brought up to the Mets from Buffalo in 1963, was sent down and brought up again in 1966. Jones and Agee had been high school football stars in Mobile, Alabama, and the two ex-stars were delighted to play with the New York organization.

Al Weis weighed only about 155 pounds but had been a mainstay at short and second base for the White Sox for six years. In 1965 Weis hit for a .296 average and seemed on the verge of developing into one of the stars in the league, but in a fierce collision on a play at second base, Al had been knocked down and out by Frank Robinson of the Orioles in an attempt to break up a double-play. The collision was a brutal one. Robinson, a big, tough player, barrelled hard into Weis and both players were hurt. Robbie suffered a concussion, while the accident knocked Weis out of action for most of the season.

But Hodges had scouted Weis in the fall Instructional League, noted that Al's bad knee had fully recovered, and asked for him to be included in the Agee trade. Hodges liked Weis's play and his spirit and wanted him as a utility man for Bud Harrelson.

Tug McGraw, now 24 years old and out of the Marines, was back at camp. But his control was non-existent and he was sent back to Jacksonville for further work. But he would be back, soon.

The most heartwarming development in 1968 was the rejuvenation of 35-year-old Ed Charles. Ed became the most popular man in the Mets clubhouse with his poems, high jinks, and most important, his solid clutch hitting.

There were also a number of good-looking young players brought up from Jacksonville: Amos Otis, Rod Gaspar, Duffy Dyer, and a touted pitcher out of Arizona State University, Gary Gentry, who arrived for spring training with a huge St. Bernard that consumed five pounds of meat a day. The Mets also picked up the promising young infielder Wayne Garrett in the winter draft.

Talking to the press, Tom, who called himself "the supreme optimist with that touch of reality," said, "Maybe we'll finish third, more likely second. We can beat Pittsburgh, Philadelphia, and Montreal. The only team we won't be able to take is St. Louis, but we've got a good chance of beating Chicago for that second spot."

In private talks, however, "the supreme optimist" was sure that not even the St. Louis Cardinals were going to be able to stop the Mets from taking the Eastern Division title.

In Las Vegas, however, the odds-makers were in complete agreement with the view of the sports-writers. They put the Mets at 100–1 to win the division crown. And there was nobody, just nobody, who was willing to lay down a bet on the Mets, even at those odds.

At the beginning of the season, with their old error-prone habits in the field and lackluster hitting, the Mets made the sportswriters and the Las Vegas gamblers look good. On May 4, they had only 9 wins to show against 14 defeats and had lost 13 of their last 20 games. In one of those games the Mets lost, Tom Seaver gave up three home runs.

Dejected over the loss, Tom began to think about his pitching. Were the hitters digging in at the plate, knowing that he was too good-natured, too much the All-American clean-cut type to throw at them—to drive them back with pitches at their heads? A few days later those thoughts were confirmed. Jack Fisher, a former Mets pitcher now with the Reds, told Tom that he had heard other players talking about Seaver: "You can dig in against Seaver. He'll never throw a knock-down pitch. He's too much of a gentleman." On the way to Chicago, Tom decided that he had to choose between a nice-guy image or a winning-pitcher image. He did not take too much time in reaching a decision.

In the first game against the Cubs, before a

rooting, hostile crowd, Seaver faced Ron Santo, the Cubs' dangerous cleanup batter, who a week earlier had hit one of those three home runs off Tom.

Tom's first pitch was a high, hard fastball right at Santo's head, and Ron quickly flattened himself to the ground to get away from the pitch.

The huge crowd booed, but Santo got the message. "Don't dig in against me, or I'll throw another one."

In the Cubs' dugout, Leo Durocher, who was a noted authority on beanballs, just looked at his pitcher, Bill Hands. Leo looked and nodded his head and Hands went out to the mound. When Seaver came up to hit, Hands hurled the first ball right at Tom, the ball just striking Tom's arm as he fell back.

In the fourth inning Tom retaliated with a pitch up and in to Hands so tight that it hit the Cubs pitcher in the chest. Players from both sides poured out onto the field in a wild melee, but the umpires quickly squelched the budding riot. Seaver was warned by the umpire and fined $50, but it was worth the price. Santo and the rest of the Cubs were most careful as they came up to hit. And there were no homers off Tom that day as the Mets took the ball game by a 3–2 score.

But after the game there was a special feeling in the Mets locker room, a oneness of spirit, a camaraderie that fired the players up.

Later Tom and Larry Merchant of the New York *Post* discussed the ethics of a pitcher throwing at a hitter. "I tried to brush Santo back from the plate in New York," said Tom, "but I didn't do a good job. He was really hitting me hard. Possibly he's taking the bread out of my mouth. I had to make sure he respects me. You just cannot let a hitter dominate or intimidate you.

"The hitter shouldn't intimidate the pitcher, and by the same token, the pitcher shouldn't intimidate the hitter; each has to respect the other. I had to let Santo know, once and for all time, that I knew what he was doing to me.

"One small brush back pitch can let your opponent know what kind of a competitor you are. I have a reputation as a good competitor, if I have anything. But I also have a reputation as a cordial pitcher, and there are players in the league, and they know who they are, who have taken advantage of me. They have taken more liberties than they should. And I'm not going to let them keep doing it."

"This is the pitcher's code," said Merchant in his New York *Post* column, "and it is highly unethical. They are fooling around with bullets and someone can get hurt."

"I don't consider throwing a brush back pitch unethical," Tom retorted. "There's a fine line dividing throwing at a player deliberately and just brushing him back. It's the difference between good hard baseball and dirty baseball, between gaining respect and using fear. But everyone must decide for himself what is ethically and morally right. Every individual must have his own guidelines. You can't write it in a book; you can't say it's three inches or six inches or three-quarters of an inch from the batter. Every individual must put the period at the end—find the equilibrium between the pitcher and the hitter, for himself and for his ball club," said Seaver.

By May 15, the Mets were still floundering a few

games below .500, and some of his coaches, such as Yogi Berra, Rube Walker, and Joe Pignatano, thought Gil Hodges was being too nice by holding in his anger. They talked to Gil and told him to let his emotions go and not to hold himself in check, which was not a healthy thing for a heart patient to do.

That day Don Cardwell messed up a certain double play in the second inning against Atlanta. Taking advantage of Cardwell's misplay, the Braves scored three runs. The Mets made another error later that led to another run, and then there were other sloppy plays, poor base running, and poor throws, and the Braves took the game 6–5.

When the game was over and the players were back in the clubhouse, Hodges barred all reporters, locked the door, and began to talk.

Without raising his voice, Hodges reminded the players that they were major leaguers and that required all of them to make a major-league effort. He went over the several misplays simply and directly as he stood in the center of the locker room, the men sitting around him in their cubicles. This was not a democratic meeting and there was no such thing as a dialogue, because Gil Hodges did not run his team in that manner.

After the meeting, reporters anxious to get a story talked to the players.

"Gil didn't single out any individual player," said Tug McGraw. "The players he spoke about knew they were the ones being singled out. If the shoe fits, wear it," said McGraw.

"We needed that scolding," Seaver said. "I surely expect it to help us. We're mature individuals, major-league performers. We're supposed to be able to play on that level. When we don't, we have to take the gaff. The man is our manager. He's on our side. He's a perfectionist. That's fabulous. I strive for that kind of play myself."

The perfection came quicker than expected. The Mets took two straight from the Cincinnati Reds.

By May 20 the Mets had reversed their poor play and climbed back to a .500 record with 18 wins against 18 losses. Seaver won that 18th game with a three-hit shutout of the Atlanta Braves, and there was exultation in the Mets clubhouse as the sportswriters rushed in to make a big thing of it. It was a big thing. The Mets had never in all their history been at the .500 mark after playing 36 games, and the sportswriters were going to make it a historic moment for the club in their press reports.

"You're a .500 club!" they yelled. "Where in the hell is all the champagne?"

Tom looked sourly at the writers.

"Five hundred," he said. "What the hell is .500 ball? We didn't come here to play .500! I'm tired of all the old crap jokes about the Mets. We're here to win! Know when we'll have plenty of champagne?" he went on. "When we win the pennant!"

"That's great," said Maury Allen of the New York *Post*, and actually a Mets fan, "but I'll be too old to enjoy it then."

It looked as if Allen wasn't just making talk when the Mets soon lost that .500 mark, by going into a tailspin and dropping five straight games.

But they were the new Mets, and they were quick to straighten out and get back into a winning groove. Seaver started the streak off with a smooth effort in a 4 to 3 victory over the Giants. The following afternoon, the Mets once more responded with some timely hitting and a fine pitching performance by rookie Gary Gentry, as Ed Charles walloped a three-run homer and the Mets chalked up another win by a 4 to 2 score over the Giants.

On Sunday June 10, a jam-packed crowd of some 41,290 fans wildly applauded their heroes as the Mets squeaked through to a 5–4 win over the Giants for their third straight. On the next day, Monday, the Dodgers came to town, set for a Mets holiday sweep. But Jerry Koosman had other plans and shut down the hard-hitting Dodgers as the Mets pulled out another 2–1 win.

And suddenly the Mets were doing everything just right. The young pitchers were coming through with marvelous games, and each day a new batting hero emerged. One day it was Ed Charles with a game-winning homer; next day it was Tom Agee; then it was the moody Ron Swoboda driving in the winning runs. And now the Mets were above .500 and playing like potential contenders.

Young Jack DiLauro, who had just been called up from the minors, made his first major league start one to remember as the 21-one-year-old pitcher held the Dodgers to two hits over the nine-inning route. He was taken out in the ninth for a pinch hitter, and the game went on and on with the score 0–0. In the fifteenth inning Wayne Garrett singled and Agee doubled to give the high-flying Mets a magnificent 1–0 triumph.

Suddenly the Mets were winning game after game. They won 11 straight and were now firmly entrenched in second place. The baseball world suddenly sat up and really began to take stock of this phenomenal ball club.

Tom Seaver was thrilled about the way the Mets

were playing. After the eleventh straight win, Tom made a dash for the beer cooler in the clubhouse, lifted a cold beer, and began to sing, "Those were the days, my friend."

Ron Swoboda grinned.

"All my life I wished I could sing," he said to Tom. "Now I sure as hell wish you could."

But there was nothing that could dampen the spirits of this young and suddenly winning ball club.

The Mets were at Shea Stadium on the night of July 10, grimly confident as they prepared to face the high-flying Cubs led by their doughty little manager, Leo Durocher. The Cubs had such great stars as Ernie Banks, Billy Williams, Ron Santo, Fergie Jenkins, Ken Holtzman, Don Kessinger, and Dick Selma, and they were riding high in first place, seemingly invincible. Nobody could beat them.

There was no pennant race at Shea Stadium that night. No crucial series, at least for the Cubbies. The race was a walkaway. But still, any game for the Cubs in New York was just a little more exciting, with all the press involved, and Durocher a New York favorite.

There was only Tom Seaver, the perfectionist, in a Mets uniform throwing perfect baseballs.

The game was just three innings old when Rube Walker, the Mets' fine pitching coach, turned to Gil Hodges:

"Gil, I see something special out there. He's [Seaver] razor-sharp. He could throw a no-hitter tonight."

And for six innings, Tom set the Cubs down without a hit, without a walk. Eighteen Cubs batters came up to hit and Tom set them down in order.

A crowd of more than 59,000 Metsomaniacs, as

the Mets fans were called by now, sat glued to their seats in rapt attention as Seaver's fastball thudded into catcher Jerry Grote's glove with a crackle that could be heard all over the stadium.

The final two innings were almost more than the crowd could endure. Tom Seaver was having the same trouble.

"I know a thousand things were running through my mind. The fans were absolutely unbelievable," said Tom. "I grew up in Los Angeles where the fans clap softly when someone hits a home run or pitches a great game. Here the noise gets right into your system. You tingle all over. I could hear my heart pounding, feel the adrenaline flowing. My arm felt light as a feather. I know I thought about my wife, and once I looked over to where my father was sitting. And I remember sitting in the dugout and looking into the upper deck and seeing people standing, screaming in the aisles. I can't explain what that did to me. It was like being in a marvelous dream."

Now it was the eighth inning. Seaver had set down 21 Cubs batters in order and the fans were screaming for a no-hitter. It was a constant uproar.

Ron Santo smashed a long drive that Swoboda caught after a long run. One out. Ernie Banks, the effervescent Cub star, fouled off three pitches and then struck out as the crowd went wild. Two outs. Al Spangler was up to hit and he ran the count 3 and 2, then a swinging third strike and once more the crowd was up on their feet, screaming, shrieking.

"In the ninth inning," said Tom, "I paused between pitches to look the situation over. Fantastic. People were standing behind the last row of seats all the way down the left-field line and the right-field line; they were standing, yelling at every pitch.

"I peeked over once more to where my father was sitting and suddenly wondered if he remembered how I got headed in this direction during those years when the Mets were losing 737 games in seven years. And now we were actually fighting the Cubs for first place, and every sportswriter in the nation was writing stories about the Cinderella team and the impossible dream.

"Then I looked up into the stands once more, at the uproarious crowd, all up and on their feet and ready to tear the place apart. And I thought to myself, moments like these are reserved for other people: they're for the Sandy Koufaxes, the Mickey Mantles, the Willie Mayses of this world—not for the Tom Seaverses and the New York Mets."

And now in the ninth inning Randy Hundley, the lead-off batter, got the bunt sign from manager Leo Durocher and on the first pitch bunted, a slow dribbler that went to Seaver's right.

"He did me a favor," said Tom. "He's a tough hitter, always had been, for me. It was a relief to come off the mound, use my legs, do something else for a change beside pitch."

Seaver threw out Hundley. And the crowd hooted and booed the Cubs catcher as he slowly trudged back to the dugout.

The next Cubs hitter was rookie Jimmy Qualls. The Cubs called him "Quail." He was a .240 hitter and he got set at the plate as 59,000 Metsomaniacs started to scream, ready to blast the air with their cheers for a no-hit game for Seaver.

Tom wound up, kicked his left leg high in the air,

and came in with his best fastball, just a bit high to the hitter. But the rookie lashed at the ball and drove it into left field. Cleon Jones and Tommie Agee raced for the ball, to no avail. It was a clean single—and suddenly Shea Stadium was very quiet.

The huge crowd was still now, except for the booing Quaills got. He had done his job well, but he robbed Tom Terrific of that perfect game.

Tom wasn't very good at disguising his disappointment. His pretty wife, Nancy, was even worse at hiding it. She was standing at the clubhouse door and as Tom emerged, she was crying.

"What are you crying for?" he asked, near tears himself. "We won, 4 to 0, didn't we?"

That win, incidentally, took the Mets to within three games of the Chicago Cubs and first place in the Eastern Division.

Tom Seaver had won eight games in a row and nine of the last 11 he had pitched. He hadn't lost a game since May 25.

"What's turned on the Mets?" someone asked Gil Hodges.

"They've turned themselves on," said the Mets manager. "Maybe for the first time they realize it's just as easy to win as lose, even in the major leagues."

The wry Casey Stengel, retired from the baseball wars and enjoying his leisure beside the pool at his Glendale, California, home, remarked, "This club plays better baseball now. Several of them look fairly alert," he added, straight-faced.

But all the joy in Metsville suddenly came to an abrupt halt on August 13. With just seven weeks left to the season, they had dropped to seven and a half

games behind the Cubs, after suffering a horrendous slump in the last week of July and the first two
weeks of August. Still slumping badly, the Mets
dropped to third place, behind the Pittsburgh Pirates, and all the magic the team engendered suddenly seemed to evaporate. Once more they had
begun to look like the old Mets.

Four wins against the San Diego Padres in two
doubleheaders, August 16 and 17, and then a home
run by Tom Agee in the fourteenth inning of a game
against the San Francisco Giants on August 19, to
give Gentry and McGraw a 1–0 win, suddenly
turned things around again. With just a month to
go, the Mets were once again on the heels of the
Chicago Cubs, who had taken the lead at the beginning of the season and had never relinquished it.
New York was just two games behind Chicago.
Metsomania was in full swing again.

The Cubs came into Shea Stadium September 8,
still two and a half games in front, and they meant
to stay in front. Bill Hands, the Cubs pitcher, fired
his fastball right at Tommie Agee and Tommie
dropped to the ground. Hands repeated the act once
again with his third pitch. The next inning Jerry
Koosman retaliated for the Mets, hitting Ron Santo
on his right forearm. Koosman in turn had to duck
a ball pitched at his head in the eighth inning. There
was no love lost between the Mets and the Cubs,
and they weren't timid about showing it.

Between the beanballing, there was a game, and
Koosman won that game, 3–2. The Chicago lead
over the Mets was cut to one and a half.

Seaver went to the mound for the second game of
that series, and there were more than 58,000 Mets-

omaniacs in the stands to cheer him on. Tom responded in style, holding the scrapping Cubs to five hits. The Mets were just half a game out of the lead. It was four straight for the Mets, Tom Seaver's sixth straight win, and his twenty-first of the season. No Mets pitcher had ever approached that record, nor had the Mets ever been that near to glory.

September 10, the New Yorkers took the Montreal Expos 3–2, in Shea Stadium. The Chicago Cubs, that night, took a beating in Philadelphia.

"METS IN FIRST PLACE," screamed the headlines.

The unbelievable, the impossible was happening.

"You gotta believe!" shouted Tug McGraw.

"You gotta believe" became the battle cry of the New York Mets and their fans, who went about shouting from the rooftops to street corner bars, "We're number one! We're number one!" "You gotta believe!"

On the eleventh of September, Gentry shut out the Expos. The next day the Mets made it nine victories in a row as Koosman pitched a three-hitter in the first game of a doubleheader and Don Cardwell and Tug McGraw collaborated on a five-hitter to give the Mets two 1–0 wins over the Expos.

On the fourteenth it was ten straight, with Tom Seaver chalking up his twenty-second win of the season. Now, the Amazing Mets were truly Amazin'.

Tom pitched his eighth victory in a row, and his twenty-third of the season. The Mets had won 13 of their last 14 games, 29 of their last 36, and 91 in all— as many wins as they had collected in their first two years as a major league team.

The St. Louis Cardinals were eliminated from the

division race when Seaver, pitching with his head and his heart, tamed the Redbirds 3–1 to win his ninth consecutive game. The Mets, who had never clinched anything but ninth place in their history, clinched at least a tie for first place when, the next night, they took the Cardinals in 11 innings, 3–2.

September 24, 1969, with more than 56,500 Mets-omaniacs screaming their heads off, Gentry shut out the Cardinals, 6–0, and the Mets were champions of the Eastern Division of the National League.

The fans, thousands of them, poured out onto the field. They tore up great holes in the turf. They tore out home plate and tore up the pitcher's mound. One of the most daring climbed to the top of the seven-story scoreboard in center field, then slipped and fell.

The fans went completely berserk. They celebrated as they'd never celebrated before—and they paid for it.

"Casualties came in like war victims," said one of the nurses in the first-aid room, and three doctors were kept busy far into the night attending to the wounded.

The Mets themselves went a bit wild, and understandably. The hundred-to-one shot had made it.

"We're number one! We're number one!"

Tom Seaver led the run from the dugout to the locker room. He grabbed the first bottle of champagne. The champagne had been stacked high in the eighth inning. He grabbed Jerry Koosman in a bear hug, then jumped onto a table and poured a whole bottle of the bubbly stuff over the head of Gil Hodges.

Everybody and his uncle who was watching television that night saw it. Television wasn't going to miss this celebration.

"We did it! We're number one! You've got to believe!"

This was a night to remember! And for hours the Mets and their fans celebrated. It was probably the wildest and wettest celebration in baseball history.

But the celebrations of 1969 weren't over—not for the Mets, not yet. Yet to come were the league play-offs and the World Series. Celebration was to become the order of the day for the Miracle Mets of 1969!

12
PLAYOFF AND SERIES

Tom Seaver's record for the 1969 season had been phenomenal, 25 wins against 7 losses. At the age of 24, Tom was the youngest pitcher to win 25 games since the great Dizzy Dean had done it in 1935.

The Mets had closed the season with an amazing 100 victories, topping the standings in that department for both Eastern and Western Divisions of the National League and, again, Tom Seaver had brought home one-fourth of all those wins. He struck out 208 batters en route to those victories, and yielded only a 2.21 earned-run-average to opposing teams. As was expected, Seaver was named the starting pitcher in the play-offs with the Atlanta Braves, winner of the Western Division title, for the National League pennant.

The Braves had the power hitters, with Rico Carty, Clete Boyer, Orlando Cepeda, and bad Henry Aaron. The Mets had the pitchers—Seaver, Koosman, Gentry, Ryan, McGraw. During the regular schedule the Mets had handled those big Atlanta sluggers. Still, the Miracle Mets, after beating all odds in taking the Eastern Division of the National League, were the underdogs in all the betting parlors around the country.

The morning of the opening game of the play-offs, however, Tom Seaver woke up nervous. He was nervous before every game he pitched, but this was going to be the biggest game he'd ever played in. Actually, he had been nervous the whole night before.

Nancy Seaver said, "Every four days my husband stops speaking to me, and that's during the regular season.

"He gets preoccupied with things—anything, even the wallpaper in the kitchen.

"I'll call to him and ask him something like, 'How do you like the new collar I bought for the dog?' and he'll say, 'Can't you see I'm reading, Nancy?'

"Sure enough, he'll have his nose in some book. He's always reading one of those good novels or biographies, but not this time. His eyes are glued to the book but he isn't turning any pages. What's turning are all those little wheels and sprockets and gears in his head.

"From then on, we speak in a sort of code. I've learned to rely on my own special brand of ESP to break his code to find out just what's going on behind all his grunts and pregnant pauses."

What was going on, of course, was Seaver raiding his memory bank; the kind of pitches Cepeda, Hank Aaron, and company could hit. All the weaknesses of the Atlanta hitters. Tom had his little black book of notes on each batter and carefully studied every pitch, every ball he had thrown against Atlanta during the season. He memorized each man's strength and weakness, over and over, until he could actually visualize every pitch in his mind.

Still, the morning of that first game against Atlanta, Tom was unusually nervous. He just toyed with his breakfast at the restaurant, then left for the ballpark, expecting all the jitters he was suffering to disappear, as they always did, once he started to throw.

But for once they didn't go away. The fact that he had shut out the Braves, 3-0, in their last outing didn't help. His pitches kept moving up too high. His control was off. He just could not get the ball down and inside to the left-handed hitters, down and away to the right-handed batters. There was something wrong with his pitching rhythm. He struck out the first Atlanta batter, Felix Millan, but his pitching rhythm was off and he knew it. His left hip was down too low, which made him release the ball high as he whipped the pitch toward the plate.

It was all the tension.

He threw a low curveball that bounced in the dirt, to Tony Gonzalez, the second Braves hitter, then a fastball that forced Jerry Grote to leap high in the air to stop it. He did manage to retire Orlando Cepeda, but he couldn't rid himself of that unaccountable tightness in his chest and shoulder.

Three successive two-base hits gave the Braves a 3-2 lead in the second inning, after the Mets had scored twice. The Mets went ahead in the fourth, 4-3, but Tom couldn't hold the lead; Tony Gonzalez homered to tie the score. Then Hank Aaron, Tom's boyhood idol, hammered a ball over the fence and the Braves led 5–4 at the end of seven innings.

"Damn, damn, damn!"

Tom Seaver was disgusted with himself as he put on his jacket and sat down in the dugout. He just couldn't understand himself that afternoon. Worse, as he saw it, he was losing the game for the Mets.

But the Atlanta Braves weren't all nerves of steel that afternoon, either.

In the Mets half of the eighth, Wayne Garrett bounced a ball past third for a double. It was the kind of ball Atlanta's Clete Boyer always gobbled up for an easy out at first, but not this time. Cleon Jones followed with a clean hit, Garrett scoring. The game was tied once more.

Art Shamsky singled, sending Jones to third. The Braves had Cleon picked off base, but the tag was missed and Jones slid in safely at third.

The great knuckleball pitcher Phil Niekro got Boswell to tap a slow grounder to the mound for a force at second base. Ed Kranepool grounded the first pitch to Cepeda at first base, Jones tried to score on the play, and when Cepeda threw to the plate wildly, the ball bounced passed Bob Didier, the Braves' catcher, and Jones scored to give the Mets a 6–5 lead.

That wasn't the end of it.

Grote grounded to Boyer, whose only play was to first base. There were two out now, with men on second and third. Buddy Harrelson was purposely passed to get to the ninth batter in the Mets lineup, Tom Seaver. Hodges sent in relief catcher J. C. Martin to pinch-hit for Tom, and Martin promptly lined the ball for a clean single. That should have scored only two more runs for the Mets, but the ball scooted past the Braves' Tony Gonzalez and three Mets scored.

That's the way the game ended, with the Mets winning their first play-off game in baseball history, 9–5.

A sad bunch of players returned to the Atlanta locker room.

"We got five runs off Seaver," said Hank Aaron, sitting on a stool and unhappily answering the queries of the sports reporters. "That should win it for us. It didn't. There's something wrong."

"Maybe it's that Mets' magic," suggested a sportswriter.

"Mets magic can go plumb to hell," spat Hank Aaron, putting an end to his interview.

And in the Mets locker room, Tom Seaver talked like a man who had lost a crucial game, not won it, to the reporters who had crowded around him.

"I tried to control my nerves and I just couldn't," he said, waving aside the excuse he was offered and might easily have taken.

"You hadn't pitched for six full days. Maybe you were rusty."

"No," said Tom. "It was all nerves. I just was more tense than usual. I couldn't get my curveball breaking, and my fastball had no real pop. I just didn't have it. No real speed. Too tense. Much too tense."

Tom wouldn't forget that afternoon in Atlanta, not for a long time; but as far as Atlanta was concerned, that first game seemed to take all the starch out of them. They just seemed to go to pieces as the Mets walloped the Atlanta pitchers as if they belonged to them and took the next two games,

11–6 and 7–4. The New York Mets, cellar dwellers for so long, ninth in the 1968 league standing, won the National League Pennant in 1969.

The celebration in the locker room, as might be expected, was wild. They had beaten the odds again, and taken the mighty Atlanta Braves in three straight.

When their pitching faltered, the Mets batters were coming through, hammering the ball in a fashion no one would have prophesied. Tommie Agee hit two home runs and a double and had four runs batted in for a .357 average. Rookie Wayne Garrett drove out a home run, a pair of doubles, and batted .385. Cleon Jones got six hits and drove in four runs. Art Shamsky was a terror at bat as he clubbed out seven hits in thirteen at-bats for a phenomenal .538 average. Kenny Boswell, J. C. Martin, and Buddy Harrelson also provided timely hitting. Even pitcher Nolan Ryan got into the slugging act with two hits.

All that hitting promised well for the future of the New York Mets. It was something more to celebrate. But the celebrants' champagne, pies in the face, and all that were not nearly as wild as they had been at the celebration that followed their beating the St. Louis Cardinals to wrap up the National League Eastern Division championship. They were growing accustomed to winning, especially the big ones. The winning came to be expected. But there was something more to think about at this happy party, something to keep the damper down on the fires. The World Series was at hand, and that was something to think about, something to sober them up.

The Baltimore Orioles had won 109 games to take the Eastern Division title, then had captured the

American League pennant by defeating the Minnesota Twins in three straight games. With sluggers like Frank and Brooks Robinson, Paul Blair, Don Buford, Boog Powell, and Elrod Hendricks, and with pitchers like the 23-game winner Mike Cuellar, Dave McNally, and Jim Palmer, who had recently ptiched a no-hitter, they were the odds-on favorite in Las Vegas and betting centers around the nation. Three out of every four sportswriters queried in a poll had selected the Orioles to take the Mets, possibly in four straight games, for the championship.

There was tremendous excitement in Baltimore the day the World Series opened. There were parades, bands through the main streets, and the newspaper headlines read, "METS' MIRACLE STORY NEARS END."

The Orioles' powerful hitters were supremely confident. "Our pitching is better," said Frank Robinson, "and our hitters will club hell out of New York. They just don't have a chance." The Orioles were an intimidating team and they knew it.

The Mets, according to the Orioles, were a bunch of fresh nobodies who were plain "lucky" enough to win the National League pennant but still had to prove they could beat an outstanding American League team like the Orioles.

"Bring on that Ron Gaspar," said Frank Robinson.

"That's not Ron. It's Rod, stupid!" kidded Paul Blair.

"All right," said Frank with a broad grin, "bring on Rod Stupid."

The Orioles were aggressive and arrogant and perhaps just a bit too cocky. They were going to be in for a couple of surprises.

The Mets, oddly enough, were completely re-laxed. No real reason for it. They knew just how tough the Orioles were, but for some unknown reason they felt confident and calm. They felt they were destined to win the Championship.

It was 9:30 in the morning. Tom Seaver, who was scheduled to pitch the opening game of the Series, left Nancy in the hotel room in Baltimore to have his breakfast, or as much of it as he could eat under the circumstances, in the hotel coffee shop. Bud Harrelson was waiting for him at a table.

After a couple of minutes, Bud looked around the crowded shop, then said, "Let's get out of here. Let's forget breakfast. We've been here for 15 minutes and nobody has even looked at us."

They boarded the team bus and arrived at the clubhouse in the Oriole ballpark, where Tom or-dered a roast beef sandwich on white. He wasn't as nervous as he had been for that first game against Atlanta, but he was worried. He had pulled a muscle in his leg a couple of days before and he knew that his legs, so important to his pitching, weren't as strong as they should be. He wondered whether he could last through a tough World Series nine-inning game, and he was troubled about it.

Still, when he got to the locker room he was cool enough to try a screwball stunt. He got Gary Gentry to switch shirts with him, Gary wearing Tom's big 41, Tom, Gary's 39. The Baltimore sportswriters didn't know Gentry from Seaver, and when they gathered around the Mets players for their stories, Tom and Gary went into their act.

"What about Gentry?" they asked Gentry, think-ing he was Tom Seaver.

"I think Gentry is a horseshit pitcher," said Gary,

and the Baltimore scribes began to fill their note-books with quotes, ready to fill their columns with nutty stories on how Tom Seaver had ripped Gary Gentry apart.

They would have written those stories, too, if New York sportswriter Maury Allen hadn't come along, looked at the two pitchers and hollered, "You've got the wrong shirt on, Tom!"

Tom and Gary and the rest of the team got a good laugh at it. Tom was always ready to pull off some prank or other in the clubhouse, where he was something else than the All-American boy, straight as an arrow and as faultless as a true shot from a bow, which was the image the fans had of him, an image that he had helped build. Actually, he was a more complicated character, as his wife Nancy had already indicated.

But here he was, kidding around, and all the time worried about the strength of his legs and how long he could hope to be effective on the mound.

It wasn't as bad as that opening game against the Braves. He wasn't that nervous. He could put the ball where he wanted to put it. The trouble was that the Baltimore Oriole sluggers were in rare hitting form and walloped the ball all night.

After all the ritual and ceremony that precedes the opening game of a World Series, Tom walked to the mound, took his warm-up pitches, then looked across the plate to the first Oriole to bat, Don Buford.

Tom threw an inside pitch for a ball. He took the return throw from Jerry Grote and knew at once that all the nervousness with which he'd ap-proached the game was gone.

He threw a fastball. He could see it move in on the

batter, letter-high. Just a bit high, but it was a good pitch and it went where he wanted it to go, but Buford connected, a long fly ball. Tom turned, watched Ron Swoboda chase the fly in right field, saw Swoboda leap and the ball disappear—over the fence. Home run!

The fans roared; Tom was stunned. The first batter he had faced in a World Series had rifled a shot into the stands for a home run.

The Orioles kept hitting. They scored four runs off Seaver before he was taken out for a pinch hitter in the sixth inning.

As the sportswriters had predicted, Baltimore took the first game of the Series. The score was 4–1. The Mets were a sorely disappointed club in the locker room after the game, but they were far from through.

Before that first game, on television, Sandy Koufax had asked Tom, "Is God a Met?"

"No," responded Tom, the boyish smile on his face, "but He's got an apartment in New York."

It was with that same irreverent feeling that the Mets went into the second game of the World Series and, much to the surprise of a lot of people, particularly the people of Baltimore, they won the game.

Jerry Koosman and Dave McNally hooked up in a magnificent pitcher's duel, with both teams making spectacular plays in the field. There was no scoring in the game until the fourth inning, when Donn Clendenon, the tall, lanky first baseman of the Mets, stroked a home run to give the Mets a one-run lead.

This was the first of three home runs Clendenon would hit. The first baseman had come to the Mets in July on the last trading day of the season. He didn't bat for a high average, but he was a power hitter and had more than pulled his weight in the race for the division crown. With his good sense of humor, he was no little help in building the club's morale.

At the beginning of the season, when Tom introduced him to his wife Nancy, Clendenon took her hand and, in the continental fashion, kissed it. He also kissed her arm, as Tom looked on with a touch of puzzlement in his face.

"Good to be a Met," said Clendenon, who smiled and walked off.

You couldn't help liking him.

"Look who's here," he said one day when Tom walked into the clubhouse. "It's the chubby right-hander, smiling and ready to go."

Tom patted his belly. He was no boy. He weighed 207 and a lot of that was in hips and backside.

He looked at Clendenon, 34 years old, a veteran of the baseball wars for 15 years.

"I'm just a growing boy," he said. "You older fellows are just jealous."

Donn Clendenon was a great guy to have around on a ball club. He was particularly good with a bat when the team needed a solid hit in a close game. His home run was the first run that McNally had given up in 24 innings of postseason play.

Jerry Koosman was pitching the game of his life in the second game of the Series. He had a no-hitter going into the seventh inning and the crowd roared with every pitch. But Paul Blair spoiled the no-hitter with a smash through the left side of the infield. He stole second and came home on Brooks Robinson's single to tie the score, 1–1.

McNally, it seemed, was getting stronger too. The first two men he faced in the ninth were routine outs. He had allowed the Mets only three hits in the game and now Ed Charles was at bat, hopefully the last out of the game for Baltimore, the Orioles being sure they'd get to Koosman in the bottom of the ninth.

But Ed Charles hit a ball past Brooks Robinson for a single. He went to third on a hit-and-run play, as Jerry Grote singled past Mark Belanger. It was up to Al Weis, a .215 batter, to send home a run, and he did, lining the first ball pitched to him into left field. Koosman had a 2–1 lead.

That was the game. The Orioles did get men on first and second, with two men out in the ninth as Koosman lost control for the moment, walking them both. Hodges brought in Ron Taylor for that important final out.

Taylor had pitched well, compiling a 9–4 record for the season, but there was a touch of tension in the Mets dugout as Ron fell behind the hard-hitting Brooks Robinson three balls and one strike. A foul ball and the count was three and two. The tension was building, building, building. Ron hitched his belt, kicked his left leg into the air, came in with a sinking curveball that Robinson slapped to Ed Charles. Charles gloved the ball, threw to first, and big Donn Clendenon dug the ball out of the dirt for the third out that gave the Mets the ball game and tied the Series, 1–1.

Joy in Metsville: The magic was still there, and you've got to believe it.

The Series moved to New York and there wasn't an empty seat in Shea Stadium; they were standing in the aisles to see the Amazing Mets in the great magic act of 1969. The governor of the state, Nelson

Rockefeller; the mayor of the city, John Lindsay; Mrs. Jackie Onassis; and everyone else who could buy, beg, borrow, or steal a ticket to get into the ballpark was there to see and to cheer the unbelievable New York team in action. And they got their money's worth—all of them.

Tom Agee hit a home run. The young veteran Ed Kranepool hit a home run. And even pitcher Gary Gentry entered the act, walloping a double to send two Mets across the plate; all this while Gentry and Nolan Ryan combined to shut out the mighty Orioles 5–0 on a four-hitter.

You've got to believe!

It was Tommie Agee who was the superhero of the Mets that afternoon.

In the fourth inning, the Orioles had two men on base when the dangerous Elrod Hendricks drove a pitch high and deep to left center field. It looked like a triple, at least, certain to drive in the two Oriole baserunners. But Agee, sprinting across left center field as fast as he could, threw his gloved hand across his body, leaped high into the air, and grabbed the ball just as he crashed into the fence. The force almost knocked Tommie out. It was a phenomenal catch, and Agee had to look twice at the ball stuck in the webbing of his glove to believe he really had caught it. Marvelous catch.

And there was another wonderful play.

In the seventh inning, with two outs, Gentry momentarily lost control and walked three Orioles to load the bases. There was an uneasy stirring in the Mets dugout and in the stands; it wasn't necessary, not with the spectacular Agee in the outfield.

At this point in the game, Hodges brought in

Nolan Ryan to relieve Gentry. Ryan faced the hard-hitting Paul Blair, who on the very first pitch smashed a long drive to left center field.

At the crack of the bat, Tom Agee was cruising again, as the three Orioles on base headed for home. Agee, driving as hard as he could, dived high for the ball just as he reached the warning track, slid along the turf on one knee, and at the last moment speared the ball, inches off the ground.

Mets magic; even the Mets found it difficult to believe.

There were any number of heroes that afternoon, with the Mets winning their second game, 5–0, but it was Tommie Agee who topped them all with his two incredible magic catches. The Mets were all ready to take Game Four!

It was Tom Seaver to the mound in the fourth game, pitching again against the Cuban ace Mike Cuellar, but Tom knew that this time out there would be another story—no repeat of the first-game disaster.

He was rather calm the morning of the game. He checked his book and studied all the scouting reports he had jotted down on the Baltimore players. Paul Blair was a good fastball hitter; keep the ball away from him. Frank Robinson was a pull hitter; feed him breaking balls on the outside. Break stuff away to Boog Powell, or jam him with a fastball inside. And so on down the line. The scouting reports said the pitch to throw Don Buford was inside, but Tom had seen Buford strike out twice on curve-balls that were outside. Whatever, Tom, remembering the home run Buford had hit off him, wasn't going to pitch him inside.

And he got Buford, the first man up in the fourth

game for the Orioles, with a strikeout. He threw every pitch on the outside away from the dangerous Don Buford.

There had been a small but rather significant incident that morning, as Tom walked into Shea. October 15 had been declared Moratorium Day by the peace movement that was opposed to the involvement of the United States in Vietnam. There were some half-million antiwar demonstrators who would crowd into Washington and the other major cities in the country. They would all be wearing black armbands as a sign of protest.

Tom made no secret of what he felt about the Vietnam war. As a matter of fact, he had been outspoken about it. He felt that we didn't belong in Vietnam and that we ought to bring our boys home, and he said as much.

However, when he was asked to wear one of those black armbands to show he supported the peace movement, he politely turned down the request.

There were two reasons. He knew that the country was split on the issue, that probably a lot of the fans in the stands that day had brothers and uncles and maybe fathers in Vietnam right now, or had lost them in that far Asian country, and he didn't want to offend them. More to the point, however, he wanted nothing to distract him from the job he had at hand, nothing to take away from his concentration. He would need it all, facing the Baltimore Orioles that afternoon.

Tom got through the first inning easily enough, striking out Don Buford and Boog Powell. The Orioles went down in the second. Tom walked out of the dugout for a moment to get himself a Coke in clubhouse. As he was coming back to the dugout, he heard a mighty roar from the crowd.

"Clendenon hit a homer," he thought quickly— and that was it; Donn Clendenon had hit his second home run in the Series to give Tom and the Mets a one-run lead. It was a lead Tom intended to hold.

His curve was breaking just right, his slider was nipping the corners, and his fastball was moving up and in. He retired the Orioles after they got two men on base with none out in the third inning. He retired the Orioles in order in the fourth, and again in the fifth. He walked Blair, with one out in the sixth, then got the next two batters. The Orioles went down one, two, three in the seventh and eighth.

But after he gave up that homer to Donn Clendenon, Mike Cuellar was just as tough on the Mets, and Tom Seaver walked to the mound for the ninth with the Mets leading by just that one home run.

He felt that his fastball was not as lively as it had been in the earlier innings. He was tiring a bit. But just three outs to go and there'd be a World Series shutout for Tom Seaver in the record books.

It wasn't to be. Not that afternoon.

With one out, Frank Robinson and Boog Powell pounced on the ball for successive singles.

Gil Hodges walked to the mound, took the ball from Tom.

"How do you feel?" asked the Mets manager.

"A little tired, but nothing serious," said Tom.

Hodges knew that Tom stuck straight to the truth when he was pitching. He gave the ball back to the pitcher.

"If Robinson hits the ball back to you hard, go for the double play," Hodges said. "If it isn't hard, forget the double play. If you can't hold Frank Robinson on first, throw to the plate. We don't want them tying the score."

Jerry Grote, who had been standing around the mound during the conference, asked Tom how he wanted to pitch Brooks Robinson.

"There's only one way to go. My hard stuff all the way." The Orioles were threatening now. Frank Robinson was on third, Boog Powell on first, and Brooks Robinson, one of the most potent Oriole hitters, was at bat. Seaver came in with a sizzling fastball, waist high. Robinson swung hard and slammed the ball over second base. The ball rose higher and higher, then, just as the wind took it, it curved slightly to right center field. It looked like a certain triple, for Swoboda, who was after the ball, was not very agile.

The ball was now out in right center field, sinking down, down, down, now just inches off the ground.

"I remember turning, watching the ball, sure it was a big drive that would give the Orioles at least two runs and a 2–1 lead," said Seaver. "And then, my heart suddenly stopped, just for a moment, and out of nowhere Swoboda dived head first toward the flight of the ball and I thought, 'Lord, he might just catch the ball.'"

Stretched out fully extended, perhaps a few inches off the ground, Ron reached for the ball just as it headed for earth, speared the ball in the webbing of his glove, crashed into the ground, rolled over, pulled himself up, and in one great motion heaved the ball to Grote and just barely missed Robinson at the plate. The score was tied at 1–1 and that's how the game stood at the end of the regulation nine innings.

The first man up for the Orioles in the tenth

inning was Davey Johnson (now the Mets manager). Davey slugged a pitch down to Red Garrett at third base and Red booted the ball, and Johnson was safe on first base with no one out.

Tom took a deep breath. Everyone makes errors. He had made his share. Don't blame Garrett, he's made great plays too. But there was a man on first and Tom didn't feel too good about that.

He looked across at Mark Belanger, the next batter; a good contact hitter, good bunter. Undoubtedly, Mark would bunt to advance the runner to second in a scoring position.

Tom pitched high to Belanger and Mark squared away as if he was going to bunt. The Mets infielders all moved in to cover the play. Belanger, trying to bunt, however, popped the ball up near the plate and catcher Jerry Grote smothered the ball. One out.

But pinch-hitter Clay Dalrymple went for a low fastball and banged it into center for a clean single. Johnson was on second now, and Dalrymple on first, and pitching coach Rube Walker came out to the mound.

"How are you feeling?" said Rube Walker.

"Tired, Rube," said Tom, "but I think I've got a few pitches left."

"Okay," said Rube Walker. "Pull up your pants and go get 'em."

Don Buford drove a pitch that Swoboda caught in the outfield, but it was far enough for Johnson to move on to third.

One out to go. Tom knew this was going to be his last inning in the game. His arm felt heavy as lead. He was through.

Paul Blair was at the plate. Tom Seaver blazed

two fast strikes by him. And then, with every ounce left in him, he broke off a slider for strike three.

"Let's get a run," Tom shouted, back in the dugout.

Whatever makes for Mets magic must have heard him.

Jerry Grote, first up in the tenth for the Mets, hit one into the glare of the late afternoon sun and the ball fell between Belanger and Buford for a double. Rod Gaspar went in to run for Grote.

Little Al Weis, who barely hit over .200 during the season, was purposely walked. Tom Seaver was scheduled to bat, but J. C. Martin was sent in to hit for him.

Martin was to bunt, to move the runners to second and third. A long fly, then, could score the winning run. Martin did bunt, and suddenly the Mets magic was in full play.

The bunt went no more than 10 feet up the grass edging the first baseline. Orioles relief pitcher Pete Richert ran off the mound, scooped up the ball, saw he would be too late to get Rod Gaspar sliding into third, so instead he threw to first.

But J. C. Martin was in the way of the trajectory of the ball; the ball ticked Martin's wrist and, like a true Mets supporter, bounded out toward right field. Gaspar was up on his feet and came down the line flying with the winning run and the third Mets victory in the World Series.

"My God," thought Tom, utterly exhausted at the moment. "My God, I've won a World Series game."

13
WORLD
CHAMPIONS

It took a while for the Mets to calm down in the clubhouse after the Seaver win that gave them a 3–1 lead in the World Series. There was the usual post-game hoopla with the gaggle of sportswriters pushing away at the ballplayers, question after question, to get some new angle for a line of print in the sports pages.

"What do you think of your chances in the Series now?" they asked manager Gill Hodges.

"Much better than yesterday," said Gil laconically, but he smiled.

"When Brooks Robinson smashed that ball to right field, did you think Ron Swoboda had a shot at it?" they asked Tom Seaver. "Did you figure it was the end of the ball game for you?"

"Not with this ball club," said Tom. "We used to see it that way, but not anymore."

"That Martin bunt? How did you see it?" asked another reporter.

"I saw it as the winning run all the way," said Tom, and he didn't even smile.

The newsmen finally left and the ballplayers could begin to relax.

"How's the chubby 27-game winner?" asked Donn Clendenon, the big grin on this face.

"Still chubby," said Tom, giving Donn his biggest smile. "Thanks to your home run."

Al Weis came over.

"Nice game. Nice game," he said.

He was bubbling all over and, the way he had been hitting the ball, he had every right to be bubbly.

"You'll be batting cleanup tomorrow," said Seaver to the little hero, and slapped Weis on the back.

Getting out of his uniform, Tom looked at Jerry Koosman who was already getting into his street clothes.

"Wrap it up tomorrow, Koos," said Tom. "I don't want to go back to Baltimore."

"I'll get 'em," said Koos. "I'll get 'em."

Tom briefly answered a few more questions from the sportswriters, then ducked into the shower, dressed quickly and hurried to the clubhouse. His father and Nancy were waiting.

"We'll never forget this day," Charley Seaver said. "None of us will."

The three Seavers pushed their way through the crowd to Tom's car, then drove to Lum's, the Chinese restaurant, where the rest of the Seaver family awaited them.

As Tom, Nancy, and Charley Seaver walked into

Lum's, a huge crowd that had jammed this popular restaurant stood and applauded. Tom was startled, embarrassed. But Nancy Seaver cheerfully greeted the people and calmly waved at all the diners.

Nancy had become more than just a ballplayer's wife. Back in late summer, the New York *Post* had signed Nancy to write a series of feature columns discussing her particular view of the play-off games, and if the Mets won the play-off against Atlanta, the column would continue on throughout the World Series. Her picture had appeared each day, smack on the front page of the paper, and she was recognized and greeted everywhere. She, too, had her fans; many of them were here at Lum's and she waved at them happily.

Nancy Seaver made her debut as a feature reporter for the New York *Post* with this gem of a column before the first play-off game:

Every four days my husband stops speaking to me. It's not the kind of thing that makes me want to start packing my bags for Juarez, in fact, it usually lands me in places like Atlanta. But it creates some pretty weird problems.

Tom starts getting preoccupied with things like the pattern of the kitchen wallpaper on the night before he pitches. By the day of the game, he's in a mental world of his own.

And that's when the fun starts.

"George," I'll say. That's his name. George Thomas Seaver. "George, how do you like the new collar for the dog? George? George?" Then he'll say something like, "Can't you see I'm reading, Nancy?"

Sure enough, he'll have his nose buried in *The*

Grapes of Wrath. Only the pages don't turn. What's turning are all those little wheels and gears and sprockets in his head. From then on we speak in a sort of code. I've learned to rely on my own special brand of ESP to break the code and find out what's going on behind the grunts and pauses. On Saturday in Atlanta, my ESP was definitely giving me bad vibrations.

I just had a feeling that he didn't have his good stuff. I knew for sure when he went to the mound. Usually he kind of hops and skips over from the dugout, like a peppy little kid. In Atlanta, it was more of a shuffle than a hop.

You can imagine how I began to feel after Tony Gonzalez' home run in the fifth inning. And Hank Aaron's in the seventh.

Actually most baseball wives probably go through worse mental anguish than their husbands in uptight on-the-field situations. You feel so frustrated— all you can do is cross your fingers and yell your heart out.

After Aaron's homer, I kept yelling, but I mentally began preparations to comfort a losing pitcher. I'm a little out of practice at that. As I vaguely remember it, it involves pouring myself into a super-sexy dress, breaking out a bottle of Lancer's and saying soft romantic things like, "The umpire was an idiot, but let's forget about it."

Thank goodness for the Mets' eighth-inning revival. I wasn't even mad when Gil Hodges took Tom out of the lineup so that J. C. Martin could pinch-hit. It's great to be married to a superstar, as far as I'm concerned. But even superstars have bad days—and that's when an all-around great team really shows its stuff.

And I really loved the Brave in the Indian costume

who comes out of his teepee and does a war dance every time the Braves get a homer. Shea Stadium ought to have a mascot, too.

I know a brown poodle named Slider who might be interested, but he's a terrible war dancer.

In a column written on the day that Seaver faced the Orioles in the fourth game of the Series, Nancy wrote:

Tom's pitching today and everyone wants to know if I'm worried. Well I'm not. I have great confidence in his ability and I know he's not going to pitch many losing games.

Besides I'm not a losing pitcher's wife.

With all the excitement, my big problem now is seeing that he gets a good night's sleep. We have an unlisted phone number, yet the phone seems to ring all night long. Then there's the neighbors who come to wish him luck. They come in groups of 30s.

Tom isn't superstitious like so many players are, but his stomach is jumpy on the morning that he pitches so I prepare soft-boiled eggs, one strip of very dry bacon, and some dry cereal. Any other mornings he can eat like a horse.

A lot depends on today's game. If Tom pitches the way everyone knows he can, we'll be only one game away from the championship. The thought absolutely floors me—the World Champion Mets. Six months ago the thought would have made me wonder if I should consult a psychiatrist.

You just don't know how much it means to be back home among friends. The trip to Baltimore was a bad trip. The hotel was awful and we didn't have good seats to watch the game.

Here at Shea, everyone is like a family—the fans,

the other wives. You feel so different. Even Tom remarked how good it was not to be in enemy territory. After the games we sit around and rehash every play. It's like being on an incredible fast ride and we're all afraid to slow down.

Take yesterday's game. It's all like a blur in my head except for those two unbelievable catches by Tommie Agee. All the players' wives are cheerleaders and when Tommie made those great plays we screamed and jumped up and down like everyone else.

What a marvelous game Gary Gentry pitched. When he walked out to the mound yesterday, he looked so determined. I just knew he'd have a great day. That's what this Mets team is all about—we're all family and we know each other so well, we can just look and tell what the other is thinking.

Tom is thinking about that game he lost in Baltimore and like I said in the first place, I'm not a losing pitcher's wife.

In another column she wrote:

During the regular season I was uptight when Tom was pitching and I'm having fun and he isn't. We (the wives) just sit there and chat about all kinds of things.

But the World Series is something else. We probably had the loudest, wildest, kookiest cheering section in any ballpark. We were yelling ourselves hoarse.

The weekend in Baltimore was hectic, but now at home we are just going to try and get some rest so we can all be set for the games at Shea. I just know we are going to win. I just know it. I hope we can win 3 straight at Shea.

158

Shortly after Tom's win in the Series, she wrote:

> At first I thought Donn Clendenson's homer would be all Tom needed. It wasn't a comfortable lead, but he seemed to have such control of the game from the sixth inning. I thought he would shut them out. Then they tied the score in the ninth and there was that unbelievable catch by Ron Swoboda. I was sitting on the edge of my seat, screaming, yelling, wringing my hands.
>
> It all ended so suddenly. It was such a complete surprise and relief. I wanted to run right out on the field and hug Tom and tell him how proud I was of the way he pitched. . . .

Back at Lum's, after the festive dinner, Tom and Nancy said their good-byes to the rest of the family and all their friends at the restaurant and returned to their Bayside apartment.

On the front door they saw a huge sign put up by their neighbors:

"Nice going, Tom, we knew you could do it."

On the nights that he pitched, Tom usually had trouble falling asleep. He would pitch, toss, and roll and relive every mistake. But this night he was sound asleep as soon as his head hit the pillow.

In the fifth game of the Series, the Mets magic, often slow in making itself manifest, suddenly began to work.

In the top of the third inning, the Orioles' Mark Belanger slapped out a single. Dave McNally, instead of a sacrifice bunt, crossed up the Mets and surprised everyone in the ballpark by smashing a long drive into the seats for a home run, and the Orioles had a 2–0 lead. To make matters worse, Frank Robinson drove a Koosman fastball for another home run and the Orioles had a 3–0 advantage.

But that was all the scoring for the Baltimore team. Jerry Koosman, pitching magnificently, held the Oriole sluggers at bay throughout the rest of the game.

The magic began to work, at last, in the Mets half of the sixth inning.

Cleon Jones was hit by a pitched ball. The ball barely grazed his shoe. And then big Donn Clendenon picked out a fastball and drove it fully 500 feet for his third home run of the Series, and the score was 3–2, in favor of the Orioles.

In the seventh inning, the .215 hitter Al Weis had the overflowing crowd in Shea Stadium standing on its feet, cheering itself hoarse, by driving a pitch over the left-field fence. The rivals for the world championship were now tied, 3–3.

In the eighth, Cleon Jones hit one that bounced off the fence for a double. The ball had just missed clearing the wall at the 395 mark.

Swoboda doubled and Jones scored. The Mets 4, Orioles 3.

Boog Powell messed up a grounder around first base and Swoboda scored. Mets 5, Orioles 3.

Three outs to go and the Mets would have the championship.

Frank Robinson walked and Koosman was upset. A home run would tie up the game, and the power hitters were coming up.

But Koosman settled down.

Boog Powell hit one on the ground to Al Weis and Weis got the force-out at second. An easy fly ball to Ron Swoboda, and there were two outs.

No one sat in his seat in Shea Stadium. They were cheering and hollering and standing on every pitch now.

Johnson tagged a pitch, a fly ball deep, but Cleon Jones camped under it, waited for it to come down, gloved it. The New York Mets, the unbelievable Mets, the magic Mets were world champions!

Pandemonium in the stands. Pandemonium on the field. The fans ran amok, tearing up the field, trying to get to their heroes.

Mrs. Payson, owner of the Mets, cried. Old Casey Stengel, who had managed the Mets when they were Amazin', hugged Gil Hodges. And they all made a wild dash for the clubhouse before they were mobbed by the raving fans.

But there was pandemonium in the clubhouse too. Everyone was delirious. Champagne flowed into the cups and more of it over the heads of the ballplayers, the manager, the coaches, even the newspapermen who had crowded into the room.

"Don't give me that destiny stuff!" yelled Ron Swoboda, the drink in his hand. "Destiny brings you so far, but destiny doesn't win you a hundred games! Destiny doesn't win you a play-off! And destiny doesn't win you four games in a World Series!"

"It's beautiful!" yelled Tom Seaver. "Beautiful! Beautiful! Beautiful! It's the biggest thrill in my life! We played to win. We never quit. We'd come from behind to win. We did it today! Beautiful! Beautiful! Beautiful!"

"We're Number One," shouted all New York.

There had never been anything like it in the city that was supposed to be so cool, so sophisticated.

Teachers stopped teaching—the kids wouldn't be listening anyhow. Bosses closed their offices because no one could be kept at his tools or his desk. The cops didn't even try to keep order in the streets. One bus driver on the Madison Avenue line yelled, "Everyone rides free! All aboard! Everyone rides this bus free!"

The staid *Wall Street Journal* reported the story on page one, center.

> It was bigger than the celebration of the end of World War II. It was bigger than the celebration of Lindbergh's solo flight, than the celebration of the return of the Apollo astronauts.
>
> You could roll all those days together and it wouldn't compare with this.

They were hugging, they were kissing, they were drinking in the streets. New York was Number One, and New York celebrated as it never had before.

The next morning there was a ticker-tape parade from Bowling Green at the bottom of Manhattan to City Hall, the players and their wives in black, shiny, limousines, a million people in the streets to do honor to their heroes. They cheered and threw confetti as the entourage moved slowly through lower Broadway, and ticker tape showered out of the windows of the shops and offices along the way. Crowds poured off the sidewalks to stop the cars, shake hands with the victorious Mets, beg for autographs. And at City Hall, Mayor John Lindsay waited to greet them and make his speech of gratitude, to thank the Mets in behalf of all the citizens of New York, for all the honors they had brought the Big Apple.

And there was more.

All sorts of offers poured into the Seaver home, tempting Tom with all kinds of money to lend his name to some commercial product or another. He was offered $70,000 if he and Nancy would join a stock acting company in Florida for seven weeks. Tom didn't take that offer.

"I don't think I'm an actor," he said.

He did take an offer from one of the Las Vegas hotels and, with Art Shamsky, Ed Kranepool, Jerry Koosman, and a few other Mets, got up on the hotel's stage and sang "The Impossible Dream" from the musical *Man of La Mancha.*

"We set the art of supper-club singing back several centuries," said Tom, "but the money was fine."

Each of the Mets got $5,000 for the performance, which wasn't bad at all. Tom Seaver always had a proper respect for money; he also had a good sense of humor.

There were some bad strokes, however, that came with the Las Vegas appearance. Tom had naturally brought along Nancy, and the pretty young wife, remarkably photogenic, was always there when the TV cameras started to roll. That's the way the TV men wanted it. But there was some talk among the other Mets of Nancy's horning in on their glory; they resented it.

There was also some resentment about the way the big money offers were all going Tom's way. They were appreciative enough of his strong pitching down the stretch to win the division, the league, and the World Series, but they felt that everyone in the Mets lineup had done his share, that they had won as a team. For all Tom's kidding in the clubhouse, for all the cheerleading he did, for all he did to help make a unit of the club, and for all of his key role in building up the team's morale, there was the beginning of a rift that wouldn't do the Mets any good in 1970.

Of course, the sportswriters were not involved. They voted him the Cy Young award as the best pitcher in the League. Actually, they couldn't do anything less. He was edged out of the Most Valuable Player Award in 1969 by the great Giants' star Willie McCovey, but only because two writers who believed pitchers should be excluded from the voting left his name entirely out of their ballots.

But he won the S. Rae Hickock diamond-studded $10,000 belt as the Professional Athlete of the Year. The *Sporting News* named him Man of the Year and *Sports Illustrated* selected Tom as their Sportsman of the Year at their annual sports luncheon.

The Mets owner, Joan Payson, Commissioner Bowie Kuhn, and such immortals as Joe DiMaggio, Dizzy Dean, and Stan Musial were present at the affair.

"There are two things of primary importance to me," said Tom, making the obligatory acceptance speech, "and they're both in this room. My marriage and baseball. I would not do anything to jeopardize either of them."

There were tears in Nancy's eyes.

"I wouldn't have had the success I've had without Nancy's help," continued Tom. "I wish you'd thank her for me.

"Gee, I told you not to cry," Tom said.

And the tears rolled down Nancy's cheeks as all the guests at the luncheon applauded the young star and his beautiful young wife.

It had been the greatest year in the history of the Mets. It had been the greatest year in the lives of young Tom Seaver, and Nancy.

14
DISAPPOINTMENTS

It was a busy winter for the Tom Seavers. They fell in love with and bought a 90-year-old barnhouse near Greenwich, Connecticut. Greenwich is a bedroom suburb for a host of executives whose offices are in New York City. There was much to repair in the old house and Nancy and Tom spent hour on hour remodeling, painting, and, of course, redecorating. Tom added a wine cellar that he designed and built himself. The Seavers were becoming connoisseurs of expensive wines.

They rarely appeared at the usual social affairs, but they were constantly being called for public appearances of one kind or another, mostly for well-paid television appearances. Sometimes it was Tom alone; often enough it was Tom and Nancy facing the TV cameras.

The TV talk show host Alan Burke had Tom and Nancy on his program regularly. He wanted to do a regular program with Tom. On the Kraft Music Hall show Tom subjected himself to having a pie slapped into his face, for which he was paid handsomely. Rocky Graziano, that lovable ex-middleweight champion of the ring, had both Nancy and Tom on a TV pilot show. And then there were all the interviews for newspaper and magazine stories, the negotiations for endorsements of a variety of commercial products, and the public appearances in one kind of shop and another to sign autographs.

It all paid well, The checks kept coming in, and Tom was getting the kind of publicity that would have cost millions. Still, they had time enough to place a small ad in the sports pages of *The New York Times* December 31, 1969.

"On the eve of 1970," the ad read, "please join us in a prayer for peace."

The ad was signed, "Tom and Nancy Seaver."

Nancy spent time reading the best-selling novels. Tom read history, biography, and novels that dealt with the troubles and problems of the times. Tom Seaver was a thinking man and his thoughts were not limited to baseball, however devoted he was to the game. He was fully aware of the world around him, its evil as well as its good, and in his quiet way he let the world know what he was thinking.

He matured, perhaps slowly in the eyes of some, but he matured. He could still horse around in the clubhouse, but he became more and more thoughtful about values, philosophical values, and perhaps for that reason he became an even quieter person, a more withdrawn person, for the most part keeping his deeper thoughts to himself.

"I think I've become more introverted," Tom said.

There was no doubt that Tom was a changed man

in 1970, but the change was largely misinterpreted. There was the feeling, particularly among the ballplayers on his own club, that all the success he was experiencing had gone to his head.

The Mets front office signed Tom to a contract that called for $80,000 for 1970, a huge jump from his 1969 salary, and Tom said, "One day they'll be paying ballplayers $200,000."

They were going to pay a lot more than that, in time, but Tom's bit of prophecy was completely misunderstood, again particularly by his own teammates. The way they saw it, Tom was thinking only of himself as that $200,000 ballplayer.

There was no question about it. The resentment among the Mets against Tom, which had begun with their resentment of the presence of Nancy Seaver in Las Vegas, had built up during the winter of 1969 and the early spring of 1970 with every new honor, with every bit of good fortune, with every bit of publicity Tom Seaver was fortunate enough to receive.

"Following the winter of his great content," wrote one sportswriter, "the writers detected a certain aloofness in Seaver. He frequently did not have time to sit through long periods of questioning like he formerly did and there were many times he was in a hurry to get out of the clubhouse."

Nobody asked him why the hurry. Most, if not all of them, were of the opinion that Tom's hat had become too tight for his head.

This attitude didn't help to pull the team together. It certainly cut into the unity that Tom had helped bring the club and brought instead a feeling of tenseness.

There were other factors, however, that affected

the Mets in the 1970 battle for the division title and the National League pennant. Ron Swoboda put it rather well.

"It went to our heads," he said, talking about the phenomenal 1969 season. "Some stars thought they were superstars, some fringe guys thought they were stars, nobody worked hard, nobody really cared.

"Those guys who performed in Las Vegas made some extra dough, but they created some jealousies. We won because we had been a one-for-all and all-for-one team. Now we were cashing in separately. That created problems. It even created problems among that group. Seaver wanted more money than the others got and don't forget we had to play together again a few months later."

Maybe everything Ron Swoboda said was completely on target. Tom Seaver didn't want more money than the others got. Tom Seaver wanted the money he felt his pitching merited. But Swoboda was undoubtedly speaking the sentiments of a good many of the Mets ballplayers.

Whatever the feelings of some of his teammates, Tom started the 1970 season from where he had left off in 1969. He set himself a goal of 30 victories for 1970, and the way he began to pitch at the beginning of the season, the goal was a pretty realistic one.

Tom won the opening game. He was the winner in his second appearance on the mound. In his third appearance he broke a club record, tied a major league record, and established a record that still has not been matched.

The San Diego Padres had come to Shea Stadium and Tom Seaver was on a roll. He was pitching strikes and nothing but strikes, and striking out one hitter after another.

Johnny Podres, the once great pitching star for the Brooklyn and L.A. Dodgers, the man who shared the major league record for consecutive strikeouts, eight in a row, was watching in the stands, scarcely believing what he saw.

"Fantastic!" he said, watching Tom Seaver pump them across the plate. "As hard as he's throwing, he's still hitting the spots. If you don't swing at it, it's still a strike."

At the beginning of every inning, Tom didn't walk, he ran to the mound.

"Look at that guy!" exclaimed an unhappy Padre player. "He can't wait to throw the ball, he's going good."

Tom was pitching the way he liked to go, full speed ahead and damn the topedoes. The adrenaline was flowing freely and he was setting those Padres down one after another with a vicious fastball that no hitter could touch.

He got the first two Padres up in the eighth on strikes, and there was a loud noise from the crowd. He looked up at the big scoreboard and the scoreboard was flashing, "THAT WAS SEAVER'S 15TH STRIKEOUT, TYING NOLAN RYAN FOR THE CLUB RECORD."

Tom himself was a bit taken aback by the flashing sign. He hadn't thought he had that many strikeouts under his belt.

"Hell," he said. "Let's go for another one."

Up to hit was Ivan Murrell, pinch-hitting for San Diego, and Tom Seaver breezed a strike by him.

"He's pitching like a machine," said Johnny Podres, realizing that his own record of eight straight strikeouts might very well be equaled, might even be wiped out of baseball's record books.

Strike two and, quickly; Tom Seaver always pitched quickly. Strike three!

Sixteen strikeouts at the end of eight innings, and seven in a row.

Back in the dugout, Tom recalled Steve Carlton striking out 19 in a game he lost against the Mets. It was Ron Swoboda's two home runs that had done him in, beating the great pitcher 4–3.

The 19 strikeouts had set a major league record, but Tom was thinking about winning the game. Nevertheless, the record was on his mind when he went to the mound for the ninth and last inning of the game. He had a chance to match that record of Carlton's and he would give it his best try.

Van Kelly was the cleanup hitter for the Padres and he swung his bat menacingly at the plate.

"Strike one! Strike two! Strike three!"

Eight strikeouts in a row, and Johnny Podres leaned back in his seat. Seaver would be there in the record books to share the consecutive strikeout record with him. Podres knew in his bones that that record wasn't going to stand for more than a few minutes.

Clarence Gaston was the next San Diego player at the plate. Three fastballs and Gaston, his bat still up around his shoulders, was out on strikes.

Johnny Podres didn't even blink an eye. His record, set some 20 years earlier, was broken. Seaver had whiffed nine men in a row and Podres could only sit and wonder at the speed, the delivery, the artistry of young Seaver.

And Tom now had 18 strikeouts for the game. One

man more to face, one chance to equal Carlton's record, and he went at it.

Al Ferrara was the third man to advance to the plate for the Padres, and he had hit a fastball for a home run in the second inning.

"Don't throw him a fastball," said Tom to himself, standing on the mound.

He threw him a slider that nipped the outside corner of the plate.

"Strike one!"

The next pitch was a ball, the only ball he had tossed in the inning.

Tom decided to gamble with a fastball. Ferrara took a vicious cut, and missed.

"Strike two!"

Just one strike away from the record.

For a moment, Tom hesitated, If he threw Ferrara a slider, he might get enough of the ball to roll it into the infield. It would mean the game, but it would kill the strikeout record he now wanted, and wanted badly.

A fastball was what Ferrara was waiting for, he figured, and he could take the fastball out of the park, as he had done before.

"Hell," thought Tom. "I'm going with my best pitch!"

And he did.

He let the fastball rip.

It swung toward the middle of the plate.

"Damn!" thought Tom. "It should be more inside!"

Ferrara was waiting for it. He swung from his heels, and he missed!

Shea Stadium rocked with the great roar from the stands.

"Strike three!"

Tom Seaver had done it! Nineteen strikeouts to match the record of Steve Carlton. Ten straight strikeouts to create a new one for baseball's record books!

The Mets players forgot all their differences, all the petty jealousy. There wasn't a man who didn't slap the back of their star pitcher, congratulate him on a great job on the mound.

Rube Walker, the Mets pitching coach, was ecstatic.

"When Carlton struck out 19 last year," he said, "I said that no one would match that record for a long time. Well, son of a gun, this guy comes along and matches it in the very next season."

"But I tell you what," he continued, "I'll stake a lot on this prediction. I don't think anyone's going to come along for a long time and match those ten strikeouts in a row."

Johnny Podres said that Tom had pitched in a groove that was remarkable, but that he'd never throw that hard again, ever.

"That's what Ron Santo said last year," rejoined Tom when told of Podres' remarks, "when I pitched that one-hitter, that almost perfect game against the Cubs. He said I'd never throw that hard again. Maybe Podres and Santo ought to get together and have dinner."

Tom had won 13 games in a row now, beginning with the end of the 1969 season. He was starting to wonder, himself, when he'd lose a game. He won his first five starts in 1970, making it 15 in a row, and the Mets began to feel that they were a cinch to win every time Tom took the mound.

He did lose, eventually, after carrying his streak

to 6 games in a row for 1970, 16 in a row since August of 1969, when the Mets failed to score behind him in a close one with the Montreal Expos.

"You can't win them all," said Tom, "but it's no fun to lose."

He had begun to think of himself as invincible.

Four days later, he pitched a one-hit game against the Philadelphia Phillies, striking out 15 for his nine-inning stint.

"I'll take a one-hit, 15-strikeout game any time," he said, but he couldn't hide his disappointment. Once again he had missed the perfect dream, the dream of a perfectionist.

The 1970 division race was a three-club affair—the Mets, the Cubs, and the Pirates battling it out for the championship. The Mets won 20 of their 27 games from June 12 to July 9, and the New York club was in front by a game and a half. But Montreal beat them in the next three games and Los Angeles took the next two from them, and the Mets never regained the lead.

Tom lost two straight.

Bursting with anger, he stormed into the clubhouse.

The sportswriters had told Tom what Carl Morton, the Expos winning pitcher had said about it.

"We beat Seaver last week. Maybe he was trying too hard to make up for it."

"Is that what he said?" snapped Tom. "It just shows you how stupid he is."

This was another kind of Tom Seaver, a Tom Seaver the writers had never met before.

"Losing appears to be getting to Seaver," one sportswriter wrote for his column. "He is not reacting to adversity as well as he did to success. He's showing us another side of Tom, a not-so-pleasant side.

"Ever since he came within two outs of pitching a perfect game against the Cubs last July, Seaver has pictured himself as 'the perfect pitcher,' and has tried in every start since then to achieve what he narrowly missed. The moment he gives up the first hit or the first walk in a game, he immediately becomes annoyed with himself."

Tom had a word for another writer about that loss to Montreal.

"Frankly," he said, "after that game I didn't want to talk to anybody."

And then, more to explain than apologize, he added, "I've been lucky to be able to control myself on the mound and off the field, but some people think I'm not subject to everyday emotion just like everybody else. I'm not allowed to get mad at myself and show it. If you let it stay in, it'll give you ulcers."

Tom lost four straight games. His record was now seven wins against five losses. He had pitched well enough, but the Mets had collected a grand total of two hits for each of the five defeats.

Eventually, however, the Mets began to hit once more and at the All-Star break, Tom had won 14 games.

In August, Hodges asked Tom whether he would like to pitch with only three days rest instead of the customary four days. Tom didn't like the idea at all. He really needed four full days, but if Hodges insisted, he would try it. He idolized Gil Hodges and would do anything for him.

Tom went along with the idea, but it did not work out at all.

He lost his next game to the Atlanta Braves, 3–2. He was hit hard in the next game, losing to the Houston Astros 9–4. He lost to the Cincinnati Reds 7–5. His record was now 17 and 9.

The reaction of the Mets to Tom's slump was mixed. There were his good friends who tried to help him get back into form. There were others who were not too fond of him, perhaps envied him, for all the goodies that had come his way following the triumphant year of 1969.

"It couldn't happen to a nicer guy," they said sarcastically. "He didn't share the glory. We're not going to share his failure."

The feeling among a few of the Mets was that Tom cared more about himself than about the team, and Tom was aware of that feeling.

"How do you figure the pennant race?" he was asked by a newsman. It might as well have been asked by one of his less than friendly teammates.

"I haven't had time to think about it," snapped Tom, "I'm too busy thinking about myself."

He wasn't yelling words of encouragement from the bench when someone else was pitching for the Mets. His teammates made note of it and said what they thought about it to the press.

"How can I?" said Tom to the newspaper people. "Last year I would cheer the others and could help pitchers with advice. You can't contribute when you're not winning. How am I going to offer any advice when I can't win a game? I have to help myself before I can help anybody else."

Tom lost 9 of his next 11 starts, following the

August decision to pitch with just three days' rest. There was one no-decision and only one win in those 11 starts.

The Mets wound up third in the Eastern Division of the National League in 1970.

Tom had won 18 games against 12 defeats. He had led the league in strikeouts, establishing a record for right-handed pitchers with 283 K's. He had the lowest earned-run average in the league at 2.81, yet had heard himself booed for the first time in Shea Stadium. He was tired and discouraged.

Gil Hodges said, "Seaver's a perfectionist. He's always trying to be perfect, to be analytical, to be Tom Seaver."

"I need a vacation," said Tom. "I need to get away, refresh myself, and start all over."

He was tired enough, he needed the rest enough, but he wasn't through, not by a long shot. Good things were ahead, that he was sure of.

And Nancy was going to have a baby!

15
TRADES, INJURIES, AND THE LOSS OF GIL HODGES

Tom and Nancy took a trip through the States following the disappointments of the 1970 baseball season.

"We've got to get away to restore ourselves," said Tom.

With a mobile home and their dog, Slider, they traveled through New England and west through Yellowstone Park, not forgetting a stop at Cooperstown to visit the Baseball Hall of Fame. One of Tom's baseball caps was on display there. It was the cap he had worn in April when he tied the record for strikeouts. Tom and Nancy got a thrill out of seeing the thousand-and-one exhibits of the greats: Babe Ruth's uniform, Ty Cobb's glove and bat, and assorted equipment of all the baseball immortals. "It was a thrill of a lifetime," he later recalled.

The trip in the mobile home got them away but not from all of it. They traveled nearly nine thousand miles, from coast to coast, and were recognized wherever they went. If it wasn't Tom, it was Nancy who was known from all the television appearances and numerous pictures of the two in all the papers.

They were in Wichita, Kansas, sitting in a restaurant, when a young girl passing their table stopped, looked at Tom, and said, "You're Tom Seaver, aren't you?"

It was pleasant enough being recognized so far from home and Tom answered, pleasantly enough, "Yes, I am."

"I thought so," said the girl. "I recognized your wife."

For the first time since they'd been married, Tom Seaver went down to spring training in St. Petersburg alone. Nancy was back in Greenwich, waiting for her baby to come. Tom had been a good father-to-be. He had attended all the courses at the hospital for the natural birth Nancy wanted. He said, "We used to have a nice place on the beach here in St. Petersburg. Now I'm here alone, and living in a hotel alone is a drag."

He missed Nancy very much, and waiting for the call that would send him flying back to Greenwich when the baby was to be delivered had him on edge. The horrible slump in 1970, when he was the winner in only one of the last fifty games of the season, was on his mind, too, but Nancy and the coming infant were his top concerns.

The call from Connecticut came at last. Actually, there were three calls.

At two in the morning, it was Nancy on the phone.

"Tom, I think I'm having the baby."

At four in the morning it was, "Tom, I'm still in labor."

At six, as calmly as she could manage it, Nancy said, "I'm going to the hospital to have the baby."

Tom Seaver was on the next plane.

He landed at the Newark airport in a blizzard. He drove to the hospital in Greenwich. He got into surgical clothes as fast as he could, and walked into the labor room.

He was tan with the Florida sun and looked as fit as a young "Mr. America." Nancy was white and perspiring, uncomfortable.

"You make me sick," she said to him.

Tom laughed.

There was a baby coming, his first child, and Nancy was going to be all right.

He wiped the perspiration from her face, gently.

"Everything is going great," he said to Nancy.

"I quit," said Nancy.

"You can't quit now," said Tom. "You can't quit." And gently, lovingly, encouragingly, he did everything he was supposed to do in the labor room, as he had been taught in the natural childbirth classes, and Nancy delivered their child, Sarah Lynn Seaver.

Tom hugged and kissed Nancy, kissed the new baby, handed out cigars and then, after five marvelous days with his beautifully expanded family, headed back to his job, to spring training.

Just prior to the start of the 1971 season, Gil Hodges traded Ron Swoboda to the Montreal Expos. Ron, always the extrovert, had rubbed Hodges the wrong way on a number of occasions and it had been rumored that he was slated to go.

At various times Swoboda looked like one of the

finest young prospects in baseball, but he was not consistent at the plate, and despite his sometimes long-distance clouting when he did hit, he had tailed off until he hit a mediocre .233 in 1970, and he and Hodges were not comfortable with each other.

As he left for Montreal, Swoboda took a jab at Seaver. "Tom Seaver and I have never been the best of friends," Ron told a New York *Post* sportswriter. "We come from different backgrounds. He has no feeling for people other than himself. He's completely self-centered."

Tom laughed at Swoboda's remarks. "I guess Ron's angry and I can't blame him. I'm really sorry to see him go."

When the season opened, things didn't go well in the first half of the season—for the Mets or for Seaver. The team played erratic ball. The pitching was off and the hitters just seemed to fade away; there was not one .300 hitter on the team. Consequently they dropped game after game. By July the Mets had lost 20 of their last 29 games.

Seaver's record of 11 wins and 8 defeats was one of the few bright spots, but it was not a record that Tom was too happy about.

Now it was early August and the sportswriters were writing Tom Seaver's obituary.

"This is not Tom Seaver's year," a noted New York writer said. "He's lost his fastball. He's through."

One writer, Maury Allen of the New York *Post*, did note that Tom was getting little support from the Mets hitters. He had given up three runs or less in five of those losses. One of the games he lost by a 3–1 score, twice by 3–2, once by 2–1 and one game was lost by a 2–0 score. With all those defeats, however, he was leading the National League in strikeouts with 202, and had the second best ERA average at 2.55.

"There are times this year when I just don't have my fastball," said Tom, as always analyzing his own performance on the mound, "and I have to fight to find it."

And find it he did. By mid-September he had improved his record to 18 wins against 8 defeats. He didn't lose a game in August, winning 7 straight. His streak was finally broken in Pittsburgh when the Mets were shut out in a 1-0 game.

"I pitched well enough," said Tom quietly in the clubhouse. "But I didn't win. And that's all that counts, winning."

Buddy Harrelson, looking at his obviously un-happy road roommate across the room, said, "It doesn't matter how good he pitches or how good things have been going for him, if he loses he just can't take it. He really gets dejected when he loses."

Tom beat the Pirates in his next outing, 3-1, striking out 10. That made it 19 victories for 1971. He wanted to make it 20.

"It takes 20 victories for people to recognize you as a great pitcher," said Tom Seaver.

With those 20 victories in sight, Tom, never over-modest but never the real egotist, said, "I've been looking through the records and I don't think I've had two bad days all year. I've been very consistent and, quite honestly, I feel I've pitched as well as ever. I feel I'm the best pitcher in baseball. I really do."

It wasn't boasting. Tom Seaver wasn't given to boasting. He was making an honest observation of his pitching, and only after he had studied and analyzed all those records as objectively and as carefully as he could.

Tom got the coveted 20th win for 1971, beating the St. Louis Cardinals at the end of the season 6–1, striking out 13 of the Redbirds. It was a wholly personal triumph. The Mets hadn't been able to manage more than 83 wins against 79 losses, and finished the year tied for third, 14 games from the top of the league; but for Tom there could only be applause from the fans, and they gave it to him eagerly as he left the mound, after his last victory of the season.

He had lost only two games after the All-Star break. He had led the league in strikeouts with 289, breaking his own record of 283. He also led the league in earned-run average, giving up only an average of 1.76 earned runs a game.

No one could ask more of a pitcher, except Tom Seaver himself. No one demanded more of himself, as a performer and as a winner than did "the perfectionist with a touch for realism," Tom Seaver.

Thoughts turned now to the 1972 baseball season, but before it could even get started, the baseball world was in for a couple of sharp jolts, and certainly one great shock for everyone in the game, and especially for the New York Mets.

On April 1, 1972, the baseball players went on strike. Again, it was the pension question. But it would be settled and baseball would go back to its normal routines.

However, there was no going back to the normal routines after the headlines that hit the sports pages on April 2: "GIL HODGES DEAD."

On Easter Sunday, Hodges had gone off to play golf with his Mets coaches, Rube Walker, Joe Pignatano and Eddie Yost. On their return to the Ramada Inn where they were all staying, Hodges suddenly collapsed and fell backward, his head hitting the stone pavement. He was unconscious, perhaps already dead, before any help could be summoned. It was a heart attack and the great Gil Hodges, idol of Brooklyn, idol of so many baseball fans around the country, was dead just two days before his forty-eighth birthday.

The outpouring of sympathy was universal. Few men in baseball had been so respected, so admired, so much loved.

The night of Easter Sunday, with perhaps insensitive haste, the Mets front office announced that Yogi Berra would take over as manager of the Mets. Yogi was and is one of those great lovable characters in baseball. Everyone had expected that he would be given the managerial job in Shea Stadium when Casey Stengel had retired, but he was bypassed. His appointment at this time came as no surprise and was even welcomed; but everyone thought, too, that Bob Scheffing and M. Donald Grant, the big guns in the Mets organization, might have waited a little while in their announcement, waited at least until Gil Hodges had been carried north to his hometown and properly buried.

Actually, though the newspapermen knew it soon enough, the announcement of Berra's appointment wasn't made public until the day after Gil Hodges' funeral. There was another announcement made that same day, simultaneously. Ken Singleton, Mike Jorgensen, and Tim Foli had been traded to Montreal for the popular hard-hitting redhead, Rusty Staub.

Staub was a good outfielder, who could hit the ball out of the park at any time. He was certain to add to the offense, an offense that had been so sadly lacking in the 1971 lineup.

Yogi Berra wasn't a Gil Hodges. Nor was he the clown that so many baseball fans imagined. He was one of the greatest catchers in baseball history for 18 years for the Yankees. When he retired as an active player he became a Yankee coach, then managed the Yanks; when he left the Yankees, he joined the Mets as Casey Stengel's right-hand man in the Mets organization. He would not inspire a team to come from behind to victory, but he was a solid, efficient, and down-to-earth guy whose utterly modest sincerity could perhaps bring back the unity that marked the championship team of 1969.

The players' strike didn't last too long, but it did delay the opening game of the 1972 campaign by six days. The delay, however, didn't seem to affect the ballplayers at all. They were ready to go with the first cry of "Play ball!"

Tom Seaver, in marvelous form from the very start, pitched a shutout in the opening game, blanking the Pirates 4–0. The Mets lost the next two but then went on a seven-game winning spree. On May 21 the Mets were six games in front, leading the Eastern Division of the National League with a 25–7 record. Tom Seaver had won more than one-fourth of those games, coming home a winner seven times while losing only one.

And during that streak, Willie Mays, the great Willie Mays, put on a Mets uniform and was back playing in New York.

Listening to the wisdom of the Old Professor, Casey Stengel, who managed the Mets from 1962–65.

The 1965 University of Southern California baseball team, for which Seaver had to go to Fairbanks, Alaska, to prove himself before he could get a scholarship.

Seaver and his mentor Gil Hodges, the Mets' manager
from 1968–71.

Nancy Seaver gives Tom a pregame rubdown on the arm that won
25 games in 1969, the season the Mets
crept ahead of the Cubs to
win the division, the
pennant, and the World
Series.

The newest Mets fan, Sarah
Seaver, with her dad.

"Sorry guys, I haven't learned this pitch yet."

Always at ease with the press, Seaver fielded a daily avalanche of questions, questions, and more questions from anxious reporters.

Nancy rewards her husband for setting a record of ten straight strikeouts and tying a major-league record of 19 strikeouts in one game, against the San Diego Padres in 1970.

At age 25, Seaver was awarded the S. Rae Hickok "Professional Athlete of the Year" award, a diamond-studded belt valued at $10,000. Seaver won with the highest point total in the twenty-year history of the award.

Spring training 1971: Seaver received fan mail before the season even opened.

Check this out: Mets Yogi Berra, Willie Mays, and Seaver arrive in California for Game 1 of the World Series against the Oakland A's. Fortunately, they wore their uniforms, not their sportcoats.

Ready . . .

Aim . . .

Fire!

Seaver picked up his second Cy Young Award in 1973, which he earned with a 19–10 record, 251 strikeouts, and a league-leading 2.07 ERA.

Tom Terrific is greeted by Japanese fans as he and his teammates arrive in Tokyo for an 18-game exhibition series against Japanese teams in 1974.

The expression of a man who has just taken a $34,000 cut in pay, from $170,000 to $136,000 after a tough 1974 season and an 11–11 record.

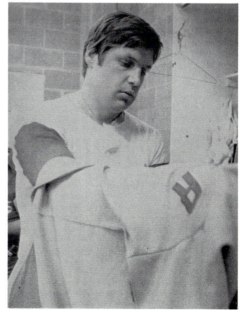

A new jersey: Seaver puts on the uniform of the Cincinnati Reds for the first time, after he was traded by the Mets for four players on June 15, 1977.

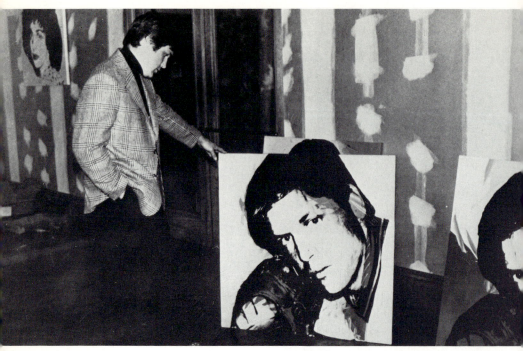

In 1977, Seaver was one of ten top athletes painted by pop artist Andy Warhol. Warhol painted six portraits of Seaver, each "slightly different."

Not only did Seaver pick up his 17th win of the 1977 season, but he also hit a home run, his third as a Red. The scoreboard flashes the message, and Pete Rose offers congratulations.

Tom reports for spring
training, hinting that
he'd like to prolong
the off-season.

1981: Seaver acknowledges a standing ovation after throwing a called strike three to St. Louis Cardinals' first baseman Keith Hernandez to record his 3,000th career strikeout, only the fifth pitcher in baseball history to reach that mark.

Future Hall-of-Famers Johnny Bench and Seaver get off to a slow start in 1982 spring training. It would be Tom's last season as a Red.

Seaver returns to New York in 1983 to post a 9–14 record and a 3.55 ERA. Following that season, the Mets failed to protect Seaver on their roster, and the Chicago White Sox picked him up.

Seaver won his 300th game as a Sox player, but by 1986 he was looking for a trade that would bring him closer to home in the east.

Willie Mays was a living legend in baseball. But the Willie Mays who had played stickball in the streets with the kids in Harlem, the Willie Mays people called "the greatest ballplayer," was certainly long past his prime when he joined the Mets in 1972.

He had sore knees and numerous other physical aches and pains that come with the years. He was 41 years old now. He couldn't throw accurately anymore and he hadn't hit .300 in seven years. True, in 1971 he'd had flashes of his old great form. He stole 23 bases in that season and was a key figure in the San Francisco Giants' winning the Western Division title. But his batting average that year had dropped to .271, and he had hit only 18 home runs.

Nevertheless the fans made a holiday of his return to New York, and the talk around town was all pennant talk.

"Willie Mays," they said, "is pennant insurance."

The Mets weren't all that sure. As a matter of fact, there were many Mets who grumbled, thinking Willie Mays might very well prove a liability to the club, though nobody said as much in public.

Willie Mays the legend could undermine the authority of manager Yogi Berra, just as he had undermined the authority of several managers in San Francisco. He couldn't swing a bat with his old authority. He could no longer cover the vast area in center field as he once did. Still, with fans yelling for Willie in the lineup, Berra had to insert him, wherever and whenever Willie asked it.

He did slug a home run in his first game, and against his old team, the San Francisco Giants. Willie did manage to get on base 14 times in his first 27 at-bats for the Mets. Three of the hits in his first

185

12 at-bats won games. But at 41 years of age there was no consistency to his play in the field or at bat. It was a joy to have Willie back in New York, but he was anything but pennant insurance.

Nevertheless by June 1, the Mets had a record of 30 and 11. They were setting a torrid .732 pace, leading the division by four games. There was some reason to hope for the beginnings of pennant fever in New York, but that hope soon disappeared.

Injuries can slow the progress of the best team in baseball, and the Mets began suffering more than their share. On June 3, George Stone, the Atlanta pitcher, hit Rusty Staub with a darting fastball on his right hand. Rusty stayed in the lineup, but could not swing a bat properly and stopped his effective hitting. Two weeks later X-rays revealed that a small bone near the wrist had been fractured. For all practical purposes, it was the end of the season for the hard-hitting outfielder of the Mets.

Jim Fregosi hurt his shoulder on June 9, and then his leg. He was gone for the rest of the season.

June 16, Cleon Jones collided with Joe Morgan of the Cincinnati Reds and he was nowhere near his form for the rest of the season.

Tom Agee injured his ribs. Buddy Harrelson developed a bad back. Pitcher Gary Gentry was suddenly afflicted with shoulder trouble. Jerry Grote, the star catcher for the Mets, injured his right shoulder and sat out most of the year. He needed an operation to remove bone chips in his elbow, but waited until September before he turned himself in for surgery. Without a first-rate receiver it was impossible to mount a challenge to the league leaders.

The injuries mounted and took their toll, sapping

the morale of the players, and by the end of July the Mets found themselves some 11 games behind the division-leading Pirates.

A number of insiders believed that Yogi Berra had allowed the Mets too much leeway. Players came into spring training overweight and never took off the necessary pounds to play good ball. There were no bed checks throughout the season; players came and went on their own. Problems with Cleon Jones, Tommie Agee, and Willie Mays hampered club discipline.

Yogi was an easygoing guy and the players took advantage of him. There was nothing like the atmosphere that Gil Hodges had created; consequently there was a letdown all the way around.

Despite the injuries that plagued the club, Tom Seaver took his regular turn on the mound every five days, but with all the mounting problems and a few of his own, Seaver had a difficult time, and had to be relieved on several successive occasions. He was struggling for the consistency that he believed was the essence of a great pitcher. Yet despite all the problems, Seaver kept coming back on the mound single-handedly attempting to put together a winning streak.

In a game against the Pirates on August 20, Seaver went the distance for only the third time in 13 starts, but it was one of his finest games. He struck out 15 Pirate hitters, the final 6 in succession, allowed the talented Bucs only five hits, and picked up a 4–1 win. It was Seaver's finest effort of the season and gave him his 18th win against 12 losses.

After the game Tom was in a happy frame of mind.

"When you struggle all season long, and then start

coming on strong like today, it feels great," said Tom. "When you have a good, live fastball late in the game, it's a real luxury, and it makes the team come alive, too. We really needed this game."

Tom achieved win number 19 on September 24 in a brilliant duel against Steve Carlton and the Phils. And once again, Seaver went the entire nine innings, allowing the hard-hitting Phils only five hits, and came away with a 2–1 victory.

One week later Tom produced the pitching gem of the year with a magnificent two-hitter against the Pirates. Tom struck out 13 Pirates to register his 20th decision, and on October 1, Tom collected his 21st win with another outstanding effort as he fanned 10 Expos in a 5–2 triumph.

Twenty-one victories was one game more than he won in 1971, but Tom wasn't especially elated with his stats. There was no doubt that if the Mets had stayed reasonably healthy, Tom could easily have won 25 games, perhaps more, and possibly the pennant as well.

Considering the team's numerous problems, the incredible number of injuries to key players, it was indeed a miracle that the Mets finished the season just three and a half games behind the second-place Chicago Cubs.

There was one consolation that gave manager Berra hope for a better tomorrow: "It was my pitchers," said Yogi. "Seaver, Jon Matlock, and McGraw did one helluva job for me this year. And if they can repeat next year, and if we can stay healthy, we'll give everybody a helluva lot of trouble next year."

It is doubtful that Tom Seaver took as much

consolation as the front office from the fact that the Mets finished above the .500 mark for the season, and that he finished the year with a 21-12 record, including 249 strikeouts and a fine 2.92 ERA. He didn't consider 1972 a bad year. Whatever else, there was Nancy, and there was the baby, Sarah Lynn Seaver; and the baby was enough to bring joy to the Seaver household through 1972 and the many years to follow.

16
THE METS MIRACLE
RETURNS

Spring training time 1973, and a number of the leading players were not reporting to camp. It was another of those labor-management hassles that did not take very long to settle. But Tom Seaver and some of the other players weren't waiting to begin their own training for the season.

Down in Jacksonville, it was Seaver who took over and organized the conditioning program.

"Your turn to throw, but for only five minutes," he said to pitcher Jim McAndrew.

"I want to get a haircut and I want you to get one after this workout," he kiddingly said to Bud Harrelson.

"Fat chance," said Harrelson.

"I'll fine you," Tom warned.

Bud Harrelson laughed. He was glad that he had joined Tom and the other players in this unofficial camp. It was fun being with them all, especially with that great guy Seaver.

Jon Matlack, Jerry Koosman, and Duffy Dyer were all there, along with Tom, and he led them through their calisthenics and wind sprints.

For 10 days, Tom Seaver was the unofficial manager of the Mets.

Dick Young of the New York *Daily News*, who wasn't one of Tom Seaver's best friends, was impressed.

"One of the most organized camps I've ever seen was Seaver's Underground," he wrote. "No doubt if he chooses," he added, "Tom Terrific will be a manager of the future."

He wasn't the first and he wouldn't be the last to recognize Tom Seaver's managerial potential.

When the players reported to camp, following the settlement of the labor-management dispute, Yogi remarked, a little surprised by the condition of Tom's boys, "His guys are ahead of our guys! What do you know?"

Tom Seaver, incidentally, signed a one-year contract in 1973 for $140,000. He signed it for just one year because his eyes were on the paycheck Hank Aaron was getting, and Hank was the highest-paid man in baseball with a salary of $200,000. Tom had that $200,000 mark well in mind and felt he deserved it as the best pitcher in baseball. Another good season in 1974 and he would ask for it.

And the potential for a winning season was there, with the club that Yogi Berra brought north for the pennant wars. John Milner, at first base, had slugged 17 home runs in 1972. Felix Millan was an excellent second baseman and a solid hitter.

Bud Harrelson, who had become one of the finest

shortstops in the league, was healthy and back at his position. Jim Fregosi was a question mark at third. But the outfield with Staub, Cleon Jones, and Willie Mays could be one of the hardest-hitting outfields in Mets history, and the catching with Jerry Grate and Duffy Dyer ranked with the best in the league.

Potentially, the pitching staff was the finest: Jerry Koosman, Jon Matlack, Tug McGraw, George Stone, Ray Sadecki, Jim McAndrew, and the ace of the staff, Tom Seaver.

So the potential was all in place. If the team could stay healthy, they could win it all.

Seaver won the opening game of the season, shutting out the Phils 3–0. They won the second game and Seaver went back to the mound to win the Mets' fourth straight with a 2–1 win. Everything was coming up roses until, as in 1972, a plague of injuries struck.

Milner, Millan, and Cleon Jones were hit by injuries that would keep them out of the lineup for weeks at a time. Harrelson damaged a shoulder and he was on the bench. The Mets hadn't been hitting too well before the spell of injuries. Now with all the regulars out of action, the subs couldn't hit at all.

Tom lost his third start, 1–0. He dropped the next one, 2–1. In the next game he lost 2–0. He had pitched 40 innings in 1973, given up only five runs and all he could show for it was a mediocre 2–2 record.

The Mets were floundering, going nowhere, but Tom suddenly began to win the close games. He posted five straight victories for a 7–3 record. As a matter of fact, in one 21-day period in May and June, Tom was responsible for the Mets' only four wins.

"I just don't know where in hell we would be in this league without Seaver," said Yogi to sportswriter Terry Shore.

I know where you'd be," said the writer. "In last place with a 17-game losing streak and certainly out of any division race."

At the end of August, Tom's record was 15 and 8. He led the league in strikeouts and owned a remarkable 1.70 ERA.

The Mets were at the bottom of the division at this time, seven and a half games behind the leading St. Louis Cardinals, but Seaver's marvelous pitching had kept the team within striking distance of the league leaders.

Buddy Harrelson, back in the lineup for the second time after coming off a disabling injury that had him sidelined for a good part of the season, said, "We should be out of first place by at least 25 games, the way things have gone for us this season. But Seaver, George Stone, Matlack, Harry Parker, and Jerry Koosman have kept us close. We still have a helluva chance," he added.

All season long Berra had said, "All I wanna do is to have the guys stay healthy. If they are not hurt, we got a real shot, we'll be right up there."

All of a sudden, by early August the pennant picture took on an utterly brand-new and astounding look. There was a complete turnaround by the Mets. With Harrelson darting about at shortstop with his customary flair, grabbing those "sure base hits" away from the enemy and catcher Jerry Grote back behind the plate, the Mets started to win game after game.

"You have no idea," said Seaver, "what it means for a pitcher to have an outstanding receiver like

Grote back there behind the plate, thinking like you do."

On August 12 the old Mets magic, missing for two years, suddenly made its appearance again. The Mets swept a four-game series with the Padres and headed for a showdown series with the league-leading Cardinals, who were just five and a half games ahead of the Mets.

"It's beginning to feel like 1969," said Jerry Koosman.

"You gotta believe!" shrieked Tug McGraw. "We're gonna do it again." And in the space of a ten-game streak, McGraw saved six and won three other games. "We may be the first team ever to be last in August and win the pennant."

"I been tellin' you," said Berra. "In this division anything can happen. We're the only club that hasn't had a hot streak. Maybe we're gonna have one now. But remember," said Yogi, coining his most famous phrase:

"It's never over . . . until it's over."

On August 30 Seaver lost a heartbreaker to the Cardinals by a 1–0 score. He had pitched his heart out, striking out nine tough Cardinal hitters, but St. Louis punched across a single with two outs in the tenth inning to take a bitter battle, and now the Mets were down at the bottom of the division again.

Now there were only twenty-three games left to play, and the Mets were still five and a half games behind the Cards. It looked as if they were done. Out of the race.

Seaver won the next game and Ray Sadecki won one. Now they had climbed out of the cellar into fourth place.

The Mets were three games behind the first-place

Cardinals; two and a half games behind second, and half a game behind third-place Montreal. They took four of their next six games and were just two games behind the league leader. St. Louis had slumped and it was the Pirates who were on top in the standings, and the Mets were scheduled to play five games against Pittsburgh. It was a do-or-die series against the Pirates, who had one of their great teams.

The Pirates knocked out Seaver in the third inning of the first game and won easily. They had the second game apparently locked up, 4–1 in the ninth inning, but the Mets rallied for four runs and then Tug McGraw came in to stop the Pirates and the Mets pulled out a dramatic 6–5 win.

It was McGraw now, in game after game, pitching like a Cy Young winner, holding the enemy at bay, during the final stretch that made the Mets magic come alive.

Back in Shea Stadium, the Mets took the Pirates 7–3. In the second game, Cleon Jones made an unbelievable catch of a ball against the wall in the thirteenth inning. The Mets then scored in their half of the thirteenth to make it two wins in a row over the league-leading Pirates. And now the rip-roaring Mets were just one-half game out of first place, and on fire.

Tom Seaver was on the mound with only three days' rest (Tom volunteered for the pitching assignment). The last time he faced the slugging Pirate hitters, they tore into Seaver, drove him out of the box. Not this time. This day Tom pitched a five-hit gem, holding the aggressive Pirates to two runs as Johnny Milner, Wayne Garrett, and Rusty Staub connected for long home runs and the Mets took the crucial game 10–2.

Was VICTORY in sight?

THE METS WERE IN FIRST PLACE!

Here is how the race shaped up in the National League East after the Mets had taken two games from the Pittsburgh Pirates and five clubs steamed into the final nine days of the season:

Team	W	L	PCT.	Games Behind
NEW YORK	79	77	.506	
Pittsburgh	77	76	.503	½
St. Louis	76	80	.487	3
Montreal	75	80	.484	3½
Chicago	75	80	.484	3½
Philadelphia	69	87	.442	10

With only nine days remaining in the season, any one of the five ball clubs could be the winner. Yogi Berra was trying to give his starting pitchers a breather. He had to worry that Seaver was tiring— he showed the ill effects of pitching with only three days' rest. He won a big game against the Pirates, but looked beat after the game. Tom had pitched 2,000 innings during the past seven years and was on a ragged edge. And Yogi had every reason in the world to worry the night of September 26, when the Expos battered Tom for three hits and five runs in the first three innings and the Mets lost, 8 to 5.

But nine days was a long time in 1973; it was a lifetime. There was still time for the Cards, Cubs, Expos, and of course the second-place Pirates to make a final run for the division championship.

The Mets held on, and it wasn't until the very last day of the regular season that the championship was finally decided in a race that went right down to the wire.

Still a half game ahead of the Pirates on October 1, the Mets flew into Chicago for the final three games of the season. A win over the tough fifth-place Cubs would give the Mets the division title, and Berra promptly announced that Tom Seaver would be his pitcher for "the biggest game of the season."

There were Mets who voiced their opposition to Yogi's choice of Seaver.

"He hasn't pitched that well in his last four starts," said Matlack. "I don't want to be negative, but I'm a bit leery. After all, it's the biggest game."

"Seaver got us here," said Bud Harrelson, "but he's got to be very tired. If he doesn't win this one, I've got to sympathize with him."

The day before the big game, Tom was questioned by a corps of sportswriters. "I'm happy to try to get this game for us. I'm not going to pressure myself," said Tom. "I'm going to pitch like I always do. I'm going to give it 100 percent of myself and I think we can win it."

The next day Tom Seaver readied himself on the mound, looked around at his outfield and his infield, nodded to his catcher Jerry Grote, and was set to pitch to the first Cubs hitter, Rick Monday. Seaver recalled his notes on Monday: "A solid .290 hitter. Has a good, powerful swing. Hit 26 homers during the season. Could be dangerous. Have to come in low and inside. Careful, just nibble at the corners."

Tom got Monday to pop up, struck out Don Kessinger, the Cubs shortstop, and then got Billy Williams on a long fly to center field. It was one, two, three.

In the Mets half of the second inning, Cleon Jones slammed the ball into the bleachers and the Mets had a 1–0 lead. In the second and third innings Tom was using his curveball and slider. He didn't have the strength to rely on his fastball, but did visualize the pitch to show the Cubs hitters that his fast one was alive, and that he could bring it in when he needed it.

He was now pitching with his head and his heart—no strikeouts—that took too much out of a pitcher. He was slipping in his fastball, then teasing the hitters with the change-up, a curve, or the slider. He was getting the Cubs to hit ground balls for easy outs, and some of the hitters were driving long fly balls to the outfield, where they became easy outs.

In the fourth inning, with three Mets on base, Jerry Grote singled home two runs and now Seaver had a 5–0 lead to work with. He could take it a bit easier.

But Tom was tiring now as the fifth inning came up, and the Cubs jumped on his offerings for four successive base hits. Now the score was 5–2 and Tom was struggling. He got by the sixth inning on sheer guts and determination. Up in the stands you could hear Seaver grunt with the effort of every pitch. Now it was the seventh inning; only three more to go as the Cubs came out to hit.

Dave Rosello, the Cubs' second baseman, singled to lead off the inning and Rick Monday stepped in to hit. Tom stared at Monday, stared hard, and then came in with a twisting slider for his first pitch. It was a good pitch, low and inside. But Monday calmly lashed at the ball with a terrific swing and drove a home run far out into the center-field bleachers, and now it was a 6–4 ball game.

Yogi Berra slowly walked out to the mound, took the ball from Tom Seaver, patted him on the back and called for Tug McGraw, his ace relief pitcher.

Tug came in with that peculiar stride of his, cocky, arrogant, and sure of himself, and took his warm-up pitches.

There were still three innings and nine outs to go before the Mets could claim the division championship, but McGraw, the "you gotta believe" young southpaw who pitched brilliantly down the final stretch of the season, blazed his fastball across the plate, giving up just one hit in three innings for the victory, and the New York Mets were the division champs one more time.

"You gotta believe!"

The celebration in the clubhouse couldn't match the bedlam of 1969, but the champagne flowed everywhere. They threw Yogi Berra into a cold shower, they hugged each other, they slapped each other, and the great Willie Mays who couldn't drink had one sip of champagne and got sick.

You gotta believe.

"You gotta believe!" yelled the cocky Tug Mc-Graw.

"If you had told me in August we would make the play-offs and had a chance to be in the World Series, I would have said you were crazy," said Tom Seaver. "You've just got to believe!"

And if the race for the division title had been exciting, the battle in the play-offs and the struggle in the World Series were certainly not going to prove anticlimactic!

17
NATIONAL LEAGUE CHAMPIONS AGAIN

The Cincinnati Reds had been comparatively easy winners of the Western Division title. They had one of the most powerful lineups in baseball in 1973. Considering the offensive difference between the light-hitting Mets and the powerful Red machine, the New York pitchers were faced with a most difficult task in the play-offs.

Switch-hitter Pete Rose and left-handed Joe Morgan were the number one and two batters in the Reds' lineup, and they were not only powerful but consistent hitters. Moreover, both were outstanding baserunners. Tony Perez and Johnny Bench were third and fourth in the lineup, and both were dangerous long-ball hitters. Cesar Geronimo, Darrel Chaney, Ken Griffey, Dan Driessen, Andy Kosco—there wasn't a poor hitter in the entire Cincinnati ball club.

Offensively, the Mets couldn't match the Reds.

Once again, victory or defeat would have to depend on the New York pitching staff, and Tom Seaver, the Mets ace, was a big question mark as the play-offs got underway. He hadn't done too well in the final weeks of the drive for the division championship, and there was considerable question about his arm. He had won two of this last four games, but had not been the overpowering Tom Seaver. There was talk around the baseball world that Tom couldn't win the big ones.

Tom heard enough of that kind of talk, maybe too much, but he wasn't thrown.

"Some people may have forgotten," he said, "that I won my last 10 games in a row down the stretch, when we won the pennant in 1969."

But Tom felt an uncomfortable stiffness in his right shoulder. Dr. Peter LaMotte, the team physician, said it was a slight inflammation that he had treated with a shot of Butazolidin.

"I'm not particularly fond of the treatment," said Dr. LaMotte. "I won't be giving him another shot unless it's absolutely necessary."

The morning of the opening game of the play-offs, Tom was out at the ballpark testing his arm. He threw easily for a few minutes, then tried his fastball and his change-up. His arm felt good.

Yogi watched him warm up, studying his every movement.

"How does the arm feel?"

"Great, no pain at all."

"Good!" beamed Yogi. "You're pitching!"

There were 52,526 fans in the Reds' Riverfront Stadium and they watched anxiously, excitedly, as Tom Seaver handled the favored Cincinnati Reds easily, setting the hard-hitting Reds down in rapid-fire order; one, two, three, without a hit.

Jack Billingham, the ace of the Reds' pitchers, walked Bud Harrelson to start the third inning. Seaver was the hitter and no real threat; or so Billingham thought.

Billingham came in with a fastball and that was a mistake. Tom, a good hitter for a pitcher, slammed the ball with the fat part of his bat and the ball took off like a rocket into left center field. Harrelson dashed home with the first run of the play-offs and Seaver was on second base with a ringing double.

That was all the hitting the Mets did for the rest of the day, but the way Seaver was pitching, it looked as if the one run that Tom had driven home would be enough to bring home the first game of the play-offs.

The Reds got two men on base in their half of the second inning, but Tom Terrific struck out Cesar Geronimo and Darrel Chaney to end the inning.

With a runner on second in the fourth, he struck out Johnny Bench and Ken Griffey. Again in the fifth, again with a runner on second, he struck out Pete Rose to shut the door on the Reds.

And now Seaver was bearing down with every pitch, his face grim and determined. He was tiring, but he meant to stay—he had to get this game.

In the seventh inning Seaver struck out his tenth batter, tying a play-off record; then his eleventh batter to set a play-off record.

He struck out pinch hitter Hal King to ring up his twelfth strikeout in the eighth inning. He didn't, however, get Pete Rose.

Pete wasn't particularly a long-ball hitter, but he came up with the long ball often enough.

"When I get out in front with a bat," he said, "I can hit as far as anyone."

With the count two balls and two strikes, he got

203

hold of a fastball that Tom had thrown. The pitch came in low and fast, a good pitch, one that Rose liked, and he promptly slammed the ball over the right field barrier in Riverfront Stadium. The score was tied, 1–1. Tom Seaver got his thirteenth strikeout of the ball game in the eighth, but the damage had been done.

The Mets got nowhere in their half of the ninth. Tom walked to the mound to face Tony Perez, then Johnny Bench.

Perez was an easy out on a routine grounder to Buddy Harrelson. Bench took his first pitch for a ball. Tom was throwing fastballs. He had thrown fastballs tight most of the afternoon, with good effect. Not this time. This time Tom made a mistake and came in with a fastball that was just where Bench likes a pitch. John went down with the pitch and cracked it on a line over the left-field fence. Score: Reds 2, Mets 1. The first game of the play-offs belonged to Cincinnati.

Tom was off to the clubhouse before that drive by Johnny Bench cleared the outfield wall. He knew the game was lost. He was furious. How the hell could he have given Bench that good pitch?

He paced the floor of the clubhouse, he walked away from the sportswriters. He sat down for a moment, then burst away from all the newspapermen who came at him, questions popping.

For perhaps 15 minutes in the stunned silence of the Mets clubhouse Tom Seaver walked alone, his head down, his face without expression, avoiding the newsmen who waited for him to talk about the game.

He stood in a corner with a paper cup in his right hand, wearing his sweatshirt, underpants and blue stockings. He walked from the trainer's room to the manager's office, to an empty corner of the clubhouse, then back up past the open lockers.

Finally, after about 15 minutes, he stopped at his locker and began to strip the tape from his stockings. He took off his long white understockings. He changed into a dry sweatshirt.

"Is that what you had to replace, Tom, that pad?" a newsman asked, pointing to the arch of Seaver's foot. "That foot pad?"

Tom didn't look up. He turned and walked to the other end of the clubhouse. He returned in a couple of minutes with a can of beer in his hand. He sat at his locker and looked up. At last, he was composed enough to hide his deep disappointment.

"Did your foot problem bother you?" a newsman asked.

"That was not a factor at all," Seaver replied. "I just put a pad on in the dugout. It was not a factor."

"What were the pitches to Rose and Bench for the home runs?" a newsman asked.

"Rose hit a pretty good pitch. Bench hit a nothing pitch, nothing in it," said Tom.

"Did you get tired out then?" said another reporter.

"I didn't feel like I was getting tired," said Tom, looking up. "But I might have been."

"Is it frustrating to get only one run and have to knock it in yourself?"

"You never feel that way," said Tom. "You feel the team is going to open the game up. I thought we'd get to Billingham. We had the bases loaded in the first inning. But he got out of it."

"You pitched well, you had 13 strikeouts," said a reporter.

"I had a good fastball, but big deal. We lost 2–1."

"You had some overpowering stuff," said another reporter.

"What the hell difference does it make? We lost, 2 to 1. What difference does it make if I was throwing change-ups?" said Tom. "We lost the game."

Tom was angry enough about the Mets once again failing to score behind him. He was more angry with himself for giving up those two home-run balls, losing the game he was sure he had in his hands.

But for all the anger that seethed in him, Tom Seaver hoped that he'd have another crack at the Redbirds; and he did.

The next day Jon Matlack held the big Red hitters to two hits, both singles by Andy Kosco, while Rusty Staub homered in the fourth inning and the Mets added four more runs in the ninth inning. It was a two-hit shutout win for Matlack and the play-off, tied at 1–1, moved to New York for the third game. The noise started and mounted to a crescendo when Rusty Staub homered in the very first inning. In the fourth inning Rusty once again powered a home run with two men on to give the Mets a big 6–0 lead.

The Reds scored twice in the third, but the Mets, on a roll now, simply kept driving in runs and by the fifth inning had piled up a 9–2 lead.

In the fifth inning, Pete Rose barrelled into Bud Harrelson at second base and the force of Rose's smash into Harrelson sent Bud sprawling. When he arose, he said something to Pete and suddenly both players were at each other in a frenzy, and players of both teams poured out to separate the two men.

According to Rose, Wayne Garrett and Matlack were the only players to actually throw any punches. The other players simply pushed and shoved each other to no avail.

"The films of the play show only Garrett and Matlack in actual combat. They are the ones who threw punches at me when I was down," said Rose.

From his position, flat on the turf, he couldn't see Pedro Borbon of the Reds and Buzz Capra of the Mets both leave their bullpen areas and begin to whale away at each other on the fringes for the main event of the afternoon.

This event promised to be a better fight than the Rose-Harrelson set-to and the cooler heads turned their attention to it fast before the situation turned into an uncontrollable free-for-all.

It took fully five minutes before these cooler heads and the umpires could establish any sense of order on the field. The players were hot.

Borbon, with two of this teammates holding on to him, picked a baseball cap off the ground and fixed it on his head angrily.

"Hey, man," said one of his escorts, "that's a Mets cap you've got on your head."

Borbon snapped the hat off his head, dug his teeth into it and ripped off a piece. Apparently Borbon was seeing red, because the Cincinnati caps were red, the Mets caps blue; Borbon was one angry man not to have seen the difference. But Borbon's anger was nothing compared to the anger of the Metsomaniacs.

The moment the Reds took the field for the Mets half of the fifth, Pete Rose in left field was met by a barrage of apples, beer cans, paper, anything that was handy and loose. One projectile hit a Cincinnati bullpen pitcher in the face. Pete Rose angrily picked up a bottle and shot it back into the stands. The debris kept coming out of the stands. Pete caught a fly ball off the bat of Wayne Garrett and the abuse and refuse from the stands increased in tempo. Something hit Pete's leg. He called for time and started to walk to the Cincinnati dugout. Sparky Anderson, the Cincinnati manager, came out to meet him.

"I can't play with all that stuff going on out there," said Pete.

"I don't blame you," said Sparky, and he called in all of his players.

"I'm pulling my men off the field until you can guarantee their safety," he said to the umpires.

The umpires conferred among themselves. They spoke with Bob Scheffing, the Mets general manager. It was decided to send a delegation of Mets players to the left-field side of the stadium in an effort to quiet the fans down.

Yogi Berra and Willie Mays led the parade. Cleon Jones, Tom Seaver, and Rusty Staub joined them.

The fans cheered at the approach of their heroes. The players waved back. Willie Mays gave them the peace sign with his fingers and the fans roared, but it was most of 10 minutes before the crowd calmed down enough for play in the field to be resumed.

After it was all over and the Mets finished the day with a 9–2 victory and a 2–1 lead in the play-offs, the newspapermen finally got the real lowdown on the cause for the brouhaha at second base. It seems that Bud Harrelson had cast some slur on the Reds' hitting, or lack of it, in the two-hit shutout Jon Matlack had pitched against them in the second game.

"What's Harrelson," came back Rose, "some sort of batting instructor?"

Pete Rose had shown Buddy Harrelson what he thought of his remarks more concretely with that slide into second base.

That sort of thing, along with the beanball, happens all the time in baseball. It may give some release to some boiling anger; it rarely, if ever, wins games. What does win games is that big hit, and Pete Rose answered all the torments of the Mets fans with that big hit in the twelfth inning of Game Four of the 1973 play-offs.

The Mets took a one-run lead in the bottom of the third inning, but that was all they were going to score as three Redleg pitchers limited them to three hits in the 12-inning game. Tony Perez hit a home run in the Reds' seventh inning to tie the score. Pete Rose blasted one for all the bases and the ball game in the twelfth. The play-offs were tied 2–2. The National League pennant would go to the winner of the fifth and deciding game of the hot series. Except for the role of Tom Seaver, the game would prove anticlimactic.

Tom was the Mets' money pitcher. If it were just one game to decide who took home all the marbles, it would be Tom Seaver that Yogi would send up to the mound. Yogi knew Tom was tired; he had pitched a long and exhausting season, and Yogi knew that Tom's fastball had lost some of its early season velocity. But he also knew that Tom didn't have to rely on his fastball to win a game, that he could pitch to spots with devastating accuracy, that he knew how to set up a batter, that he was driven by the will to win, and that, given any support, he would bring in a win and the National League flag.

Early on in the deciding game, Tom knew that he didn't have his fastball.

"I might be throwing you some sinkers," he said to Jerry Grote. "I'll give you the big body motion, but that's all that will be big," said Tom.

Behind the plate, Grote just nodded his head.

A vicious sinker, with two men on base, and Tony Perez tipped the pitch and it stuck in Grote's glove for out number two in the first inning. Bench walked to fill the bases, and then Tom fooled Ken Griffey, the next batter, on a low slider, and an easy out on a short fly ball to center.

Ed Kranepool promply gave the Mets a two-run lead with a sharp single into left that sent two Mets across the plate.

Tom continued to rely on his sinker and breaking stuff. He wasn't striking them out the way he did in the first game of the play-offs. In the third, the Reds scored their first run; they tied up the game 2–2 in the fifth.

Again, in their half of the fifth, the Mets' offense came to life, with a bang.

Wayne Garrett opened with a double. Billingham pounced on a bunt by Felix Millan and snapped the ball to Dan Driessen, but Driessen tagged third instead of the runner and the Mets had men at the corners. Cleon Jones promptly doubled, Garrett scored, and the Mets led again, 3–2.

That wasn't the end of it.

John Milner walked, loading the bases. Yogi sent in Willie Mays to hit for Ed Kranepool. The stands in Shea Stadium went absolutely wild.

Anderson took Billingham out of the game and Clay Carroll, the right-hander, came in to pitch to the right-handed Mays.

Willie Mays was 42 years old. Now, the Metsomaniacs cheered, asking Willie for one last hurrah, and he gave it to them. It wasn't a screaming liner out of the park; it wasn't even a liner. It was a chop, a high bouncer, and before it could come down there was another run for the Mets and Willie Mays safe on first base. It was Willie's last hit in a National League game.

And the inning was still not over.

An infield out and a single by Bud Harrelson, and the Mets were leading the Reds by a comfortable 6–2 margin.

Cleon Jones made it 7–2, banging in the seventh Mets run of the with a clean single. It was Tom who came in with that seventh run, after smashing a double past the outstretched glove of, of all people, Pete Rose.

Tom went into the ninth, his lead intact, the fans already moving down from their seats and into the aisles, ready and crazy to celebrate. Tom had pitched his heart out; he was struggling to maintain his rhythm but he was dead tired now. Two walks, a single, and the bases were filled.

Yogi came out to the mound once again. Tom gave him the ball and Berra patted him on the back.

Tug McGraw came in to relieve Seaver and the noise in the stadium began to heat up again.

Cocky as ever, Tug McGraw set down the first two batters he faced. He also set down the third and final Redleg—and pandemonium broke loose in Shea Stadium.

The Mets streaked for the clubhouse, ran for their lives through mobs of screaming, clutching fans. The Reds had to use their bats to keep the Metsomaniacs from inflicting bodily harm.

"We're Number One! You gotta believe! We're Number One!" they hollered and screamed, tearing everything loose and a lot of things that weren't loose in the park.

"Whooo-eeee!" yelled Tom Seaver in the club-house.

The photographers tried to get pictures of him. It was an almost impossible job.

"It's been a long uphill fight," he hollered, "and by God it's good to get here!"

Then, looking around, "I feel like somebody pulled a cork off the top of my head and it's all pouring out! I'm glad it's over," said Tom. "I never worked so hard in my life."

Lifted to a platform for a TV interview with Ralph Kiner, he caught sight of Tug McGraw somewhere in a corner of the clubhouse.

"You gotta bee-lieve!"

They both raised the bottles of champagne they were holding and, together, they shouted at each other, "You gotta beee-lieve!"

The New York Mets were once again the cham-pions of the National League; they would play against Oakland in the World Series for the Baseball Championship of the World.

18
"I LOST A GREAT MANAGER—A GREAT FRIEND"

He was a big man, silent and so intense; an understanding man, and he died much too young.

Tom Seaver was sitting in the dugout just before the start of the 1973 World Series against the Oakland Athletics, but his mind was a million miles away, in another time and another place and in another ballpark.

It was 1969, the year of the Miracle Mets and their manager Gil Hodges.

Tom remembered the day he was summoned to Hodges's office. "We were all scared to death of him," Tom said. Hodges had the young pitcher sit down. He asked one question.

"Do you ever look at your wife in the stands when the game's going on?"

Tom wasn't sure what to say. He knew that no one ever lied to Gil Hodges and that sometimes he would test his players.

"Yes sir, sometimes when I'm on deck. I look up in the stands. I see her and I tip my hat. She's a kind of inspiration to me," Seaver answered.

"OK, that's all I want to hear," said Hodges. Tom left the office mortified.

The next day Hodges summoned Seaver into his office again.

"There was a time," Hodges said," when I was in the worst slump of my career, something like 0 for 30. One day before I went to the ballpark, my wife told me I was having some little thing wrong when I was hitting. That day I tried correcting that 'little thing' and hit a home run."

With that Hodges pulled an 8-by-10-inch photograph out of the drawer. It was a picture of him crossing home plate after a home run.

"As his foot was touching the plate, he was blowing a kiss to his wife," Seaver said. "I just said, 'Thank you,' and left his office."

There was a certain closeness that opened between Tom Seaver and his second manager. Wes Westrun was his first. There was an understanding between the young kid pitcher and Hodges, the man who was so physical, so silent, so feared by all.

The Mets had reason to fear Gil Hodges. Seaver remembered an incident in the clubhouse. Catcher Jerry Grote had been quoted in the newspaper as saying he was tired and that day Hodges came to the ballpark in a rage.

He believed that his players were professionals, that they didn't need to make excuses. Furious, he called a team meeting.

"When he was like that we all just sank away back in our lockers," said Tom.

Then, from across the room, Ron Swoboda spoke up. The outfielder defended Grote.

We all gasped," Seaver said. "Hodges just stood there, his eyes getting wider and wider and that vein in his neck that always stuck out swelling."

Near him sat a laundry basket filled with clothes.

"Gil kicked that laundry basket and it sailed right over Swoboda's head. Then he charged at him, was really going to kill him, when Rube Walker stepped between them. Rube told Hodges to go to his office and cool down . . . and he did.

"The physical strength of the man was legend. And he knew more baseball than anyone I'd ever met," said Tom. "There was this game where Ken Boswell, our second baseman, was struck on the right wrist with a pitch, only to have the umpire rule that the ball had struck the bat, not the batter.

"Hodges charged out of the dugout and grabbed Boswell's arm. 'You mean to tell me the ball hit the bat? How can you say that?' Hodges roared.

"For a full two minutes he stood there arguing and getting more and more angry, all the while holding Boswell's arm in his grasp.

"Finally Hodges pulled the arm forward. 'Look at this,' he said. 'Take first base,' said the umpire.

"Gil had cut off the circulation to the injury. It was all swollen and you could see the seams of the ball," Seaver said.

But there was patience too. Tom remembers one of the worst experiences. Atlanta had one out, second and third were occupied, and Bob Tillman, a catcher, was the batter.

"It was one of those days when I really was in command and my fastball was moving," Seaver

215

said. "I got two strikes on Tillman and knew just what I wanted to do—throw him a fastball inside.

"I got ready to pitch and I looked and Grote is flashing the sign for a curveball. I don't know what happened, but I was so intent on the pitch that I had decided to throw, that I went ahead with it.

"I threw a fastball just where I wanted it. The pitch buzzed right past Grote to the screen and the umpire call it strike three.

"All of a sudden everyone is running and I'm coming to the plate and I can't understand what's happening. I struck the batter out and Grote gets the ball and a run is trying to score and he throws the ball to me and I don't even see it. It goes right past my head.

"All of a sudden the field is empty and I'm standing there and all I can see is Grote flashing the curveball signal and I know what I've done."

Seaver expected to be killed by Hodges.

"He didn't say a single word to me," Seaver said.

But there was another time. "I was on second base," said Tom, "there was one out, when Boswell lofted a fly ball to right field. I should have gone halfway to third, instead I went to tag up. The ball hit the wall for a double, but I could only get as far as third base. It was a bad blunder.

"I got to third base and I looked into the dugout and Hodges has a bat in his hand and he's smashing it against the steps. The bat is in splinters shattered by his tremendous strength.

"I was standing there on third base rooting like hell for my own teammate to strike out. There was no way that I was going into the dugout with Hodges smashing that bat around. Finally our guys made out and I never did go to the dugout. I had someone bring my glove to the mound."

One heart attack produced a change in Hodges, mellowed him, and he was much easier in the dugout and smiled once in a while. But after having given up cigarettes for several months, he started smoking again and before long he was dead.

"I lost a great manager . . . a great friend," said Tom Seaver, "and I think about him. I miss him. He was so much of an inspiration to me. I think about him now and it gives me a tremendous feeling about this Series."

19
A WORLD SERIES
TO LOSE

The Oakland A's had a powerhouse of a lineup with Bert Campaneris, Joe Rudi, Sal Bando, and Reggie Jackson. They also had one of the top pitching staffs in the league, headed by three 20-game winners— Ken Holtzman, Vida Blue, and Catfish Hunter. And Rollie Fingers was one of the finest relief hurlers in the game. The odds-makers considered the Mets' record and made the A's the Series favorites. They figured Oakland was a good bet at 13–10. They might have figured better odds, but they remembered the Amazin' Mets who beat all the odds right through the World Series in 1969.

Jon Matlack pitched the opening game of the Series in Oakland. The Mets brain trust decided that Tom Seaver needed more rest. After all, he had pitched the final game of the play-offs; he was tired after a long and arduous uphill climb to the division championship. Better save him for the third game of the Series, when they'd be back at Shea Stadium.

Matlack pitched a marvelous game in the opener. In his six-inning stint he allowed the Oakland A's only three hits and two runs; and Tug McGraw, in his two innings of relief pitching, gave up only one hit to the A's. But in typical Mets fashion, the hits weren't there when the New York club needed them. The Mets actually outhit the A's, 7–4, but they left nine men on base, scored only one run, and Oakland had the first game of the Series by a 2 to 1 score.

The second game of the classic was anything but that. Jerry Koosman was hit hard. So was the Oakland ace, Vida Blue. The relief hurlers weren't any better. The Mets got 15 hits; the A's 13. Oakland scored twice in the ninth to even the score at 6–6. They played into the twelfth inning and it was the old, old Willie Mays who singled home the tie-breaking run.

Four runs crossed the plate for the Mets in that twelfth inning; the A's rallied but all they could manage was one run, and the Mets won the long, four-hour game 10–7, to even the Series at 1–1.

It was Tom Seaver against Catfish Hunter when the A's and the Mets took the field for their third set-to.

"It is generally conceded that Seaver is the best pitcher in baseball," wrote one sportswriter. "It is generally conceded that Catfish Hunter is the best pitcher in the American League."

Everyone in the ballpark expected an old-fashioned pitchers' duel, but Wayne Garrett opened the very first inning against Catfish with a home run. Felix Millan and Rusty Staub hit Hunter for singles and Millan came home on a wild pitch. Mets 2, A's 0.

But, again in the Mets fashion, they couldn't get another man across the plate the rest of the way. Nine Mets were left on base in their first five innings.

Tom Seaver was invincible on the mound. He struck out nine A's batters in those first five innings, five of them in a row, just one short of the World Series record. In the sixth inning, however, Tom's weariness was evident.

A long drive by Joe Rudi was caught at the fence, but a longer drive by Sal Bando was good for two bases. Reggie Jackson was up at the plate. Tom had already struck him out twice. He struck him out a third time; but Gene Tenace hit a line drive for two bases and Bando scored the A's first run and the Mets led 2–1. Seaver pitched to three consecutive pinch hitters in the next inning. Pat Bourque flied out, Jay Alou grounded out, and Deron Johnson struck out on three of Seaver's best fastballs, down low and away from Deron. It was Tom's eleventh strikeout.

In the eighth the A's suddenly struck. Bert Campaneris led off and sliced Tom's first pitch, blooping it just over first base for a fluke base hit. Seaver tried to keep Bert close to the bag, but then Campy tore into second base, just sliding in, barely beating the tag for a stolen base.

Tom threw a breaking pitch to Joe Rudi. Joe was fooled by the big curveball, but he swung and sent a grounder to first base that barely skidded by Milner for a single as Campaneris raced home and the game was tied, 2–2.

Seaver then fanned Gene Tenace for his twelfth strikeout. But Berra, peering at him from the dugout, thought Tom looked very tired. "What do you think, Rube? He looks like he's had it," said Yogi.

"Yeah," said Rube Walker, the pitching coach. "He's thrown 112 pitches—that's enough."

Yogi sent in a pinch hitter for Tom in the bottom of the eighth inning and brought in Harry Parker to start the ninth inning.

In the eleventh inning Parker walked Ted Kubiak and struck out pinch hitter Angel Mangual. Mangual swung and missed the third strike, but the ball zipped past Jerry Grote's glove, rolled to the backstop, and Kubiak hustled to second base.

With two outs, Campy Campaneris laced a clean single to center field and Kubiak raced home for what proved to be the game-winning run.

In the locker room after the heartbreaking loss, Tom avoided the reporters, who insisted on talking about Jerry Grote's passed ball. When he did respond to their questions he said, "I had very good stuff. Certainly the 12 strikeouts proved that point. My shoulder did get a little stiff, but that's to be expected in this cold weather and after pitching so many innings this season."

In the fourth game, the Mets hitters who had been silent for Tom Seaver went to work for Jon Matlack, and the Mets again evened the Series with an easy 6–1 victory. In the fifth game, it was Jerry Koosman pitching a shutout against the A's that paved the way for a 2–0 win for the Mets and a 3–2 lead in the Series. One more win. One more win . . . and the Mets would once again be champions of the baseball world; and Tom Seaver was the pitcher nominated to bring home that victory as the teams moved to Oakland for the finale of the October classic.

But it wasn't to be.

The A's got to Tom in the first inning for one run,

222

and another in the third. The Mets, in the tradition when Seaver pitched, were impotent at bat.

Meanwhile Catfish Hunter was in top form, setting down the Mets in order.

In the eighth inning, Seaver left the game for a pinch hitter. The Mets scored once; the A's came back to score their third run of the game, this time against Tug McGraw, and that's how the game ended, A's 3, Mets 1. One game now would settle the battle for the World Championship.

It wasn't much of a game; at least it wasn't much of a game for the Mets. Campaneris and Jackson both clouted two-run homers in the third inning, and that was it. The Mets managed to collect two runs but that was not enough. The Oakland A's took the game, 5–2, and the Championship, four games to three.

The Mets lost the Series, but lost none of the respect they had won across the country.

Reggie Jackson said it for the A's:

"I have nothing but respect for all of them. Seaver's the best pitcher in baseball. Matlack's almost as good. McGraw is out of sight. They got a hell of a team."

As for the Mets themselves, of course they were a bunch of dispirited young men. They had come so close to repeating the Miracle of 1969, and had missed.

John Lindsay, mayor of New York, was on the plane with them on the way back to the city.

"We'll come back," he kept saying to them, walking up and down the aisle of the plane. "We'll kill them next year."

Suddenly, in all the dour silence, Tom Seaver stood up and let go a yell.

"How many days till spring training?" he hollered.

Everybody in the plane turned to look at him, and laughed.

"We did all right," they said to each other.

"We won the pennant, didn't we?"

"We made a lot of money!"

"We're good! We showed them we're good!"

And, echoing the Mayor, "We'll beat the hell out of them next year!"

Tom Seaver was once again the cheerleader of the Mets, the man who could bring them together, the man who could inspire them to victory.

And he had a good year to look back on, personally. He had won 19 games. His ERA was the best in the National League, 2.08. He led the league in strikeouts for the third time in four years with 251. In fact, Tom's performance throughout the year was a record good enough to have the Baseball Writers of America vote him the Cy Young award for 1973.

Only three pitchers in baseball history had won the Cy Young award more than once. One was Sandy Koufax. Another was Bob Gibson. A third was Denny McLain. Thomas Seaver made four.

The season over, Tom went back to Nancy and his daughter. He took a correspondence course in geology, another in physical education, aiming for his bachelor's degree from the University of Southern California; and he played golf with his buddy, Buddy Harrelson.

20
200 STRIKEOUTS
A YEAR

Everything was going Tom Seaver's way in the first few weeks of 1974. Trading on the second Cy Young award he had won, he was able to negotiate a contract for $170,000.

"Why not?" asked Bob Scheffing, who with Don Grant ran the Mets front office. "He is the best pitcher in baseball, isn't he?"

That's what everyone in baseball, and particularly the men who came up against him at the plate, were saying.

The $170,000 contract made Tom Seaver the highest-paid pitcher in the history of baseball.

"How long do you expect to be pitching?" one sportswriter asked him.

"I guess I can go another seven seasons," said Tom. "Till I'm 35."

"And what do you intend to do when you're 36?" followed up the newspaperman.

"Pitch one more season," said Tom, and he laughed that infectious high-note laugh of his.

Things went well in spring training camp as well, and Tom was primed to go to the mound for opening day, as usual. Yogi was looking forward to another great year from his Cy Young award hurler. It wasn't to be. Tom Seaver, who hadn't had anything close to a losing season from the day he began to pitch professional ball, came mighty close to it as the season wound down to a very unhappy conclusion for the New York Mets.

It was in and out for Tom throughout the season. There would be an impressive five-hit game against the Montreal Expos, when he would strike out 13, then a night when he wouldn't last more than five innings.

"Tom Seaver is not all that terrific this spring," wrote one newspaperman. "He still has the same terrific-looking wife and he is still terrifically handsome and still has a terrific personality, but his fastball is only a sometime thing."

Another writer had it, "The velocity is there, but Seaver's fastball is tailing off, there's no hope to it anymore. He's lost something."

Tom just shook his head.

"The frustrating thing," he said, "is that I can't figure it out. Some games I have my old speed. In others there's nothing there."

He struck out 16 Dodgers in one game, then got hammered in his next appearance on the mound.

"My trouble is in the head," said Tom Seaver. "I concentrate so much on trying to hit one spot that I literally forget to put stuff on the pitch."

On June 1, he struck out 11 Astros and brought

home a 3–1 win, but his won-lost record was an abysmal 3–5.

"I wanted to go back to basics," said Tom after the win in Houston. "Keep the ball low and throw strikes. That's what's been hurting me lately. I've been getting the ball up too much."

On June 21, with a 2–0 lead against the Philadelphia Phillies, Tom had to limp off the mound. There was something wrong with his hip. One way or another, that hip injury was to keep him on the sidelines for 11 days before he took up his regular pitching rotation. But the hip was to plague him for the rest of the year.

Toward the end of July, he pitched a four-hit shutout against the Cardinals, only to be battered out of the box five days later against the Pirates in the fifth inning.

"He wasn't as fast as he used to be," said captain Willie Stargell, who had started the bombardment against Tom with a towering home run. "There were a few good fastballs, but nothing consistently. I think Seaver's hurting," said Stargell.

On October 1, Tom asked manager Yogi Berra for the pitching assignment for the next-to-last game of tne Mets schedule, against the Phillies. Seaver had not pitched for several days, but wanted the assignment when his troublesome hip showed some slight improvement. He had to know the extent of the problem.

It was a typically marvelous Seaver pitching outing for Tom as he went the distance for the first time in weeks. He allowed the hard-hitting Phils but four base hits, and struck out 14 hitters. The Phils collected three hits and two runs in the first inning, but Seaver held them scoreless during the remainder of the game. But the Mets, helpless against the equally fine pitching of Jim Lonborg, collected just four hits and could only manage one run, and once again Seaver was beaten by a 2–1 score.

"Even though we lost the game," said Tom, "I had to pitch. I needed something good to carry me through the long winter months, after this horrible year."

Tom wound up the poorest year of his career with a won-lost record of 11–11 and a 3.20 ERA. If he could take any comfort in the 1974 season, it was in his strikeout record. For the seventh successive year, Tom Seaver had struck out more than 200 batters. Seaver shares that incredible honor with one other pitcher, the immortal Walter Johnson. Seaver and Johnson are the only pitchers in baseball to have achieved that remarkable pinnacle of pitching greatness.

There were plenty of good years ahead for Tom, but he wasn't particularly happy about his performance in that painful year of 1974.

"The season was frustrating, long, and difficult," he said. "I was grouchier at home than usual. When a team is losing, there's also a lousy attitude in the clubhouse. Losing and being happy is a facade.

"But if you sit and worry about the end of the world," he said, "you won't come up with the answers to the problem."

He wouldn't worry about the problem; he would attack it.

"How does it feel to be 30 years old?" one reporter asked him.

"A helluva lot better than being 40!" said Tom, and he laughed.

That was Tom Seaver close to his thirtieth birthday at the end of the 1974 season. Nothing had been right for him for six months, but there were lots of months ahead.

"A bad year comes to all of us," his father had said.

In September of 1974, Tom went to see a doctor about his aching hip. Dr. Kenneth Riland, after a careful examination, immediately diagnosed the trouble.

"Your pelvic structure is out of balance," he told Tom. "Your hips are tilting forward."

"Can you fix it?" asked Tom, thinking that perhaps he had come to the end of his career.

"I think we can straighten it out," said the doctor; and the good doctor did.

Tom wasn't as certain as his physician.

"He pulled me around, manipulated and twisted me, and it felt like being pulled around by a bulldozer," Tom said. He had to test his arm before he could tell for certain how much the doctor had done for him, and he would learn that soon enough.

Off season, Tom spent hours studying the movies of his pitching performances in 1974. He saw his mistakes but he saw something more. He realized for the first time that he never threw the same pitch twice. There was always something slightly different to each pitch he threw.

"I wasn't a machine out there on the mound," he said, "throwing the ball mechanically."

No, each time he threw a ball it was a new invention. Each pitch a new creation.

There was an excitement in his discovery and it made him more eager than ever to try out his arm again, to find out for certain whether the doctor had really taken care of the misaligned hip that had plagued him throughout the long and painful season of 1974.

In spring training, 1975, he threw the ball and there was no pain. He threw it again and again and again; no pain. He was ecstatic. But he was also realistic and thought, I just hope that hip stays healthy.

"I would like a long career," he had said.

He was going to have it.

There was something else for Tom in spring training. He worked on a new pitch.

"Watch this," he said to Jon Matlack.

Matlack watched.

Tom wound up and let the ball fly. He threw with a big body motion, just as he would in a game. Jon Matlack braced himself for one of Tom's exploding fastballs, but the ball took off and just seemed to float in midair. It was a half-speed pitch.

"You've got it!" yelled Matlack. "Great change-up! You got it!"

That was another pitch to add to Tom's repertoire. In addition to his fastball, slider, and curve, he now had a great change-up. It was a pitch that he would use after the batter had a look at his fastball. It was a pitch that he would rely on in a given situation, and he would use it again and again in the years to come.

"Tom's looking sharper than he has in the last few years," said pitching coach Rube Walker as he talked things over with manager Yogi Berra.

"He doesn't have his curveball yet," said Yogi. "But Seaver ain't any problem. He's like another coach on the field. I just hope we keep healthy," said a worried Berra.

"I got into some bad habits because of that peculiar hip injury," said Seaver. "I'm just trying to get back into that smooth, effortless motion."

He was tense and uncertain about how long his hip would hold up, even though he was assured by Dr. Riland that the hip was as good as new.

The problem had actually begun about a year earlier. After the exhausting 1973 season he had a sore shoulder, which didn't surprise him. And when he began spring training in 1975, Tom was careful not to overstrain it. So he eased up and threw easily, carefully. Convinced from his earliest days that his legs were most important, he neglected the exercises needed to strengthen his arm. He was sure his pitches would naturally come around when he needed them.

But as spring training progressed, the pitches seemed to elude him. He went into his tight, compact, fluid windup as always, but nothing much happened. His fastball had no zap, and as a pitcher who constantly challenged hitters in a contest of power, he had to throw the ball harder and harder.

He overstrode to get more speed, and because of that he landed on his left heel instead of the ball of his foot. That minuscule difference in his motion put the constant pounding and strain of each pitch on the wrong part of his body and threw his hips off balance. Consequently, the muscles in his back pulled down and pinched the sciatic nerve, and that resulted in terrible pain on every pitch.

Opening day, 1975, saw Tom open the season against the Phillies. He pitched carefully, and as he began to mow down the strong Philly batters, his confidence slowly returned. By the fifth inning he was pitching with his old speed and strength. He looked fast and accurate, as he struck out nine, while limiting the Philadelphia club to just five hits. It was Tom's 147th career victory and certainly one of the most rewarding.

"I felt no pain at all," Tom said after the game, "and I knew I pitched the way I'm capable of throwing. Sure I'm tired, but I feel absolutely great."

The Mets, though, were having problems. Berra, though well liked by most of the players and a fine baseball man, seemingly had lost control of the club as the Mets dropped some ten and a half games behind the league-leading Pirates. On August 6, after the Mets had lost four out of five travel games, Yogi was replaced and Roy McMillan, a former Mets shortstop and a 16-year major leaguer, took over as interim manager of the club.

But 1975 was one of Tom's finest years in baseball. He won 22 games, but none was more exciting than his twentieth win of the season.

Tom trudged to the mound on September 2, 1975, to face the Pittsburgh Pirates. There were two things on his mind: the coveted 20-game winning season and a strikeout record within his grasp. He had already chalked up 194 strikeouts; he needed 6 more to make it 200, and 200 or more strikeouts eight years in a row.

There were 52,410 Metsomaniacs in the stands that afternoon in Shea Stadium, every one of them aware of what was on the line for Tom. They cheered at every one of his pitches. They began to stand and cheer when Tom slipped a pitch past Willie Stargell in the sixth for his 199th strikeout of the year. In the seventh, with Dave Parker on first base, Manny Sanguillen stepped up to the plate—

232

and he didn't want to be, in any way, the strikeout victim to give Tom Seaver the record.

Tom worked fast. He always worked fast. He fired a fastball over the plate.

"Strike one!"

It seemed that everyone in the park knew what was coming. Nobody was warming his seat.

Tom, too, knew what was coming. He didn't waste a moment.

Two more fastballs cut the plate, and Manny Sanguillen never had a chance.

The stands exploded.

"Strike three!"

The fans roared, and they wouldn't stop their cheers until Tom raised his cap, acknowledging the cheers and showing appreciation their support.

"It was really a very emotional experience," said Tom. "You try to divorce yourself from it, and you simply can't."

Two hundred strikeouts for eight consecutive years.

He had shared the record with two immortals of the pitching mound, Walter Johnson and Rube Waddell, with 200 strikeouts for seven years in a row. Now he was there alone in the record books.

Tom added to that strikeout record in what remained of the 1975 season. He wound up the season with 243 strikeouts, and a total of 22 wins. He was by far the best pitcher in the National League, and that's how the sportswriters saw it. By a vote of two to one, for the second time in his career, he was voted the National League's outstanding pitcher.

Robin Roberts and Bob Gibson were the only two pitchers who had won that coveted award twice before. The great Dodger star, Sandy Koufax, and

Warren Spahn had won it four times. It was something to achieve.

There was icing on the cake. For the third time in the past seven years, Tom Seaver was voted the Cy Young award. The only man in baseball history equally honored was the great Sandy Koufax.

Tom Seaver had attained a pinnacle on the diamond and he had just turned 31. He only wished the Mets could have finished higher than third place in the Eastern Division, four games behind the second-place Phillies and ten and a half games behind the Pirates.

21
TROUBLE WITH MANAGEMENT AND A TRADE

The Seaver's second child, Ann Elizabeth, was born in December 1975. Also that month Tom, with 168 victories under his belt, thinking of reaching the 300 pinnacle. It was not a completely impossible goal, but the way the Mets were going, with their perennial weakness at the plate, there weren't many among the baseball experts who thought Tom Seaver would ever make it.

Tom Seaver, however, started out in magnificent fashion as the 1976 season got underway. By the end of April he had won three consecutive games and was leading the National League in strikeouts with 35.

But now there was some turmoil in the Mets front office. There was a hassle with Donald Grant, the man who controlled the purse strings, about his contract. Grant had called Tom an "ingrate." Tom felt his salary should be increased, and brought

235

more into line with what a good number of free agents were receiving. Here he was considered "baseball's greatest pitcher," and he felt there should be an adjustment in his contract.

It became a nasty affair, but salary wasn't the only issue annoying Tom. These were the years of the free-agent draft, and Don Grant was making some feeble attempts, or none at all, to secure the kind and type of players that would vault the Mets into the pennant race.

Tom was not alone. Other players were upset by Grant's refusal to strengthen the pitiful Mets offense. Jerry Koosman and Jon Matlack, top-notch stars, along with Tom Seaver, lost game after game because of the paucity of runs their teammates produced. Matlack and Koosman were so disgusted with the situation, they asked to be traded.

Tom struck out 235 men in 1976, leading the league in that department for the fifth time in the past seven years, and had a magnificent 2.59 earned-run average, yet his statistics for the year were just 14 victories against 11 defeats. Seaver let everybody from M. Donald Grant to the press know how he felt. Grant kept attacking Seaver for his lack of gratitude and loyalty. The writers who covered the Mets, almost to a man, sided with Tom. There was one, however, who was a very loud and, often enough, obnoxious supporter of Grant. An explosion was due, but it would wait for a little while. Meanwhile there was another incident in 1976 that soured a lot of people, and especially the Mets players.

Cleon Jones, a nine-year veteran, had remained in Florida after spring training to work his injured knee into shape. Early one morning, Cleon was arrested. He had been discovered in the back of a van with a woman who wasn't his wife. Grant organized the scenario after the press reported the incident in a front-page story that made glaring headlines.

He had Cleon Jones and his wife, Angela, at a press conference, where Cleon read a letter of apology to the fans.

The press responded as might have been expected. It charged Grant with humiliating Cleon and Angela, both black, and accused him of paternal racism.

Grant demurred. "They agreed it was the best thing to do," he said. "Angela walked to the press conference holding my hand. I'm not a sonofabitch who likes to hurt people. I like to do nice things."

When Angela Jones was apprised of Grant's statement, she is reported to have replied, "He told you that? That's a lot of baloney. I have to believe if it was Seaver or Koosman he might have handled it differently."

Grant's retort to that was, "Mrs. Jones doesn't talk that way. She is a very nice person. I don't believe it."

The whole affair didn't sit well with the Mets players, but it wasn't until 1977 that the top blew off the kettle. And it seemed that the sportswriters took over center ring in the struggle between the combatants, management and labor.

Dick Young of the *Daily News*, one of the most powerful sportwriters in baseball, took up the cudgels for M. Donald Grant. Almost everyone else in the newspaper business took up arms for Tom Seaver and company. And no one pulled his punches. It was a raw, angry, and, often enough, vicious battle of words in every New York paper.

Jack Lang, whose column generally appeared on

the same page as that of Dick Young, wrote, "Grant is so pompous he thinks he's God."

Maury Allen of the New York *Post* wrote, "When you have the best pitcher in the world, you sign him. You don't humiliate him. Grant can't stand opposition from Seaver or anybody. He'd sooner lose a pennant. Grant is cold and pompous. He has alienated the fans and the press with his stodgy boorishness. He must go."

Grant told his players to stop bitching to writers like Allen and Lang.

When Grant ordered the Mets to win the annual Mayor's Trophy game against the Yankees, forgetting that the Mets were just going nowhere in the pennant race, Tom Seaver called Grant "a bleeping maniac."

Tom apologized for that remark, but there were no apologizers among the sportwriters.

"No team wants Seaver," wrote Dick Young, "because he's a troublemaker."

He accused Tom of flying off the handle, and "in his undisciplined rage, he put down his teammates. They were not worthy of playing behind him."

Matlack, whose locker was next to Tom's, said he had never heard Tom bad-mouth a Met.

Dick Young, when pressed on whether he had talked to the Mets players or just to the Mets management, said he spoke to Matlack often; but Matlack said that Young hadn't spoken to him once in 1977.

The question of facts, however, didn't seem to bother Young. He continued his attack on Seaver.

"Tom Tewwific," he wrote, "a pouting, griping, morale-breaking clubhouse lawyer poisoning the team."

The men who had played with Tom Seaver during

the nine years in which he had lifted the Mets out of the cellar to win two National League pennants and a World Series couldn't understand Young's attitude. They simply said that he was an apologist for the Mets front office, and let it go at that.

Pete Hamill, the noted columnist, was to write, "Young has been functioning as a hit man for the Mets management, and demeaned his own talents."

Young's answer to that was, "Very unprofessional. You get a guy like Hamill, he's standing off ten miles away making comments about things he doesn't know a damn thing about."

Dick Young suggested that Maury Allen see Donald Grant for the truth.

"What's the point of seeing a guy who gives you a lecture instead of information?" said Allen. "All he'll do is bullshit me. He's a very abrasive personality who talks down to you. When I asked him how much Mets stock he owned, Grant screamed, 'That's none of your business!' "

In the middle of June there was a conference between Tom Seaver and Donald Grant. Each had a different story about that meeting.

According to Grant, he never looked for a trade as long as he could satisfy his star hurler.

"I talked to Tom," he reported, "and told him I had visualized him winding up as president and part owner of the club."

Tom's version was a bit different.

"I gave them a contract proposal I thought was fair, and I had to go back to them after five days because they didn't even respond. After ten good years with a club, why not the courtesy of a yes or no? They were trying to intimidate me by threatening a Sutton trade if I didn't sign."

Don Sutton was a free agent, and a top pitcher.

"Joe McDonald said," went on Tom, speaking of the Mets general manager, " 'Nobody is beyond being traded. I have one deal I can call back on right now.' "

"I said," went on Tom, " 'Pick up the phone and make the damned trade.' He didn't move. But then it began to dawn on me how fast ten years could go out of the window."

June 15 was the date of the trading deadline. On June 7, Seaver pitched an 8–0 shutout against the Cincinnati Reds, as the fans kept rocking Shea Stadium with "Sea-ver! Sea-ver! Sea-ver!"

Tom struck out ten Reds in that game. He moved past Sandy Koufax in career strikeouts in that game, became number 13 in the list of all-time strikeout artists in the National League. And the fans went wild when that item was flashed on the scoreboard, giving Tom a standing ovation that just kept going strong for a full five minutes; and M. Donald Grant, in his box alongside the Mets dugout, was on his feet, too, applauding the best pitcher the Mets had ever had on their roster, the best pitcher in baseball.

Grant came back into the clubhouse after the game to shake Tom's hand and to congratulate him, but the situation would not change.

Joe Torre, then managing the Mets, suggested that Tom call Grant once more. It was June 10. Tom called and they spoke for an hour. No change.

On June 12, Tom pitched and beat the Astros. He knew it was his last game for the Mets.

He was misty-eyed, having dinner in a nearby restaurant with his two old pals, Bud Harrelson and Jerry Koosman.

"I'm gone," he said. "I don't think anything can save it."

On the fourteenth there was a number of calls between Tom and Lorinda de Roulet, who had inherited the Mets on the death of Joan Whitney Payson, and it seemed that a last-minute compromise was about to save Seaver for New York.

But the morning of the fifteenth there was another vitriolic column by Dick Young in the *Daily News*:

"Nolan Ryan is getting more money than Tom Seaver and that galls Tom because Nancy Seaver and Ruth Ryan are very friendly and Tom Seaver long has treated Ryan like a little brother."

The column was read to Tom as he was sitting at poolside at the Marriott Hotel in Atlanta.

For a couple of moments Tom didn't seem to react; the thing was churning his mind, and an anger was burning in the pit of his stomach.

Suddenly he was up on his feet and bolting out of the room. He was looking for Arthur Richman, the Mets public relations director.

He found him.

"Get me out of here!" he yelled. "Get me out of here!"

"The attack on my family," he said later, "was something I just couldn't take."

June fifteenth, Tom Seaver was traded to the Cincinnati Reds.

They called it the Wednesday Night Massacre. It was the night Dave Kingman was traded to the San Diego Padres for rookie pitcher Paul Siebert and Bobby Valentine, who was hitting .172. And it was the night that the Franchise was traded to the Cincinnati Reds for utility infielder Doug Flynn, pitcher Pat Zachry, and two minor-league outfielders, Steve Henderson and Dave Norman.

The reaction of the fans was immediate, violent,

and obscene. The switchboard at the Mets front office was flooded with calls, a stream of abuse heavily weighted with the most foul words in the American language.

"This place is a madhouse!" exclaimed an exhausted switchboard operator. "It's insane! The people are calling up and screaming and cursing!"

At the ballpark the next night, the fans who did not boycott the game marched in with banners flying high:

"M. DONALD DUCK"

"TRADE GRANT"

"BRING ME THE HEAD OF GRANT"

"GRANT MUST GO"

"BURY GRANT, BRING BACK TOM"

Outside the gates, the boycotters collared everyone they could, urging them to stay out of the park. Others passed out leaflets demanding that the fans stay out of Shea Stadium until Tom returned with his new team, the Cincinnati Reds. "On that occasion," the leaflet read, "we urge all true Mets fans to attend the game to show Tom Seaver our appreciation for the many magnificent performances he has given us."

Tom made his final appearance in a strange scene in the Mets clubhouse beneath the first-base grandstand. He faced a horde of some 125 newsmen and television cameramen as he sat dressed in a three-piece (vested) suit. But he also sat facing 25 empty lockers in which clean white Mets uniforms had been hung, for the later arrival of the players who were to fly home from Atlanta to open a series against the Astros.

Tom had not seen his teammates since the night before, when he quietly slipped out of Atlanta Stadium just as the Mets took the field there.

The trade involving four Cincinnati players had not been officially announced yet, but everybody knew that something was coming, and before leaving for the airport Tom left a note in Jerry Koosman's locker asking his friend to "tell each and every player individually" how Seaver felt after 11 great years, "because I don't think I can stand to tell each guy myself."

When Tom arrived at La Guardia Airport at 10:30, he was met by Nancy, who said later, "This whole thing has torn Tom apart." Instead of going home to their converted barn in Greenwich, they drove to the Warwick Hotel in Manhattan so Tom could appear on an early morning television program and also appear at Shea Stadium to gather his belongings.

"I don't know if I really want to ride back through the history of all this," Tom said to the reporters, "but it all goes back to my signing my contract last year.

"Things were said then and written by Dick Young. My loyalty was attacked. Then a couple of days ago, I was talking to the club and there was a little discussion about a new contract. They did not want to renegotiate, and I can understand that," said Tom. "But my proposal was to play out the next two years under the current contract and talk to them about the three years after that: 1979, 1980, and 1981.

"But then, the very next day," said Seaver, "Wednesday, Dick Young dragged my wife and family into it and I couldn't take that. I called the Mets office and said, 'That's it. It's all over. This alliance or whatever between Young and the Mets chairman is stacked against me.' "

On his new job with the Reds, Tom said, he would

be paid at his current rate of $225,000 per season. However, his contract with the Mets provided for certain incentives both ways—if he won so many games, more money, if he didn't, less money. "And those negative parts of the contract have been taken out by the Reds," he said, "because they bring too much pressure on both sides."

For awhile, Tom seemed to keep his cool under a constant barrage of questions, then:

"What am I going to do with all my blue Mets sweatshirts?" he asked Ron Swoboda, his old teammate, now a sports broadcaster for a television station.

"You're going to use them for softball in the park, right?" Swoboda answered.

There was a hollow laugh. No one in the clubhouse was going to feel happy that night.

"Do you think you've gained anything, being traded to Cincinnati?" asked one reporter.

"I don't have to pitch to Johnny Bench, Pete Rose, and Joe Morgan," quipped Tom.

Then someone asked him how he felt about leaving the Mets fans. That stopped all the joking, all that was left of any laughter in the room.

Tom lowered his head. He tried to answer. He couldn't.

"Give me a couple of minutes," he said, and he got up from his chair.

"I need a break," he said, and there was dead silence as he walked out of the room.

It was fully 10 minutes before he came back and sat down on his stool again.

Ron Swoboda said quietly, "They watched you grow up, Tom."

"As far as the fans go," said Tom at last, "I've given them a great number of thrills, and they've been equally returned. The ovation I got the other night . . ."

He couldn't continue. He lowered his head again. He began to sob.

"Come on, George," he said to himself, tapping his heart; but he still couldn't say what he wanted to about those loyal Mets fans.

"Let me have that book," he said, taking a notebook from one of the newspapermen. "I'll have to write it down."

No one spoke as the ballplayer wrote what he couldn't speak: then he asked another reporter to read what he had written.

And the newspaperman read, slowly and quietly, " 'And the ovation I got the other night after passing Sandy Koufax's record, that will be one of the most memorable and warm moments in my life.' "

That was it. Tom Seaver collected his gear and left for home. The clubhouse had never experienced as sad, and perhaps as profound a moment.

The story in Cincinnati was, of course, quite different. The Reds were hot on the heels of the Los Angeles Dodgers for the lead in the Western Division of the National League. Sparky Anderson, the Reds' manager, beamed. With Tom Seaver in a Cincinnati uniform, he could see a third straight World Series championship in the books.

"With Seaver joining those other guys out there in the clubhouse," he said, "I feel now just like I know I'm going to feel when I walk into Yankee Stadium July 19 as manager of the National League All-Star team.

"I'll bet those Dodgers will down a few Dramamines when they learn we got Seaver," he added. "They'll feel the boat rocking."

Pete Rose, captain of the Reds and head of the

welcoming committee for Tom Seaver, spoke for his teammates.

"I just hope Tom is as anxious to come here as we are to have him."

"This takes the pressure off the other pitchers," said Larry Shepard, the Reds' pitching coach, "like Sandy Koufax did for the Dodgers."

"This gives us the premier pitcher in baseball," added Sparky Anderson. "It will be like fielding an All-Star team. Seaver may be the all-time all-timer before he is through."

At the opening session of Ohio's House of Representatives, the Reverend Kenneth Graimes, concluding the prayer that traditionally comes before the legislators begin their state business, said, with all the profundity that comes with prayer, "And thank the New York Mets for us."

There was sadness, along with angry protest, in New York. There was joy and expectation in Cincinnati. And Tom Seaver was off to Ohio with all the beautiful possibilities waiting for him there, pitching for a club that surely could promise him that cherished goal of 300 victories in his pitching career.

22
CINCINNATI

Tom Seaver's first pitching stint for the Cincinnati Reds was a masterful three-hit shutout in Montreal. He set down the first seven Expos to come to the plate; then, after yielding a single to Larry Parish in the third inning, he retired the next nine batters in a row.

"Slow down, man," said Joe Morgan to the ace pitcher as they trotted back to the Cincinnati dugout. "You look like you're nervous."

He was nervous. He was anxious to look especially good as he continued to keep the Expos off the base paths, and he added to his delight by getting two hits in his four times at bats, his single in the eighth inning sending two Redlegs across the plate.

"I'm starting the second part of my career," said Tom. "It's going to be beautiful. I'm gonna be called, 'the hitting pitcher,'" he said to Pete Rose. Pete looked at him, and both men roared with laughter.

"I just hope Jerry Koosman was watching on TV," he said, "and saw those two hits."

His first home game for the Reds was on July 9, and it seemed as if Cincinnati had declared a universal holiday. The business section of Cincinnati's Main Street seemed deserted. The walkway across Interstate 75 was jammed with fans heading for Cincinnati's Riverfront Stadium more than three hours before game time.

"I've never seen anything like it," said Brook Smith of the Red's front office.

It didn't take an hour for the fans to grab up the 1,000 standing-room tickets once the office was opened. "It's like we're playing the World Series," said one of the office staff.

In the stadium there were banners all over the place.

"WELCOME TOM TERRIFIC"

When the public address announcer introduced Tom, a thunderous standing ovation rocked Riverfront Stadium as the pitcher trotted to the mound.

"Are the Dodgers worried about Seaver?" a reporter asked slugging Steve Garvey of the Los Angeles club.

"Worried?" repeated Garvey. "Why should they be? He has never beaten us before at Riverfront Stadium, has he?"

It was a joke, a lame sort of joke. Of course Tom had never pitched against any team but the Reds in Cincinnati.

Garvey, however, made good his boast. Tom Terrific held the slugging Dodger bats to three runs, but three runs were enough to spoil Tom's debut in home territory, as all the Reds could muster were two.

"Where were all the runs that were promised?" he chuckled in the clubhouse after the defeat.

"You just stick around all year, Slick," said Johnny Bench.

And Tom said that he wasn't going home just now.

The Reds liked Tom's humor as well as his pitching.

"How are you feeling?" Sparky Anderson asked Tom before he went out to beat the Atlanta Braves, 7–1, five days later.

"I've got work to do, Sparky," responded Tom. "I'll kibitz with you tomorrow."

"Right then," said Anderson, "I knew I didn't have to worry about Seaver for the rest of the year. I knew he was no prima donna. He came to the park to win. That's my kind of ballplayer."

Tom's sense of humor and his clubhouse pranks gave a lift to everyone in the club, including Bernie Stowe, the Reds' equipment man.

Stowe was just a little taken aback when one afternoon Tom Seaver stalked into the clubhouse after the second inning of play and began to take off his uniform.

"If I had known it was going to be so damn hot in this town, I'd never have agreed to the trade. I'm through for the night. I can't take it any longer. I think I'll go home."

A stunned Bernie Stowe just watched as Tom got rid of his sweat-soaked uniform. He didn't notice at all that Tom was getting himself into a clean, dry one.

"Well," said Tom, fixing himself fresh, "the third

inning must be about ready to start. I might as well go out and watch."

"Who's pitching?" stammered Stowe.

"I think it's Pedro Borbon." (Seaver was pitching.)

And all this with a straight face. It made a good story back in the clubhouse after the game; and it certainly boosted morale and helped keep the players loose and happy.

When Tom returned to Shea Stadium to pitch his first game against his old teammates, the ballpark was jammed. Every time he appeared anywhere on the field, even just to take batting practice, the fans gave him a standing ovation. And Tom gave his old fans one more thrill, limiting the Mets to six hits, one run, striking out 11, as the Reds beat his old club 5–1.

"I'm glad it's over, very glad," said Tom.

After the game the usual gaggle of newspapermen surrounded him in the clubhouse. "I'm exhausted physically and emotionally. It was no fun at all pitching against those guys: Harrelson, Stearns, Randle, Mazzilli, Henderson."

Tom could control his emotions when he was in there on the mound, pitching. It was something else when he dealt with those emotions in retrospect.

"This game . . . was the the end of a tradition," he said, as if he were trying to clear himself of all that the Mets had meant to him over the many years.

"That's the first time," he said quietly, meditatively, almost to himself, "that's the first time I ever beat the Mets."

But later, a month later, in his red-trimmed Cincinnati uniform and red socks trimmed with white, Seaver had adjusted.

"I feel," he said, "like a real member of the Reds now. It's no one thing, but just being with this club day after day, understanding the new people.

"I think a lot of the guys thought I was dead serious," Tom said, laughing. "They didn't know I'm crazy.

"John Bench is still on me for hitting a home run the other night," he said. "I hit it to right field, too, way out there, and when I got back to the dugout I looked down at the other end, where the water cooler is, and there was Bench flat on his back with all his catcher's gear on, like he'd passed out from the shock.

"This is a hitting-conscious team," said Tom, "and they even let me hit at the batting cage. They don't make a lot of noise in the dugout until something happens, until somebody does something first. And they're always needling each other about those cheap hits—John Bench, Joe Morgan, Pete Rose especially. Any time there's a cheap hit it's a 'Judy,' like in Punch and Judy. With these guys if you get a cheap hit you may get it in the record book but not in this clubhouse. You hear about it in the club-house.

"When the Reds lost four games in a row," said Tom, "I chewed everybody out. I told them, 'Damn it, I didn't come over here to lose.' I meant it, but they knew I was having fun too, trying to loosen them up. I think I surprised Sparky Anderson too. I think he thought I was all briefcase and seriousness. Sparky is very much like Gil Hodges was as a manager, in that he commands respect. But he's much more open than Gil was."

Tom Seaver talked about his new teammates.

"Pete Rose is a very quiet guy," he said. "Everybody is under the impression that Pete is a real chatterbox, but he's not. There are no real chatterboxes on this club. That Joe Morgan is amazing. When you need a run in a tight game, he lines a double down the left-field line, and the game is tied.

"You watch Morgan, Rose, and Bench, you're watching three fine professionals play. Concepcion is a super shortstop. And George Foster, Griffey, and Dan Driessen are outstanding young hitters. Foster is so strong. He hits the ball so far, so easily. He hit three home runs the other night—three monsters. And in center field, Cesar Geronimo catches everything hit in that area. These guys are great. They hit, they run, and they throw."

The Reds never did catch the Los Angeles Dodgers in the race for the Western Division title, but 1977 proved another great year for the pitching ace of the National League.

On April 17, while still in a Mets uniform, Tom pitched his fifth one-hit game. It was a record shared by only four other hurlers in National League history.

His record with the Mets, before he departed for Cincinnati, was seven victories against three defeats. With the Reds, he won 14 while losing three, to give him 21 victories against six defeats for the season. It was the fifth season in which he had won 20 games or more. When he beat the Dodgers on September fifteenth of the same year, he joined Ferguson Jenkins, Gaylord Perry, Jim Kaat, and Catfish Hunter as the only active pitchers with 200 or more victories to their credit.

One of the greatest and perhaps most exciting feats in the baseball career of Tom Seaver, however, was yet to come. Friday, June 16, 1978, was a day Tom Terrific would never forget.

Tom got off to the worst start he had ever experienced in the major leagues as the 1978 pennant race got underway. In his first six trips to the mound, he lost four games. He didn't win a game in the entire month of April. The Cincinnati fans became restless. Tom wasn't getting the cheers; he was getting the boos; disenchantment comes easily to baseball afficionados, and yesterday's hero becomes today's goat.

Was the great Tom Seaver concealing an arm injury?

Was Tom the Terrific through?

"I'm throwing super. I feel terrific," Tom said. "I'm not as frustrated as a lot of people seem to think. Why? Because every athlete goes through it. There things happen. Do you expect me to become manic-depressive about it? You try to be objective, recognize the problem, find out what's wrong, and try to rectify it."

Everyone from his old Mets teammates to his mother to his wife's grandfather called to commiserate with him on his poor start and to offer him advice. Even Reggie Jackson called him and offered some smooth words of encouragement.

Jerry Koosman called to say, "You're over-throwing."

Nolan Ryan said, "You're opening up your left side too quickly. When you do that you lose some velocity and some control."

His mother, as she had been doing for years now, ever since Tom was a Little Leaguer, advised him to take it easy.

"Slow up, Tom. Slow up. And don't spit on the

mound," she laughed. "Too many people are watching on TV."

Nancy's grandfather, a tough Kansas farmer, said, "Your finger is in your butt and your mind is in Texas."

"He's the one who had it," said Tom. "It's all in the concentration."

This season, for the first time in 10 years, Seaver's concentration seemed diffused, and it seriously affected his pitching.

Driving to a Mets-Reds game, he said, "I don't know, it just goes. My mind will wander and I'll throw well for a spell, then throw a horseshit pitch that hurts. I'll get ahead of the batter, say 0–2, and then instead of wasting a pitch, I'll throw a mediocre fastball right down the pipe. I know it's a matter of concentration, but I still can't seem to maintain it. That's what's disturbing me."

It was apparent that Tom had gone into the season looking forward to the best year in his career, with the powerful-hitting Reds. He could never do that with the Mets. In New York he concentrated on one game at a time. Now, as he let his thoughts wander far into the future, his present suffered.

One of the problems, of course, concerned his family life. When he was traded to Cincinnati in midseason of 1977, Nancy went with him and he had her constant companionship. But this year, Nancy and his two daughters remained at the Seaver home in Greenwich until school ended. And Tom found it difficult, almost impossible, to concentrate on his performance in Cincinnati while missing and worrying about his family back in Greenwich.

The cynics assumed that Tom was hiding an arm injury, but he insisted he was not. Several pitching coaches detected flaws in his delivery as he hurried his pitches, and this he acknowledged. But linked to his tendency to hurry his motion was perhaps the real reason for his problems: his unfamiliarity with a team that was expected to be fighting for first place this early in the year. Not that he couldn't cope with that responsibility, but he had not yet adjusted to it.

"I got so jacked up over the winter," said Tom, at his locker during an early season game. "I got so excited about our chances, I wanted to win the pennant in one day."

Over the winter, optimists had been speculating that Tom might win 30 games for the Big Red Machine his first season, 25 at least. "He'll be fortunate to win 20 now," said a well-known Cincinnati sportswriter.

Pitching for the Reds involved a completely different psychology from pitching for the Mets, whose two National League titles in 1969 and 1973 developed rather suddenly in September when nobody was looking. In contrast, the Reds start every season with all the media watching, particularly in their battles with the Dodgers, their annual rival for the title in the Western Division.

Seaver had a 14–3 record after joining the Reds the previous June, but once again, the psychology was different then. The Reds were never a challenger to the Dodgers that season. This year Tom knew his role was to get the Reds off fast and on top of the league. Instead, he was in the worst tailspin of his career.

Perhaps another reason for Tom's eagerness was

that 1978 was the year he wanted to justify a multi-million-dollar contract. He was making an estimated $250,000 with the Reds for the season, the last of a three-year contract with an option for 1979. When the season ended, Tom would want to talk about a new deal. How high the Reds would be willing to go would depend on how successful he and the team were this season.

"Tom's the best I've ever seen at not taking one game to another," said Bud Harrelson, his best friend and former roommate, now with the Phillies. "But this must be a very difficult time for him."

It's April 29 and Tom Seaver hasn't won a game and his guts are burning. But he won't let you analyze why he's pitching so badly.

"Obviously, I'm not very happy," Seaver said. "But I have to be realistic, get out of this mess as quickly as I can. It's strictly mental. The other night against the L.A. Dodgers I was throwing super, and then I just threw two lousy pitches; then Lopes came up and I threw the ball right where he likes it, and bang, it's out of the park. Can you believe how dumb that was?

"After I threw that pitch to Lopes," Seaver said, "I said to myself, 'Why would I ever throw a pitch like that?' So I turned around and threw another one to Russell. A nothing fastball inside. And that was back-to-back home runs.

"Where is my mind? If I knew the answer to that," Tom said, laughing, "you wouldn't be asking me that question." He laughed some more.

It wasn't until May 6 that Tom won his first game of the season, as he pitched six scoreless innings against the Montreal Expos before giving way to

Pedro Borbon. Borbon held the Expos and Tom was credited with win number one as the Reds took the game 6–2. On the seventeenth, Tom was his old terrific self as he fanned 13 Expos, scattered six hits, and pitched his first complete game of the season to post an impressive 5–1 victory.

Suddenly, as if by magic, Tom was back on track. His fastball literally jumped at the opposing hitters and then tore into his catcher's glove; his slider was a thing of beauty and drove the hitters crazy as they swung wildly, driving the ball into the ground for an easy putout. He had it all back now and bowled over all opposition.

By June 11 Tom Seaver had won six games in a row. On June 16 he would ring up his seventh in a row, and this would be a historic victory for Tom. For on that date, Tom Seaver would make the record books once again, this time with a brilliant no-hit-no-run performance.

Five times the elusive no-hit game had escaped him. Back in April 1977, Steve Ontiveros of the Cubs had broken up a no-hit game for Tom with a single in the fifth inning. Tom had gone into the ninth inning with a no-hitter on three occasions. The first was on July 9, 1969, when another Cubs outfielder, Jim Qualls, got a hit.

Tom's closest brush with a no-hitter came against those same Cubs in 1975. There were two outs and two strikes on Jimmy Qualls, but he singled to spoil the no-hitter. The game went into extra innings and Seaver allowed two more hits in a no-decision game for him.

A third-inning single by Mike Compton of the Phillies on May 15, 1970, spoiled another no-hit bid.

Vic Davalillo spoiled another Seaver no-hitter with a seventh-inning bunt in a game against the Pirates, September 26, 1971.

In a game against the San Diego Padres, Leron Lee got a ninth-inning single, once again frustrating Seaver's bid for a no-hitter. The game was played July 4, 1972.

But June 16, 1978, was different. It was a big game against an old perennial rival, the St. Louis Cardinals. In the second inning of the memorable game, Keith Hernandez walked, stole second, and went to third when Don Werner, the Cincinnati catcher, made a wild throw. But Tom struck out Jerry Morales and, after walking Ken Reitz, induced Mike Phillips to bounce out.

In the fourth inning Joe Morgan made a diving one-handed stop of Hernandez's ground ball far to his left, then got the ball to the base in time for the putout.

Hernandez came as close as anybody to spoiling the no-hit game when he smashed a ball right at Seaver. The ball bounced off Tom's glove, but Dave Concepcion was right there; like a cat the lanky shortstop pounced on the ball and threw to first for the putout.

By this time the crowd was aroused, up and on its feet, cheering every strike Tom whizzed across the plate, every putout made. The sight and sounds of a no-hitter were in the air and the excitement of it increased with every pitch.

In the top of the eighth, Jerry Morales hit a high hopper to third. Ray Knight, at third base for Pete Rose, took the ball waist-high in a defensive move, and a quick throw to first got the speedy Morales.

Tom had retired 19 in a row when he walked to the mound for the ninth inning. The crowd was on its feet in a standing ovation for the "greatest pitcher in baseball."

"If anyone tries to bunt," said Sparky Anderson as Tom began to leave the dugout for his ninth-inning chores, "don't worry about the left side of the infield. Ray will cover that. You take care of the right side and be sure to cover first if one gets past you."

Those were the first and only words Sparky spoke to his pitcher during the entire game.

Pitching coach Larry Shepard was about as tense as anybody in the park. His hands were soaked with sweat.

Tom? Tom Seaver was cool. He knew he had the possibility of a no-hitter. He didn't need the roar of the crowd or the ovation to tell him that.

"You're always aware of it," he said, "when you haven't given up a hit in a game."

But Tom walked the first man he faced in that ninth inning, pinch-hitting Jerry Mumphrey, and he took a moment to pause and consult with himself.

"Wait a minute, pal," he said to himself, as he later related the story to the newsmen. "You can lose this game."

He was thinking of the game and not the no-hitter.

He pitched carefully to Lou Brock. The count went to two balls and one strike. Brock fouled off the next four pitches, then sent a fly ball to George Foster in left field.

One down!

Garry Templeton was next, and on the third pitch

he bounced to Dave Concepcion, who tossed the ball to Joe Morgan for a force-out at second base.

Two down! One to go!

George Hendrick, the clouting Cardinal center fielder, was at bat, there to do his best to spoil the no-hitter.

Tom whipped the ball over the plate.

"Strike one!"

Then a ball, and another strike.

One strike away from the record books!

Tom took his windup, brought the ball down as he glanced at the Redbird on first base, and pitched.

It was a good pitch. Hendrick smashed hard at the pitch but topped the ball.

The ball bounced to Dan Driessen at first, Driessen gloved the ball and stepped on the bag, and the game was over.

The crowd roared. The entire Cincinnati ball club poured out onto the field to shake the hand, slap the back. Johnny Bench embraced "the greatest pitcher in baseball." Tom Seaver had finally done it, pitched the game he had always dreamed of pitching—the no-hitter.

As for his reaction to the superb performance, Danny Driessen said, "He had a super smile on his face when I stepped on the bag.

"I offered to sell him the ball," Driessen continued, a big smile on his own face, "but he wouldn't buy it."

Of course the first baseman gave the ball to the man who had earned it, Tom Terrific.

Outside the clubhouse, waiting for her husband to emerge, Nancy Seaver was wiping the tears from her eyes.

"Tears of joy," she said. "I burst out crying when Dan Driessen stepped on first base for that last out."

And Tom?

"I was aware of the possibility of a no-hitter in the third or fourth inning," he said. "If it happens, it happens, I thought. If you pitch long enough with enough good stuff, you are bound to pitch a no-hitter sooner or later."

"As for the 'victory ball,' Tom said, "my daughters, Sarah and Anne, can probably use it."

"A month from now it will be covered with tape. I can hear it now. 'Sarah, where's that ball I brought home last month?' 'Oh, it's in the pool, Daddy.' "

"He had the best curveball I've ever seen," said the Reds' pitching coach ecstatically.

Don Werner, who caught the game because Johnny Bench was out with a back strain, said, "The key was, he never gave in to the hitters.

"Before the game I said to myself," reported the rookie catcher, " 'Let's catch a no-hitter tonight.' "

And Tom to Werner after the game: "Here you are, half a year in the big leagues and you catch a no-hitter. I'll be damned."

What to do for an encore?

"Now I'll try to get Number Two," said Seaver.

One writer suggested that he might go after the record Johnny Vander Meer set in 1938, pitching two no-hit, no-run games in a row.

"I wouldn't bet against it," said another sportswriter in the Reds' clubhouse. "The way Seaver is going, I wouldn't be a bit surprised."

Tom Seaver was the perfectionist; he was also the realist with a fine sense of humor.

"They'd love you in Las Vegas," he said, referring

to the men who make up the odds for that type of bet.

Pitching a no-hit, no-run game is the crowning glory for any pitcher who tosses a ball in any kind of organized league—particularly, of course, in the major leagues and now Seaver had set that crown firmly on his head.

But he had something else to say about that no-hitter and about his pitching philosophy in general.

"It was marvelous to pitch a no-hit game," said Tom, "but that's only part of the game. Pitching is what makes me happy. I live my life around the five days between starts. It determines what I eat, when I go to bed, what I do when I'm awake. It determines how I spend my life when I'm not pitching. If it means I have to come to Florida and can't get tanned because a burn would keep me from throwing for a few days, then I never go shirtless in the sun. If it means when I get up in the morning I have to read the box scores to see who got two hits off Steve Carlton last night instead of reading a novel, then I do it. If it means I have to remind myself to pet dogs with my left hand or throw logs on the fire with my left hand, then I do that too. If it means in the winter I eat cottage cheese instead of chocolate-chip cookies in order to keep my weight down, I might want those cookies, but I won't eat them. Now, that might bother some people, but it doesn't bother me. I enjoy the cottage cheese. I enjoy it more than I would those cookies, because I know it will help me do what makes me happy.

"Life isn't very heavy for me. I've made up my mind what I want to do. I'm happy when I pitch well, so I only do those things that will help me be happy. I wouldn't be able to dedicate myself like this for

... money ... or glory, although they are certainly considerations. If I pitch well for, say, fifteen years, I'll be able to give my family security. But that isn't what motivates me. What motivates some pitchers is to be known as the fastest who ever lived. Some want to win 30 games in a season. Some want to win a World Series game. And there are some who want to pitch just one no-hitter in their lives.

"All I want is to do the best I possibly can ... day after day, year after year.
Pitching is the whole thing for me.
I want to prove I'm the best ever."

23
LOSING THE PLAYOFF

The Cincinnati Reds fielded a powerful team in 1979 and, with Tom Seaver as the dean of the pitching staff, manager John McNamara, who had replaced Sparky Anderson in the winter of 1978, had every reason to believe he had a good chance of taking his club all the way up to the World Series.

True, he had lost Pete Rose, who became a free agent and signed with the Phils, but he had Dave Concepcion, recognized as the best shortstop in the National League; Joe Morgan, who had twice been named Most Valuable Player in the league; George Foster, who had hit 52 home runs in 1977 and been named the MVP; Ken Griffey, who had all the earmarks of a superstar; Cesar Geronimo's bat; and the slugging catcher, a four-time winner of the Gold Glove, Johnny Bench. This was an all-star lineup that could strike terror any time it took to the diamond, anywhere.

Among the more optimistic and excited ballplayers on the Cincinnati roster was Tom Seaver. He had been involved in two pennant races, two pennant victories, and one World Series victory. He could sense another pennant victory, and perhaps a second World Series championship.

"Sure," he said, "I'm thrilled about being in another pennant race. When I'm sitting on the bench," he added.

"I get nervous when I'm not pitching," he said. "I'm always moving up and down the dugout, back into the clubhouse. My heart's beating. I'm yelling. I love it!"

But as the 1979 season got underway, Tom had severe and almost constant back problems. His lower back was not functioning properly.

"Most of my injuries have been to the lower part of my body," said Seaver. "That's because I keep the strain off my arm and put it on the legs and buttocks.

"Some guys," he added, "are arm pitchers. But if you want to pitch for a number of years, you can't put that much strain on your arm, so you have to distribute that strain somewhere else."

Tom had been pitching in the Major Leagues for some 13 years. The legs, the thighs, the buttock muscles weren't going to cooperate forever. His fastball was bound to lose some of its velocity. He would have to count more on his curveball and his off-speed pitches. He would have to use the slider only when necessary, for the pitch took a lot out of him.

No one was more aware of these factors than Tom himself.

"I'm throwing more breaking pitches than I used

to," he said. "I'm still a power pitcher," he added, "and the fastball is my best pitch, but I'm not as overpowering as I once was.

"That doesn't mean," he continued, "that I don't have the fastball when I need it. It means the percentages of fastballs to breaking pitches have changed somewhat. To what extent, I don't know. Pitching is the utilization," he went on, acutely diagnosing the art of pitching, "and application of what you have that particular day. For me, that may change in the context of the game."

Tom was exceedingly good in the analysis of his craft, but no kind of analysis is going to make a great pitcher, not when he has problems with his back.

From late in April of 1979 through early May, Tom Seaver was out of action because of pulled buttock muscles. When he finally did get to the mound again, he was not very effective. As late as the first week in June, all he could do for Cincinnati was to win two games while losing five.

It wasn't until the ninth of June in 1979 that Tom Terrific began to give some evidence of a return to his old mastery and then, all of a sudden, he was off on a phenomenal streak of victories. With his start on June 9, he was almost unbeatable. Eleven times he went to the mound, and 11 times he came in a winner. With his back healed and buttock muscles finally in shape, he was completely in control and Cincinnati was in the thick of the battle for the Western Division title.

In his last 15 trips to the mound, as the season wound up to its climactic finish and pennant fever was running high in Ohio, Tom lost just one game and brought home 14 victories for the conquering

Redlegs. Despite his horrendous start at the beginning of the year, Seaver wound up the 1979 season with another fine record of 16 wins against six defeats.

That record doesn't tell the entire story. He led the Reds' pitching staff with five shutouts, with 131 strikeouts, and with the most complete games (nine). It was generally conceded that a healthy Seaver could easily have achieved his sixth 20-victory year. And there was no doubt that, just as he had led the Mets to their two pennants and a World Championship, so he had led the Cincinnati Reds to the top of the heap in the Western Division.

Pennant fever ran high in Cincinnati. Cincinnati fans are among the most rabid, and loyal. They are also among the most vocal, and Tom Seaver became almost as much a hero in Ohio as he had been in New York. No city, of course, would worship Terrific Tom, could worship him, as much as did the city of New York.

Did Tom feel the excitement that filled the air in Cincinnati as the Reds prepared to battle the Pittsburgh Pirates, winners in the Eastern Division, for the National League pennant? Of course he did, but his excitement, tempered by his years on the diamond, was more controlled.

"It's exciting, all right," he agreed. "You can feel what's going on. But I try not to let it affect me. All I want to be is consistent. I try to stay at a very stable level. You can't be up and down emotionally and you can't let environmental circumstances affect you. I try to shut out everything else but pitching."

Always thinking. Always analyzing. Certainly he was as excited as the next ballplayer going into the play-offs, thinking of the possibilities of a pennant and a World Championship. But Tom's mind was on the Pittsburgh roster, on how he was going to pitch to every one of the Pirate sluggers he was going to face. Captain Willie Stargell, Dave Parker, Phil Garner, and Bill Madlock and company were all great hitters who terrorized the division all season long.

The concentration was there, as Seaver took to the mound for the opening game of the best-of-five play-off for the National League pennant, but Tom had trouble keeping the ball down. He often had trouble during the early part of the game until he could settle down into his pitching groove. In the first inning of the opening game, he walked Parker and Stargell in succession before getting John Milner to pop to second for the final out of the frame.

The Bucs, however, were not to be completely denied by the Reds' star hurler. In the third, Phil Garner led off with a home run; Dave Collins slipped, going after a sinking liner by Omar Moreno, and Moreno tore into third base with a triple; a sacrifice fly by Tim Foli and the Pirates had two runs off Tom Seaver.

That's all they were going to get that afternoon off Seaver. Pitching in beautiful rhythm, Tom held the hard hitting Bucs to but five base hits in the eight innings he pitched.

The Reds managed to even the count as they scored two runs in the fourth inning, but John Candelaria, who had won ten of his last thirteen starts for the Pittsburgh club, was just as tough as Seaver. There was no more scoring, for either club, until the game had gone into extra innings.

By that time Candelaria was out of the game, after a seven-inning stint. Seaver had gone out of the game for a pinch hitter in the ninth.

In the eleventh inning the Pirate bats began to find the range again. Tim Foli and Dave Parker led off, against relief hurler Tom Hume, with back-to-back singles. Tom Hume hadn't given up a home-run in his last forty-two relief appearances, but he hadn't had to pitch to that potential Hall-of-Famer Willie Stargell. On his very first pitch to Willie, the mighty Stargell swung, connected, and whacked the ball out of the park for a three-run, game-winning homer.

If Seaver was disappointed by his performance, or by the Reds' loss of the opener, he didn't say. Nor did he say very much as the Pirates took the second game of the play-offs to take the series and the pennant.

"We had our chances," Tom said and that was all he said as, with the rest of his teammates, he packed his bags and went home.

There is no joy in losing a pennant when it lies within your grasp, no joy in losing the chance of another World Championship, but Tom wasn't one to dwell too long on either victory or defeat. His mind almost always moved to the next square in the game and how to prepare for it. He would spend the winter studying ways and means of avoiding the kind of muscle injuries that had affected him so painfully in early 1979. He would go over the movies of his pitching performances during the year, searching out the errors he might have made, thinking of how to avoid repeating those errors. He would think, too, of a new pitch he might develop to give himself a greater arsenal on the mound, work

270

on it, and try to perfect the pitch. Perfection was still and would always remain the goal of Tom Seaver.

Following the brilliant manner in which Seaver closed out the 1979 season, 16 wins against 6 losses, Cincinnati fans understandably expected Tom to start the 1980 season with a rush and to lead the Reds in a runaway from the rest of the teams in the Western Division. Seaver wasn't thinking in terms of a runaway. He knew that no one man could carry a team to the top, that there were too many variables, accidents, to predict anything in baseball with certainty. But he did look forward to a very good year in 1980. Unhappily both the Reds and Tom Seaver were in for a bit of disappointment.

This time it wasn't the troublesome back or hip that gave Tom Seaver trouble and kept him out of the lineup; this time, for the first time in his career, it was an ailing shoulder. Tom had pitched in 35 games and at least 250 innings in each baseball season ever since he first pitched for the New York Mets, 13 years in all. What is amazing is that he was suffering arm trouble, or close to it, for the first time in his career.

It hit him hard. For almost two full months he had to sit by and watch the others take up the struggle for the division championship. And when at last he was able to take his turn on the mound, he wasn't the old Tom Seaver. The two months on the bench had dulled the sharp edge of his pitching. He didn't suffer a losing season, he had yet to suffer a losing season, but the best he could do was to turn in a 10 and 8 record and the highest ERA (3.64) of his career.

Tom Seaver certainly wasn't a happy man, packing his bags and going home to Connecticut as the season ended. But he wasn't downhearted either. He would think the year through, study the films again. Most importantly, he would work on his physical condition; particularly, he would work on his shoulder muscles and try to prevent a recurrence of the injury that had crippled his 1980 season.

Taking the suggestion of Bill Fischer, the Reds' pitching coach, for the first time in his career Tom spent the winter throwing the ball regularly, to keep his arm loose.

"I worked with weights every day, too," said Tom, "and did some running. I've always done some running," he added, "but never as religiously as I did that winter."

The ritualistic exercises and the way Tom went at them paid off, but not quite at the start of the 1981 season. There was a thigh muscle injury that limited his activity to the sidelines for a 10-day period, and he missed a couple of starts on the mound. By mid-June, however, he was healthy and had already posted seven victories for the Reds, against one defeat.

Just how many wins Tom Seaver might have registered for Cincinnati in 1981, if it had been a normal baseball season, is a little difficult to say. For sure, he would have had one more 20-game-victory year to add to his skein of 20-game years. But 1981 was not a normal season; it was by far the most abnormal season in all of baseball's history. It was the year of the strike, a strike that threatened to cancel every scheduled game not already played and cut the season in half. The strike did last for a full 50 days, the longest baseball strike ever.

When the players and the club owners finally came to an agreement and the strike was ended, the owners added a further complication to the already strange season. They voted, not unanimously, but by a majority, to split the 1981 season into two halves, as they do in the minor leagues. And, again as in the minor leagues, the winners of each half season were to meet for a three-game set-to to decide the division championship.

Ironically, both the Cincinnati and St. Louis club owners voted against the two-half decree and both were to suffer for that decree. When the strike was called, the Reds were coming on strong and were just half a game behind the leading but faltering Los Angeles Dodgers. If the strike had been delayed just a couple of days, it is more than likely that the Cincinnati club would have finished first instead of second in that arbitrary first half of the season, with a sure place in the play-offs. The situation being what it was, however, and beyond their control, the Reds had only one way of getting into the play-offs, and that was by winning the second half of the arbitrarily established ruling for 1981.

The Reds tried. They couldn't be faulted for lack of effort. And certainly Tom Seaver gave that try everything he had. Despite the 50-day layoff, he came back strong and pitched magnificently, pitched some of the best games in his career. He wound up the first half of that year with seven wins against one defeat. He repeated that performance in the second half of the year to end up at 14–2. His won-lost percentage for the entire year was an amazing .875, the best in either league. And on the way, incidentally, on the 8th of April of that year, he struck out the slugging Keith Hernandez to become only the fifth pitcher in baseball history to reach the 3,000 mark in strikeouts.

But the Reds came in second again in the second half of the season. Their overall record for 1981 had them four full games ahead of the Los Angeles Dodgers with the second-best record for the year. But overall records didn't count in 1981. It was the Houston Astros who topped the Western Division in that strange second half, and it was the Astros against the Los Angeles Dodgers for the division title. All that was left for the Cincinnati Reds was the memory of a strange year. For Tom Seaver, despite the disappointment that comes with not getting into the play-offs and perhaps the World Series, there was something more.

He had been voted the National League Pitcher of the Month in September, the month in which he posted five victories against no defeats.

He had that 3,000 strikeout mark to remember.

United Press International named him the Comeback Player of the Year for 1981.

And he just missed, by one vote, being named the Cy Young award winner for the fourth time in his career, losing it to that amazing rookie of the Los Angeles Dodgers, Fernando Valenzuela.

Both Valenzuela and Tom Seaver received eight first-place and six third-place votes. The difference came in the second-place voting: Valenzuela eight, Seaver seven.

Close enough.

Tom could look back on the 1981 season with considerable satisfaction. Perhaps his performance wasn't as perfect as he would have liked, but he certainly was thrilled with his comeback.

He surely would have cherished that fourth Cy

Young award and it was too bad to miss it by so small a margin, but it was good to know the respect the baseball world paid to his pitching. Yes, Valenzuela was voted the best pitcher in the National League for 1981, but there was no one in baseball yet who challenged his title as the greatest pitcher in the game.

24
A BAD YEAR—AND A GREAT TRADE

Nineteen eighty-one had been a brilliant year for Seaver; not only had he established himself once again as the premier pitcher in the sport of baseball, but he also repeated his performance as the ultimate clubhouse leader. He was the ringmaster, the prankster, the advisor, the jokester.

When a couple of small-town radio reporters were creeping around the clubhouse asking stupid, uninformed questions, Seaver stuck close by, pretending to be chatting with other players until the reporters turned on their tape recorders. When they opened their mikes, Tom would scream the worst vulgarities he could think of at the top of his voice.

Once he was filming a TV commercial when suddenly, after several run-throughs, Tom suddenly stopped his action, clicked his heels together, and in a perfect German accent barked to the German TV director: "You vill fix ze light, yes, Verner? And zen you vill do ziss right. Do you hear, Verner?" The act broke up the entire studio.

And then there was the time in the clubhouse when a player doing a crossword puzzle asked Seaver for a five-letter word for *pig.* "Can't think of the word," said the player. "Can you, Tom?"

Seaver looked over his shoulder at his catcher, Johnny Bench, two lockers away, winked at him, and replied, "B-E-N-C-H."

"Tom Seaver is exactly like me," said Pete Rose, the rough and tough eternal youngster of the diamond wars. "He's tough and he's hard-nosed. If it's the right thing to do, he'll put you right down on your ass. But he's a gentleman. Tom will always take the time for the younger ball players."

It was typical of Tom Seaver to give advice, and good advice, to the younger pitchers off the field, in the dugout, and while the game was in progress.

"Listen to me," he would say to a young pitcher going in to relieve. "I've never been a relief pitcher, but when you go into the game, as you walk to the mound, you decide on three things right then: what you're going to throw on your first pitch, what you're going to throw if you get ahead, and what you're going to throw if you get behind. OK?"

But behind the tough exterior and fatherly advice, Seaver was having a tough time. Early in 1982, during spring training, he began to have a problem with his left thigh. More seriously, he was hit by a severe case of the flu. It was more than two weeks into the regular season that he made his first appearance on the mound for the Cincinnati Reds. Considering his ailments, it was a very good performance: his fastball lacked the old velocity, but he limited the hard-hitting Giants to five hits and four runs before he was relieved and was charged with a 4-2 loss.

He wasn't really any more effective in his next two starts, losing to both the Houston Astros and the Chicago Cubs. In fact, he didn't pick up a victory in 1982 until May 4, when he gave up only four hits and one run to the Astros in a seven-inning stint. It was a strong performance and his teammates greeted it with more than a bit of enthusiasm. For one shining day it looked as if the real Tom Seaver was back on the mound.

But the enthusiasm didn't last long. In his next five starts, Tom came away with two no-decisions and three losses.

There were days when Tom was his old self again. He beat the San Diego Padres, giving up only five hits and two runs in eight innings. He beat the Atlanta Braves, allowing only three hits and one run in eight innings. But that was about it.

Early in July he began to have problems with his right shoulder again, and after the All-Star game he appeared in only four more games for the Reds.

His last victory in 1982 came on August 5, when he gave up four hits and a single run to the Padres in the six innings that he pitched. It was one of the better performances in what must have been one of the most disheartening seasons of his career. His last appearance of the season was against the Astros on August 15, when, after giving up two runs in the first inning, he was forced to leave the mound because of his right shoulder.

Tom's record for the year: five wins against 13 losses. It was a disastrous year both for Seaver and for the Reds, who lost 101 games, stamping the 1982 team as the losingest Reds team in the history of the club.

But while Seaver and the Big Red Machine began to show signs of mechanical difficulties, the story was quite the opposite for Tom's former team, the New York Mets. After finishing season after season at the bottom of the standings, there was finally a ray of hope for the Mets. The team had been purchased in 1980 by Nelson Doubleday and Fred Wilpon, for a record-breaking sum of $21.1 million, and they immediately announced that they were in the market for the top names in baseball, that they were ready and willing to compete for the free agents. "And," said Wilpon, "we bought the Mets for $21 million, and we propose to spend that much or more to bring back the 'Mets Magic.' "

A new general manager was elected to run the club, Frank Cashen, who had been the mastermind of the Baltimore Orioles, the man who developed the youth movement that led the Orioles to six division titles, four AL pennants, and two World Series victories. He was the man Wilpon wanted, and Wilpon got him.

Cashen wasted no time in rebuilding the "new" Mets. Dave Kingman, the sensational home run slugger who banged out 48 homers for the Cubs in 1979, was brought back to the Mets in a 1981 trade for Steve Henderson. But Cashen wanted Seaver back in a Mets' uniform, as well.

He offered the Reds a young pitcher named Mike Scott in exchange for Tom Terrific. Cincinnati general manager Dick Wagner didn't jump at it, but he didn't close the door, either.

The fact of the matter was that the Reds were in

trouble. One hundred and one losses in '82 after winning six divisional titles and two World Series in 12 years was quite a letdown. Top players like Pete Rose and Joe Morgan left Cincinnati as free agents. And the ace pitcher, Tom Seaver, didn't look too promising: a virus, a sore shoulder, a damaged big toe, and a 5–13 record. Suddenly, the 38-year-old pitcher was something less than unbeatable.

So in December 1982, when Frank Cashen offered pitcher Charley Puleo, catcher Lloyd McClendon, and outfielder Jason Felice for Seaver, the Reds accepted.

Tom Seaver was coming home.

Back in New York City, Mets fans were delirious. No one talked about the 5–13 season. No one talked about his injuries, his flu, or his age. They talked about his 14–2 season in 1981, his 264 career victories, his 3,137 strikeouts, his lifetime 2.68 ERA. They talked about his 93 mph fastball and his great slider. They talked about his Cy Young awards, his no-hitter, and the niche that was being carved out for him in Cooperstown. And they talked about going to Shea Stadium in April to see number 41 bring that magic back to the Mets.

"Tom Seaver has come home," wrote sportswriter Stephen Hanks, "and we are, all of us, young again."

In March of 1983, when Tom Seaver arrived at the Mets' training camp in St. Petersburg, his welcome was no less hearty or enthusiastic. The enthusiasm, however, was somewhat guarded. Manager George Bamberger, coaches and players, too, could not forget that Tom Seaver was no longer the young hero; he was a mature man of 38. Nor could they forget that Tom, for all his brilliant past, had experi-

enced physical problems that had severely affected
his efficiency on the mound. And that 5–13 record
of 1982 was on their minds. Sure, he could bring the
winning spirit to the Mets and inspire the younger
pitchers on their staff, but how much of the young
Seaver could he take to the mound?

They watched him carefully as he began his
conditioning program. They observed him cau-
tiously—hopefully—as he began to bear down and
throw with his old velocity. They worried when his
thigh muscle began to act up, but they were delighted when he pitched shutout inning after shutout inning in the training camp games.

But while everyone had their eyes on Seaver, he
had his eyes on the bullpen. He knew that his ability
to go the whole nine innings of a game had lessened.
Did the New York club have the relievers to finish
the games that he started?

"No pitcher can win and no team can win without
a good bullpen," said Seaver. "Look at Rollie Fingers, Bruce Sutter, Rich Gossage, and Tom Hume,"
he said. "Those are the people who put the game
away for you. And if I can go seven innings most
times, I'd be happy to turn the game over to someone else."

He continued to work with and guide pitchers Ed
Lynch, Craig Swan, Carlos Diaz, and particularly,
Jess Orosco. And he continued to be critical of his
own slow progress.

He pitched seven scoreless innings against the
Boston Red Sox in a Grapefruit League game,
March 22, but he wasn't very happy with his per-
formance.

"I struck out the pitcher on a bad pitch," he said,
and he made no bones about being bothered by that
pitch. "I was working on a slider," he continued,

"and it was up but he missed it. It would have been a bad situation in a game if I had thrown it to a different kind of hitter. It was high in the strike zone."

Always the thinking man, Seaver had some words about the form of his teammate Neil Allen, a fine relief pitcher.

"I wanted to tell him that he was moving his shoulders horizontally," he said. "Your shoulders should be driving in what feels like almost a 45-degree angle; his shoulders were rotating flat to the ground. You can't drive the ball through the strike zone like that. No way."

As for his own pitching, "I don't know how fast I'm throwing."

Actually his fastball was moving in on the plate at about 87 miles an hour. When he was younger, it had moved in at the speed of about 90 miles an hour.

"I can throw just as hard," said Tom. "The ball just doesn't go that fast."

Whatever he said, and however he said it, the Mets were thoroughly pleased with his performance, and with his condition, too. Tom Seaver was going to be their pitcher on opening day.

There were a number of reasons, of course, for scheduling Seaver as the Mets' opening-day pitcher. For one, he was still the premier pitcher in baseball, certainly the premier pitcher of the Mets' staff. Second, the fans demanded it. They wanted to see Tom back in a Mets uniform. They wanted to see Tom Terrific back in action, the big 41 on the back of his shirt, pitching for their beloved New York team. And third, Seaver promised to draw the biggest crowd ever into Shea Stadium, one that would top the record crowd of 40,000 in 1970.

The night before opening day there had been a "Welcome Home" dinner for the Mets, with Tom Seaver the honored guest. It was a warm and hearty event, with all the hoopla and all the excitement such affairs engender. But it didn't help Tom get a good night's sleep. He couldn't have slept well anyway. There was too much excitement, too much tension in the air.

He was up before seven, before anyone else had stirred in his house in Greenwich, Connecticut. He made the breakfast coffee. He walked the dogs. He bought the newspapers. He then got back into bed to rest before going to the ballpark.

Sarah, the older of the two Seaver children, was well aware of the importance of the day.

"She understands it all," said Nancy Seaver. "She's a Mets fan. She knows all the players."

Anne, the younger daughter, was less informed, less excited.

"She'll take her crayons and coloring book with her to the park," said Nancy. "When I told her we were going to the baseball game, she wanted to know how long we would be."

Tom kissed them all before going off to Shea.

"Don't rush and don't fall off the mound," said his mother. "Don't swear and don't spit."

Mothers are always mothers.

The ride to the park was uneventful, but there was plenty to make up for that once he got into the stadium.

As was always his custom, he arrived in the clubhouse a little bit later on the days he pitched. "Cuts down on a whole lot of distraction," said Herb Norman, the Mets equipment manager for seventeen years.

Exactly what Tom had in mind. He wanted to concentrate as completely as he could on the game at hand, no distractions; but the clubhouse was not the best place for the complete concentration he wanted. It never is on opening day, and it *certainly* isn't distraction-free when you're Tom Seaver returning to the New York Mets. "Say, Tom," called out Doug Montana, the Mets batboy, who was working on a newspaper baseball contest, "how many batters are you going to strike out this season?"

Tom gave the kid a friendly but quizzical smile.

"I'm not kidding," pursued the young Montana. "We get these questions right and we've got ourselves a trip to the World Series. How many are you going to strike out, Tom?"

Tom took the paper and pencil out of the kid's hands.

"Let's see," he said, and wrote down a number.

"Four hundred thirteen!" exploded the kid. "You never struck out 300! Maybe a hundred is more like it!"

"Oh, yeah?" blasted Tom, laughing, and he grabbed the kid around his chest with one arm and pretended to pound away at him with his free hand.

Distractions! Distractions!

It was only a little after 11:00, several hours before the umpire was to cry, "Play ball!" but the stands in Shea Stadium were beginning to fill up, and the banners were beginning to flutter over the railings.

"WELCOME BACK, TOM"

"WELCOME BACK, TOM TERRIFIC"

"WELCOME HOME, TOM"

"TOM TERRIFIC IS HOME"

The noise, too, began to build up in the stands.

And when Tom walked out to the bullpen in right field and began to loosen up, the roar from the crowd was enough to bring tears to the eyes of more than a few fans.

Warming up alongside Seaver was Ed Lynch, who was acquired from Texas in 1979, and had pitched well for the Mets in 1981 and 1982. He was getting ready just in case Tom's leg was acting up.

Ed Lynch wasn't the calmest man in the stadium that afternoon.

"All these people are here to see Seaver pitch," he said that day. "I could just hear the boos they'd aim at me if I had to go in and pitch for him."

Lynch paced up and down, his eyes watching Seaver's every move.

Tom noticed Lynch eyeing him, carefully. He could appreciate the kid's nervousness, but he was loose enough to make a joke of it.

"Watch this," he said to Gene Dusan, the bullpen coach, and on his next pitch, he went down to his left thigh and made that awful grimace that comes with awful pain.

"My mouth is open," said Lynch, later, "and my heart is pounding right over my tongue. I thought he pulled the leg muscle again.

"And then Tom laughs and says, 'I got you that time!' "

Tom was cool, all right. But he was all fired up inside. Then just as he finished warming up in the bullpen, the big Diamond Vision screen in Shea Stadium flashed some highlights of Seaver's great career as a Met and the stands, now jammed with a record 51,000-plus fans, ate up every star moment, their emotions building and building and building and the cheers mounting as game time approached.

The routine for the pitcher warming up in the bullpen is to walk underneath the stands and into the dugout, once his warm-ups are finished. But the Mets promotion manager, Tim Hamilton, had asked Tom to walk out on the field to the dugout.

"The fans would like that," said Hamilton.

Tom was always ready to oblige the fans. He was particularly glad to oblige the fans this opening day of the 1983 season.

He continued warming up on the bullpen, as the starting lineup was reeled off on the loudspeakers. "Playing center field, and leading off—Mookie Wilson. Batting second and playing shortstop—Bob Bailor."

Each name drew its roar of approval. "Playing first base, and third in the batting order—" blared the loudspeaker, "Dave Kingman." More cheers.

And so on down the list: George Foster, Brooks, Mike Howard, Brian Giles, and, "Catching and batting in the eighth position—Ron Hodges."

The crowd was on its feet now. The big moment, the great expectancy was at hand.

Frank Franchetti, the public address announcer, paused a split moment, then, in as matter-of-fact a voice as he could manage, said, "Batting ninth and pitching, now warming up in the bullpen, number 41—"

He didn't have to say any more.

The roar that went up in the stadium could have been heard clear across all the bridges that lead into Manhattan and Brooklyn and out east into Nassau and Suffolk. Tom Seaver was there in the flesh, on the mound again for the Amazin' Mets. He had come home again.

The rookie catcher Ronn Reynolds, who had been

warming up Tom Terrific in the bullpen, handed him the ball.

"There's a handicapped kid near the railing in the right-field corner," said Reynolds. "He asked me for a ball. Do you think you can give him this one?"

"Sure," said Tom.

He walked straight out of the bullpen for that corner in right field, handed the ball to the handicapped boy, shook hands with him, and patted the boy on his back. The crowd roared in approval.

"That showed me so much about the man," said Reynolds later. "I had tears in my eyes."

Then, with the crowd still on its feet and cheering madly, number 41 walked across the broad field of Shea Stadium to the dugout.

Mario Cuomo, the governor of New York who had once played in the Pittsburgh Pirates farm league, was in the stands. So was the ebullient mayor of New York City, Ed Koch. So were 51,000 others, including Seaver's entire family.

Tom Seaver tipped his hat to the cheering crowd, put it back on his head. He tipped his hat a second time, waved it twice, put it back on his head again. The third time he thrust it straight up into the air.

And the crowd cheered and cheered and cheered, and the cheering didn't begin to ebb until Tom disappeared into the Mets dugout.

Then Seaver went the entire length of the dugout, shaking hands with everybody on the bench, wishing each of them luck, pumping them up.

"That was what really gave me the chills," said Dave Kingman.

Then Seaver sprinted to the mound.

"It was a tremendously emotional moment," said

Tom later. "I have so many wonderful memories here. It was great to be back, but so emotional that I still had the jitters for two innings."

Tom was so fired up, he pitched nothing but 1969 fastballs in the first two innings. The first batter was Pete Rose, and the first pitch was a strike. The second pitch was even faster—another strike. When he struck out Rose on the next pitch, the roar of the crowd rivaled the clamor that went up the day the Mets won the pennant in 1973.

Joe Morgan, the second batter, walked, and went to second on a pickoff throw that Dave Kingman missed. Morgan went to third on a grounder, but then, with the dangerous Mike Schmidt at the plate, Tom came in with a snaky slider and got Schmidt to pop-up to end the inning.

Tom gave up a single to Tony Perez in the second inning, but a fast double play stopped any threat. He retired the Phils in order in the third and fourth innings and then Perez again singled through the middle for a base hit. But Seaver quickly got the next three hitters in order. In the sixth inning, Tom fanned Steve Carlton, his pitching opponent, on three quick fastballs and suddenly felt a twinge in his left thigh. He motioned to manager George Bamberger, pointed to the leg; it had been bothering him all through spring training, and Bamby alerted the bullpen to get ready in relief.

Tom struck out Rose once again, this time on a change-up. Joe Morgan singled, but while trying to stretch the hit into a double, he was thrown out by George Foster.

The Franchise pitched six strong innings, gave up just three hits, struck out five hitters, and held the

Phils scoreless. The Mets went on to win the opener, 2–0, and although the win didn't go into Seaver's record, he had done his job to perfection.

"I knew it would be emotional," Tom said later, after the game, "but I didn't think it would be that emotional. It wasn't easy keeping cool, but I was pitching and I had to keep all that emotion bottled up.

"If I wasn't pitching, I would have cried."

Of his success on the mound, Seaver said, "I just threw different kinds of fastballs, a slider, and the change-up. Just good location and a certain movement on the ball. Nothing mysterious.

"To pitch in the big leagues," he continued, offering another bit of wisdom on the art of pitching, "you have to be able to pitch inside. You have to establish that. You cannot allow the hitter to feel that he owns the plate."

Pete Rose, who was struck out twice in the game by the master, said, "He's not the blower he was when he was here the first time, but he made some great pitches, about what you'd expect of a Hall-of-Fame pitcher.

"I don't remember the last time I struck out twice in a game," continued Rose. "I only missed two pitches all spring."

"Is Seaver better?" said Joe Morgan, now playing for the Philadelphia club. "He's smarter. He knew that everybody coming back from spring training was anxious and jumping; he fed us a lot of slower speeds and guys kept swinging at bad pitches."

There could be no doubt about it, Tom Seaver was back, and with him, the promise of a great year for the Mets.

Unfortunately, that promise never materialized.

The glory of opening day soon faded, and the Mets fell victim to one of baseball's great doctrines: you can't win games without scoring runs—and the Mets weren't scoring runs. George Foster wasn't hitting. Dave Kingman wasn't hitting. And John Stearns, the Mets' fine catcher, was on the disabled list.

By the end of May, Tom's record was three wins against four losses. In three of his losses, the Mets had been blanked, and in the fourth loss the Mets had managed to squeeze just one run across the plate. In the 79 innings Tom had pitched, the Mets had scored a total of 19 runs, not quite two and a half runs per game.

"Is homecoming still that much fun for you, Tom?" asked CBS-TV's top anchorman, Jim Jensen, a former ball player with a top minor league team who was preparing a TV documentary on Seaver's return.

"Not when you lose so many times," Seaver said. "Now, mind you, I'm not ticked off, but it's no fun knowing that you can't make a single mistake and survive. But errors and no runs are part of the game and I've come to accept them.

"What gets me mad as hell is when I don't pitch well enough to cover my infielders' mistakes. I just blame myself. When I look back on my career, I won't measure my success by the numbers. And I'll never wonder what it would be like to be pitching for some other team. I've been through all that. And that's playing numbers, too.

"When I lose, it's not the losing that bothers me as much as the *way* I lose."

On June 5, Tom was in top form, pitching a superlative eight innings against the powerful Pittsburgh Pirates, who were threatening to tear the league apart. Seaver held the Pirate sluggers to four base hits, struck out six, and did not walk a batter. However, Tom tired in the eighth inning, was relieved by Carlos Diaz, and the Pirates scored a run off Diaz in the eighth for a 2–1 victory.

Frank Howard, the Mets' new manager who took over when George Bamberger resigned, said of that game, "It was a classic battle of two quality big-league pitchers. Seaver and John Candelaria [of the Pirates] are two of the finest pitchers around. We got beat because we're not hitting very well. This team has not hit well at all, and it seems that when Seaver is in there the hitting is at its worst. Tom's five and six now, but that just shows you how misleading those stats are. In at least five of those six games, we've scored less than three runs per game. You can't win in the big leagues if you can't score more runs. We simply have to put together a better attack."

And G.M. Cashen had been assembling players. The year before, realizing that the Mets' woeful hitting would never get them out of the cellar, Cashen pulled off what baseball experts called one of the biggest Met deals in recent history, when he finessed the Reds into dealing for George Foster, one of the premier Cincinnati hitters. The Mets gave up catcher Alex Trevino and pitchers Greg Harris and Jim Kern in return for the talented Foster.

Cashen and Bamberger were sure that Foster and Kingman, whom the Mets reacquired from the Cubs in 1981, would give the lowly Mets one of the most powerful slugging combinations in the National League. Kingman did produce, smashing 37 home runs with 99 RBI, although his average fell off to a meager .204. Foster, on the other hand, had the poorest year in his career, dropping off to a .247 average with only 13 home runs, falling short of the big numbers that management was certain he would deliver.

As the season progressed into a dismal May and the Mets continued to flounder, Cashen maneuvered another outstanding deal, this time for one of the leading stars of the National League, the star first baseman of the St. Louis Cardinals, Keith Hernandez. A nine-year veteran, Hernandez led the National League in 1979 with a .344 batting average. A solid line-drive hitter, Keith was also one of the top first basemen in the game, and at 30 years of age, figured to provide the Mets with the finest play at that position since the ball club was formed in 1962.

On September 10, on a cool, windy night in Montreal, Seaver was once again the Tom Terrific of old, much to the chagrin of the Expos, whose pennant express was temporarily derailed by Seaver. Flashing once more his 1969 form, his fastball zipping in and up, then baffling the hitters with his tantalizing off-speed pitches, Seaver had the Expos at his mercy, and with the aid of relief pitcher Jess Orosco, pitched the Mets to a stunning 5–4 win.

The win was number eight for Seaver against 13 losses, as he held the aggressive Expos to but four hits in the eight innings he pitched. Tom struck out seven, tired in the eighth inning, ran into trouble in the ninth, but Orosco fanned the last two Expos to put the game away for Tom. Darryl Strawberry continued to star at the plate, driving out three solid line drives, including a booming triple to raise his batting average to .245.

On September 15, Tom once more pitched his heart out in a taut, tense duel against former team-mate Neil Allen, now with the St. Louis Cards. Once again, as had been the case all season long, the Mets simply could not hit with Seaver on the mound and Tom lost a tough game, 2–1.

On September 20, Seaver, with four consecutive pitching performances that were outstanding, took to the mound against the Pirates, who were battling furiously for first place against the Philadelphia Phillies.

Tom Terrific breezed through the first four innings, retiring the first nine Pirates in order, before allowing the first two base hits. Pitching as if the Mets were battling for first, Seaver struck out six Pirates in four innings and battled John Candelaria tooth and nail for eight innings in a 2–2 game.

Seaver and Candelaria started the game as two of the top active pitchers in winning percentage. Tom was third on the list, trailing Ron Guidry and Jim Palmer, with a 272–170 mark for a winning percentage of .615. Candelaria, with a 109–69 mark, was fourth with a .612 average.

With the score tied at 2–2, the Pirates broke through for two runs in the ninth, but the Mets rallied to tie the score at 4–4. Then Mookie Wilson singled in the tenth inning and scored the winning run as Hubie Brooks brought him home on a smash base hit, and the Mets had a hard-fought 5–4 victory.

Seaver, however, had been taken out of the game in the eighth inning for a pinch-hitter, and Diaz, who pitched the final two innings, was given credit for the win.

Discussing the Mets' lowly position in late September, some 15½ games behind the division-leading Pittsburgh Pirates, Seaver tried not to be discouraged, despite his 8 and 14 record.

"We're way down and have a long, long way to go, but we've been playing much better ball the last month. There's a lot of talent on this club . . . reminds me of 1969. That youngster [Jose] Oquendo is a marvel at shortstop. He has the quickest pair of hands I've ever seen. And it looks like Strawberry could develop into one of the great stars of the future. He has a marvelous, quick wrist movement at the plate and he's only 22 years old," said Tom.

"Somehow we've got to get Foster to hit the way he really can, like he did at Cincinnati for so many years. Perhaps we can do it in '84. We've got some of the best young arms in the league, kids like Ron Darling, Walt Terrell, Ed Lynch, Doug Sisk, and relief pitchers like Jesse Orosco and Carlos Diaz. Now if Johnny Stearns can recover from his shoulder operation and give us the quality catching that he produced in some eight years, ever since 1975, we ought to be in good shape for 1984.

"With Foster hitting, and with Hernandez and Strawberry in the middle of the batting order, producing the kind of punch we need in 1984, we should be right up there in contention, all the way.

"I know just where we are going in 1984," said Seaver, "and what we're going to do to get there."

He was referring, of course, to the Mets of 1984.

Tom Seaver had known all along in his baseball life exactly where he was going. He had been able to chart his own progress from that very first day back in 1965, when, as a 21-year-old, still in school, he bargained his way into a $51,500 bonus package and a big-league career.

And when that original package deal with the Atlanta Braves was voided by baseball commissioner Bowie Kuhn, it was Tom Seaver who studied the rules and regulations, called the commissioner's office, pointed out the unfairness of his situation, and negotiated a deal with the New York Mets.

Tom Seaver knew where he was going, at all times.

That was so until the evening of January 23, 1984.

He was attending a sports convention in Chicago for one of his sponsors, Spalding, the big sporting goods manufacturer. He had spent the better part of two days being a goodwill ambassador for the company, meeting and greeting dealers and buyers attending the convention. Winding up activities, Tom was making plans to fly back home to Connecticut, completely unaware of the storm of controversy about to burst around him.

His prophecy about the Mets would come true: they would indeed be contenders in 1984. But they would do it without Seaver. On opening day 1984, Tom Terrific would be a member of the Chicago White Sox.

25
THE RENAISSANCE
OF THE WHITE SOX

The renaissance of the Chicago White Sox began late in January 1981, when two transplanted easterners, Jerry Reinsdorf and Eddie Einhorn, gained approval from the American League to purchase the White Sox for a reported sum of $20 million.

Reinsdorf and Einhorn met while attending Northwestern University Law School and became friends. Reinsdorf, in addition to his duties as chairman of the White Sox and Chicago Bulls, is chief executive officer of Balcor/American Express, one of the largest real estate syndicators in the nation. Einhorn, the president of the White Sox, is one of the most colorful and controversial executives in sports today. In 1961 he founded the TVS Television Network, the first "sports-only" channel that became so successful that he sold it to Corinthian Broadcasting for a sum in excess of $100 million.

And in April 1983, Einhorn negotiated the largest baseball TV package in the history of the sport.

The new White Sox owners made news immediately by announcing they were retaining the two top people from the former management, general manager Roland Hemond and manager Tony LaRussa.

Shortly thereafter, Einhorn and Reinsdorf signed one of the greatest catchers in baseball when they signed free agent Carlton Fisk, the Boston Red Sox star, to a multi-million-dollar three-year contract. Almost immediately thereafter, they signed Greg Luzinski, one of the major leagues' great home run hitters. Luzinski, a nine-year veteran with the Philadelphia Phillies, was returned to Chicago, his hometown, after the Sox purchased his contract from the Phils.

In Roland Hemond, the White Sox retained one of baseball's leading officials. Hemond had joined the White Sox as director of player development in 1970, and quickly established a reputation for his ability to deal with players and agents. In Hemond's first task, the selection of a new manager, he named Chuck Tanner for the job, and Tanner responded by leading the Sox to a third-place finish in 1971 and a second-place finish in 1972.

Hemond was named a vice president in 1973 and in 1981 was elevated to the post of general manager of the White Sox. Late in 1985, he moved into the front office in order to make way for Ken "Hawk" Harrelson.

Tony LaRussa's rise in the White Sox organization has been nothing short of meteoric. A 16-year veteran of professional baseball, LaRussa signed his first pro baseball contract in 1962, the same evening he graduated from Jefferson High School in Tampa, after an outstanding prep school career. He joined the Kansas City Athletics in 1963 and played in only 34 games before he threw his arm out in a play at shortstop. Tony had gone deep into the hole and made the play, but in throwing the ball to first, something popped in his shoulder.

"Everything in my shoulder got ripped up," he said. "And if you touch it today, it's still sore." Forever after he would scramble to stay in baseball, bunting when no one else could, stealing bases, living the kind of borderline existence that men with his intelligence and aspirations are supposed to be beyond.

"I played until I was 34 years old," he said. "And I should have retired when I hurt that shoulder when I was 24."

The Athletics traded Tony to the Braves, who farmed him out to Richmond. Then he was back at Oakland in 1968 and played there until 1971 when he was sent to the Atlanta Braves, where he hit .286 in a limited number of games.

For the only time in his life, Tony talked about quitting baseball, until the Cubs gave him a shot at making their ballclub. He appeared in only one game in 1973, but the money the Cubs gave him was enough for Tony to pay his tuition through law school.

In 1978, he was hired to manage Knoxville, a White Sox farm team, and LaRussa promptly led his charges to a pennant. The following season he was promoted to manage the Sox' triple-A team in the American Association. On August 2 of that season Tony was named manager of the White Sox, replacing Don Kessinger.

In his first full season as the White Sox manager, LaRussa and the Sox finished in fifth place in the Western Division, 26 games behind with a 70–90 record. In the strike-plagued 1981 season, the White Sox finished in third place with a 54–52 record, and in 1982 the Sox finished in third place once again with a 87–75 record.

But in 1983, with one of the greatest pitching staffs any team in the American League has ever had, pitchers like LaMarr Hoyt, Richard Dotson, Britt Burns, and Floyd Bannister, and with Harold Baines, Carlton Fisk, Ron Kittle, and Vern and Rudy Law driving in runs when they were most needed, the White Sox stormed to the top of the Western Division and won the championship 20 games ahead of the second place Kansas City Royals with a 99–63 record.

The championship season, however, had its hills and its valleys. On May 26, one of the darkest days of the season for LaRussa, the White Sox were mired in sixth place with a 16–24 record when Eddie Einhorn called in Bobby Winkles, director of White Sox player development, and told him "to sit on the bench, to take notes and let us know what we are doing wrong."

LaRussa seemed within days of being fired, and it wasn't a secret to anyone. "They didn't pull any surprises on me," he said. "I was kept informed by Eddie all along. I just knew that we had to start winning soon, or else. . . ."

But while it seemed that the Sox were out of the race, LaRussa kept his chin up and forged ahead. He shook up his lineup, battled with Fisk and Tom Paciorek about their lack of playing time, then moved Fisk to the number two hitting spot in the lineup, utilized the veteran Paciorek more often, and approved a trade with Seattle for the flashy defensive second baseman Julio Cruz. After Cruz's arrival in Chicago, the White Sox won 10 of their next 12 games and romped with a 71–31 record the rest of the year to win the division title.

And Tony LaRussa was named Manager of the Year by the Baseball Writers Association of America.

But the team that won its division by the most games ever in the history of the sport—20—fizzled in the play-offs, falling to the Baltimore Orioles in four games in their bid for a pennant. It was a bitter loss for Chicago, a bitter loss for the players, and a bitter loss for Einhorn and Reinsdorf, who vowed to shuffle things around just enough to get the Sox to the World Series in 1984.

It was just three months later, on that afternoon of January 23, 1984, that the offices of the Chicago White Sox at Comiskey Park were in a frenzy of excitement as Reinsdorf and Einhorn huddled with general manager Roland Hemond. The trio was studying a teletype list of ball players, a list of protected players from the roster of the New York Mets. And the name of their standout pitcher was not on the list. Tom Seaver, the three-time Cy Young award winner and one of the game's greatest pitchers, was available and could be selected by one of the two teams eligible: the Oakland A's or the White Sox, both entitled to a compensation selection from the pool of unprotected players.

"When I first checked the list," said Hemond, "I noticed Seaver's name wasn't included. I went over the list once more and then again. Then I went over the list alphabetically. Seaver's name was not there.

301

"In our opinion," said Hemond, "Tom Seaver was clearly the best player available and we notified the baseball commissioner that we were selecting Seaver. We selected him," he said, "not only because our scouts assured us he was still a top-notch pitcher, but because he is the sort of class guy we want on the Chicago White Sox.

"In 1983, we won the division championship and thought we might go on all the way to a World Series. I had our scouts watching several National League clubs that we conceivably might have to play. And our people saw Tom Seaver in a few games and they were mightily impressed.

"If we had Seaver last year [1983]," said Hemond, "we'd be celebrating a world championship instead of a division title."

Of the Mets' shock and dismay over the Sox' selection of Seaver, Hemond had this to say: "I can readily understand how people in New York might think we wronged the Mets. They probably felt that we had such a great pitching staff with Floyd Bannister who won 16 games, Britt Burns who won 10, Richard Dotson who won 22, and LaMarr Hoyt who won 24 games and the Cy Young award, that we would never select another pitcher. But Tom Seaver is not just another pitcher. He is a great one. And this was purely a business decision. It was our thinking that if we did not take Seaver, the Oakland club certainly would, and they are in our division."

The free agent compensation list which led to this dramatic turn of events for the White Sox and Seaver was created after the players' strike in 1981. Each team would set a list of players who are protected. Players not on such a list were not protected and could be picked by a team who has lost a premium player via free agency.

The White Sox lost pitcher Dennis Lamp to free agency and the Toronto Blue Jays. Thus, the White Sox were able to select Tom Seaver.

But signing him was another story.

"As soon as we notified the baseball commissioner's office that the White Sox had selected Tom Seaver, we called Tom at the Hyatt Hotel in Chicago, but there was no answer. We called again and again throughout the late afternoon," said Eddie Einhorn, "and decided that we would have dinner at the Hyatt where Tom was staying, and we would contact Tom as soon as he came into his room. We did not want to take a chance that another club would reach him.

"We called Tom's room several times and finally at about 10:30 P.M. he answered the phone," said Einhorn. "I told him who we were and that Jerry Reinsdorf and I would like to talk with him about the Mets player list that we received that afternoon.

"Tom told us to come up to his room, and when we arrived at the door we were flabbergasted when he asked us to produce some identification. It did not occur to us that Seaver wouldn't know us. Quite an embarrassment. Then, of course, he invited us into the suite.

"Now, this entire thing was a most delicate situation," said Einhorn. "Here was this truly great star, Tom Seaver, and we had to tell him that the Mets, a team that he had given his heart and soul to for more than 11 years, had not protected him, and the White Sox had selected him.

"He was in turn shocked, hurt, and angered," said

Eddie, "and after a few minutes, his first angry reaction: 'The hell with it all. Maybe I'll just retire.'

"After a while, Jerry and I talked with Tom about the White Sox potential, a potential that could easily include a great chance for another division title, the American League pennant, certainly a great chance for him to win those coveted 300 games, and last but not least, an outside shot at another World Series for him.

"When we ran through all those possibilities, he really listened and calmed down, and then we started to discuss a contract with him."

The announcement by the White Sox that they had selected Tom Seaver and were attempting to sign him was a story that shook the entire baseball fraternity; officials, fans, and players from coast to coast were shocked, and fans in New York created an immediate storm of protest, while White Sox fans whooped it up over the possibility of Tom Seaver joining a team that already boasted a quartet of pitching stars: Floyd Bannister, Richard Dotson, Britt Burns, and LaMarr Hoyt.

At a press conference in New York several days later, a disturbed and angry Seaver said, "I got more upset as things went along. I am not here to blame the Mets. They just made a stupid mistake. When I came back here to New York from Cincinnati, I expected to end my career in New York with the Mets. I still do not understand why I was not protected.

"What the Mets did," continued Seaver, "was to disrupt my family life. I did have some idea I wasn't going to be protected. Bill Murray of the *Daily News* told me I was not on the list. But I really didn't believe it. I had pitched well the entire year, and had not missed a start. I was 9 and 14, but with some help it could have easily been in reverse.

"Now I don't know what I'll do."

At a meeting with the Mets general manager Frank Cashen, Tom said, "I'm glad that Nancy wasn't here for this talk with Cashen. She's got an Irish temper. If she were here I don't think she would be as kind as I have been."

In Chicago several days later, Eddie Einhorn said that he and Reinsdorf would further discuss the situation with Seaver and his lawyer. "We're still apart on a deal with Tom, even though we've raised our offer to him. He is in no hurry. He wants time to think it over. It's been an emotional downer for him. But we want him and he has said he does want to come to Chicago."

It was not a problem of excessive pride.

Tom Seaver will never have that kind of problem.

It was a problem of the heart.

The heart of his family.

Concerned mainly about the family disruption that would result from his having to spend summers in Chicago instead of at his home in Greenwich, Connecticut, where he could commute to Shea Stadium, he waited a month before making a decision.

There were those who said Seaver wanted a sweeter contract. But Tom insisted his hesitation had more to do with his wife, Nancy, and daughters Sarah, age 12, and Anne, eight.

Early in Seaver's limbo period, when he was torn between junking his brilliant career for one in the TV industry as a sportscaster, Nancy promised delivery to Chicago. "I'll get him there," she said.

Nancy certainly had influence, but it was the

comment by 12-year-old Sarah that convinced Tom that the family ties would not be broken by a move to another city in another league. Sarah was asked by her mother how she would feel about leaving her horse and riding lessons and her friends for summers in Chicago. Sarah didn't hesitate.

"Will it be best for Daddy's career?" she asked.

"As a parent," Seaver said, "you wonder if you're doing things correctly, if you're giving your children the right ideas. I got tears in my eyes when I heard Sarah's reaction."

Finally, on February 19, Tom Seaver agreed to play for the White Sox.

"The White Sox secured Seaver's services by sweetening his existing contract," said Einhorn. The Sox also included some new clauses:

1. A no-trade clause.
2. Another option year through the year 1987.
3. A more accessible innings-pitched incentive clause.
4. The usual bonuses for postseason awards.
5. $25,000 for family visitation and moving expenses.

"I clinched the deal with Tom from the airport in Frankfurt, Germany," said Einhorn. "Tom and I and his agent were on the phone for hours. The phone bill was $1,100. But it was worth every penny for we got the greatest pitcher in the game."

Seaver appeared equally satisfied. "If I were to have picked a team myself, I couldn't have selected a more attractive one than the White Sox," he said. "From players and others I've talked with, the organization received an A-plus rating.

"I sense an immediate feeling of winning here, the same kind of attitude we had in New York in 1969. I talked with one of the players," said Tom, "who said that feeling of winning didn't just start last year, but was here a few years before that. I got the impression that all the guys wanted to keep playing in October last year. The White Sox had a taste of winning then, but not the whole mouthful. I hope I can help with that.

"I think, too, of what Carlton Fisk said: 'I feel I have 25 friends on this team.' I'm sure I'll have that feeling. One of the biggest kicks of my life was 1979 in Cincinnati when we won the division. Watching the feelings of the young players was one of those great thrills. I'd like to watch that same feeling in this White Sox clubhouse.

"As for Chicago, I think we [the family] will love it. I always felt comfortable coming into town as a player, something I could not say about all cities. It's a wonderfully refreshing city, something new to discover each and every day. We'll have to work at it, but I'm sure we'll grow to love it.

"Privately I've told people I wouldn't mind at all winding up my career here," Seaver said. "Not only have I never been in Comiskey Park, I've never been in Boston's Fenway Park, and I've always wanted to pitch in Fenway. I've been interested in the talent in the American League and the history of it. Now I'll have the opportunity to find out.

"Who knows about these things?" he said. "Maybe after all, the Mets did me a helluva favor. Now I'm with an organization that will afford me an opportunity to reach my dream goal . . . to win 300 and perhaps get into another World Series, which is, as we all know, the reason we play this game."

26
CHICAGO! CHICAGO! A WONDERFUL TOWN

Tom Seaver reported to the White Sox spring training headquarters in Sarasota, Florida, on March 7, 1984, suited up for the first time in a White Sox uniform, and began a tough regimen of calisthenics, wind sprints, and arm exercises. And when he first tossed a few pitches to his new battery mate, Carlton Fisk, a gaggle of TV cameramen, news photographers, and sportswriters descended on the two, inundating them with pleas to pose for photographs, and bombarding them with endless questions.

Standing with a reporter on the sidelines, Einhorn said, "This kind of excitement has never happened to us since I've taken over the ball club. I've been involved with the team since 1981 with Jerry Reinsdorf," said Eddie, "and during the few years we've had many thrills in baseball and plenty of excitement, but nothing to match this.

"I can remember the excitement after weeks of dickering with Carlton Fisk, then signing him for the Sox—that was a great thrill. Then getting Luzinski from the Phillies, and that was a thrill. Seeing Ron Kittle develop into a tremendous hitter was another exciting period. And then winning the division championship in 1983, the first time we had won a championship since 1959—that was an exciting period. Then the incredible excitement of the play-offs against the Orioles, even though we lost.

"But I can truthfully say that seeing Tom Seaver in a White Sox uniform has to be one of the greatest moments of my life. I've never experienced anything like it.

"Here is this great baseball star, already a living legend, a certain Hall-of-Famer, whose exploits have filled the record books and sports pages of the nation through more than 18 years. And he is one of my White Sox players. It just gives me goosebumps every time I look at him in uniform."

Seaver had been following a rigid conditioning regimen of his own before reporting to camp, and after several days of calisthenics and wind sprints he was ready to take his turn on the mound in a Grapefruit League game against the Boston Red Sox.

In a most impressive performance in the warm Florida sun, Tom pitched three innings, and the large crowd on hand for the game oohed and aahed at the perfection of his performance.

He wheeled in some carefully located sliders and curveballs that broke exactly where he wanted each pitch to go. His fastball was popping. And manager Tony LaRussa sat back on the bench and enjoyed every moment of every pitch.

"He looks like he could win a few ball games for us," said LaRussa.

Back in the clubhouse, after three innings in which he struck out four and held the slugging Red Sox without a hit or a run, Tom said he was delighted with his work, more than delighted. There had been some small technical problems, his release was a little flat at times, but that didn't surprise him, because he had been very nervous about his first pitching assignment.

"I wanted to prove to the guys on this ball club that I can help the team and do it immediately. They really don't care about previous performances and your reputation. They want to know if you still can pitch, especially at the age of 39. Now, this is a team that won a division title last year. They had a taste of victory. Just a taste; now they want more. They want a World Series.

"What this game is all about is simply proving things to your own teammates."

After several pitching stints in the Grapefruit League, it was apparent to all concerned—even to the critics who had vociferously opposed the Seaver selection by the White Sox, and there were a number of them—that even though Tom had lost some of the zap of his 95 mph fastball, he more than made up for it with his experience and his canny ability to constantly outsmart even the finest hitters.

When it was announced that Seaver would take a regular turn in the pitching rotation and would join a staff already considered the finest in baseball, experts were predicting that the White Sox were odds-on favorites to once again sweep the AL West and go on to take a pennant.

On the day of the Sox' home opener, despite the cold and constant drizzle, a crowd of more than 20,000 excited fans poured through the turnstiles at Comiskey Park. They were here to witness the much heralded debut of Tom Seaver as the White Sox, with a record of four wins and four losses, prepared to square off against the blazing Detroit Tigers, who had won five straight games.

As Seaver slowly walked to the mound for his first American League game against the slugging, rampaging Tigers, he quickly took note of his teammates on the field. They were essentially the same guys who ran off with the division title in 1983.

He studied Rudy Law in center field for a moment. Here was a guy the Dodgers shunted off to Albuquerque in 1981, where he responded by slugging hell out of the ball for a .335 average. Brought to the White Sox in a trade, Law hit .318 in 1982 and did even better in 1983 by being the catalyst in the drive for the championship by stealing 77 bases.

Ron Kittle in left field was a likable youngster. Here was one of the most dramatic stories in baseball. Another Dodger castoff. Complaining about numbness in his right arm that prevented him from properly gripping a bat, Ron was dropped by the Dodgers and signed by the White Sox after an operation for a pair of crushed vertebrae. After surgery, Kittle wore a neck brace for months, took a job in an iron foundry, was given another chance by the White Sox, and was sent to the Sox' farm team at Glenn Falls.

At Glenn Falls, Kittle powered 40 home runs in 1981 and was brought up to Edmonton of the American Association in 1982. He responded by slugging 50 home runs. Brought up to the White Sox in 1983, Kittle slammed 35 home runs and was named Rookie of the Year.

Harold Baines in right field was another great story. As a 12-year-old Little League star in Maryland, Baines was picked out as a "future star" by former White Sox owner Bill Veeck, and at age 17 Baines was the number one draft choice by the White Sox in 1977. Sent to Appleton, Baines hit .261 and was sent to Knoxville in 1978, then to Iowa in 1979 where he clubbed 22 home runs. In 1980, Harold made the "big club," slugged 13 home runs, and hit for a .255 average. His great defensive skill in the field and line-drive hitting made him a fixture at that position.

It was an outfield of fleet-footed youngsters with great arms and powerful hitters, strong enough to compare favorably with any team in the division.

Seaver looked over at Greg Walker on first base. A husky six foot three 215-pounder, Greg was one of the most promising youngsters on the team. The White Sox selected Greg as an unprotected player in the 1979 draft and in 1983, when Tom Paciorek (the Sox regular first baseman) and Mike Squires (his substitute) were both injured, Walker filled in at first base and hit .270, including 10 home runs in 1983.

Shortstop Scott Fletcher was among the leading shortstops in the American Association for the Chicago Cubs' Iowa club in 1981 and 1982. As part of a six-player trade with the Cubs, Scott became a member of the White Sox organization in 1983. He quickly improved his play and became one of the best shortstops in the league.

Vance Law over at third base was the son of Vern Law, who, as a pitcher for the Pirates, was a Cy

Young award winner. Vance was utilized as a second baseman, shortstop, and then finally shifted to third base, and in the second half of the 1983 season he hit for a .275 average. His defensive play at third saved a number of crucial games for the Sox.

Julio Cruz, certainly one of the flashiest second basemen in baseball, was acquired by the White Sox in a trade with the Mariners in June of 1983. His defensive play at second and ability to make the double play, combined with exceptional speed which saw him steal 57 bases in 1983, proved to be a vital reason for the Sox' surge.

Catcher Carlton Fisk was selected by the White Sox in 1981 and brought instant credibility to the new owners of the team. He proved to Chicago fans that the owners were sincere and would go all out in their efforts to develop a winner in Chicago.

Fisk, an American League All-Star catcher for eight years, a Red Sox star for more than 10 seasons, was one of the finest receivers in baseball history. A steadying influence behind the plate, a powerful home run hitter, Fisk had been a great influence in the drive for the championship in 1983, with 26 home runs and a .289 average.

As Seaver quickly glanced once more around his infield, he tightened his belt, wiped the cold rain from his face, stepped on the mound to face the Tiger sluggers, and said to himself: "These guys of ours all have the same kind of ability and spirit that the Mets had when we won. Maybe we can do it again."

Now ready to face the Tigers' leadoff hitter, second baseman Lou Whitaker, Seaver toed the rubber, brought his arm back down, around, and came in with a blazing fastball. Lou just stood there as the ball tore into Fisk's big glove for a strike.

The next pitch: another fastball. This time Whitaker slashed his big bat into the ball and drove it out to right field for a clean single. Shortstop Alan Trammell then lined Seaver's next pitch right to Walker at first base. Greg leaped for the ball, snared it in the webbing of his glove, and stepped on first base for the double play.

Lance Parrish, the Tigers' hard-hitting catcher, laced into Tom's next pitch, drove it on a line to second baseman Julio Cruz, and the inning was over.

In the second inning, Evans singled to start the Tigers off, and Kirk Gibson, the slugging right fielder, drove Tom's next pitch over the right-field wall to give the Tigers a 2–0 lead.

The White Sox picked up a run in the second inning and another in the third to tie the score at 2–2, but the Tigers, out for their sixth straight win, continued to connect on Seaver's pitches. Whitaker singled home a run in the fourth inning, and with two men on base in the fifth, Seaver was tiring, missing the strike zone frequently, and getting behind the hitters. LaRussa called time, walked to the mound, talked briefly with Tom, patted him on the back, took the ball out of his hand, and called for a relief pitcher.

Juan Agosta came in to pitch and he was promptly hit for a two-run double by first baseman Barbaro Garbey, and in came LaRussa and another pitching change. This time Salome Barajas came in to pitch. But the Tigers pounded Barajas for two more runs to give them a 7–3 win over the Sox.

In the dressing room after the game, a tired Seaver said, "I was ragged. The weather didn't bother me, but I would have liked it if it were a bit warmer. I just couldn't put the pitches where I wanted to. It's as simple as that.

"I'll watch the films tomorrow," said Tom. "I just feel disappointed at my first start at home. My goal every start is to go at least seven innings and to give up three earned runs or less. My job then is to keep the ball club in the game. I just didn't do it. Now I have at least five days before my next start to straighten myself out."

A huge sellout crowd of more than 53,000 fans jammed the Milwaukee Brewers ballpark on April 17 for the Brewers first home game and a chance to watch Tom Seaver once again attempt to win his first American League game.

Snow, which changed to rain, did not dampen the enthusiasm of the Brewers' crowd, as it joyously watched the Brewers score a run in the first inning to jump out and take a 1–0 lead over the White Sox.

But Seaver, warming up to the task, set the Brewers down in order in the next four innings as the Sox jumped into a 2–1 lead.

In the sixth inning, however, Tom walked Cecil Cooper, and then Ben Oglivie singled, sending Cooper to third. LaRussa brought in Barajas to relieve Seaver. The next Milwaukee hitter, Randy Ready, slugged a home run to give the Brewers three runs, and before the third out was made, the Brewers had scored six times and it was all over. A 7–3 win for Milwaukee.

Taking the loss, Seaver said, "I'm feeling a bit better because I pitched better. Milwaukee got just three runs off me. It was a much better performance than my first game. Still, it's no fun to lose. I hope next time out will be better."

After two straight defeats, Tom was determined to win his next start, and on May 4, in a game against the Boston Red Sox, he had his chance.

It was a cold, rainy day at Fenway Park. The rain came down in torrents and for an hour and forty-seven minutes, the ground crew kept the field covered. Finally, just as the chief umpire was about to cancel the game, the rain stopped, the sun came out, and the game began.

And according to the more than 30,000 fans who waited out the storm, it was worth every bit of the effort to watch Tom Seaver pitch.

He started the game by striking out Jerry Remy on three fastballs that literally whizzed past the startled second baseman. Wade Boggs walked, and slugger Jim Rice came up to hit.

Tom started Rice off with a fastball that just darted up and over Jim's frantic swing: strike one. Then another fastball, which Rice fouled for strike two. Working quickly now in the cold weather, Seaver kicked the left leg high into the air and the ball just floated across the plate to Rice, who took a mighty swing for strike three.

Going into the fifth inning, Tom had given up just three hits and two runs to the hard-hitting Bosox, while the White Sox had pecked away for three runs and a 3–2 lead.

Suddenly Seaver was tired. The fastball he had used inside and tight began to miss the mark by a fraction, and two walks filled the bases for the Red Sox.

Mike Easler, a dangerous line-drive hitter, was up. Seaver fooled him with two half-speed pitches, and when Easler set himself for another of the same, Tom quickly dispatched him with a sizzling fastball.

Now Tony Armas, one of baseball's most dangerous sluggers, was up to hit.

"Tony hit a home run off me in the fourth inning," said Tom later, "and with a man on base, and I was trying to get out of the inning with maybe just one run being scored. But I just missed with two pitches and I was behind Armas with a 2-0 count, and Tony knew I had to make a couple of good pitches."

Pitching carefully now, Seaver fooled Armas with a fastball that seemed to be just off the mark, but as it came across the plate, the ball suddenly darted up and Armas missed the pitch.

Once more Tom fired another fastball, and once again Armas missed. The count was 2-2. Now Seaver began his stretch, brought his arm up and over, a big kick with his left foot, and released the ball. It was a tantalizing half-speed pitch that seemed to float to the plate. Armas, completely fooled by the pitch, swung and missed, and Seaver was out of the inning.

Tom breezed through the sixth and seventh innings, working the corners on each batter and forcing them to swing at bad pitches. He got through the eighth inning and just as he reached the mound to start the final inning, manager Tony LaRussa called time, walked out to the mound, talked with Tom, took the ball out of his hand, and called in reliever Al Jones.

As Seaver trudged off the mound, the crowd rose and cheered the tired pitcher. He had thrown a fantastic game, allowing the tough Red Sox sluggers only six hits and two runs. He left the field with the White Sox in the lead, 5-3, and quite certain of his first win in a White Sox uniform.

"What a thrill it was to save a game for Tom," said Al Jones. "I sure as hell didn't want to mess up this game, so I got the side out without any trouble. I brought the game ball in and gave it to Tom for his trophy case. It was his first American League win."

On May 9, Harold Baines ended the first eight-hour game in major league history by hitting a home run with one out in the bottom of the *twenty-fifth inning* to lift the White Sox to a 7–6 victory over the Milwaukee Brewers. The winning pitcher of this historic game was Tom Seaver, who was making his first relief appearance since 1976, and only the seventh of his 18-year career. Tom pitched the 26th inning and was the eighth White Sox pitcher used by manager LaRussa in the lengthy game. LaMarr Hoyt was the only Sox player on the 25-man roster who did not make an appearance. Seaver allowed only one hit, a single by Jim Gantner, but then Tom finished the game strongly by fanning the next three Brewers to end the historic tussle that lasted two days. The victory took eight hours, six minutes, and two nights. Baines's 420-foot home run came May 9 after the May 8 game had been suspended after 17 innings because of an AL rule that doesn't allow an inning to start after 12:59 A.M. The game was continued the next day in the 18th inning.

The long game made a double winner of Tom Seaver, who waited 20 minutes before starting the regularly scheduled game. Tom pitched eight and a half innings and, in his finest effort of the season, allowed Milwaukee but three base hits. He struck out three and walked two hitters as the White Sox scored twice in the seventh inning to win the game 5–4. The victory marked the first time a White Sox pitcher had won two games in a single day since

Wilbur Wood in 1973, and it marked Seaver's 275th major league triumph.

May 14 saw Tom Seaver at his finest as he pitched the White Sox to a marvelous 2–0 victory over the strong first-place Kansas City Royals, in a game at Comiskey Park that was witnessed by a crowd of more than 20,000 rabid Sox fans.

The win was Seaver's fourth in a row in a White Sox uniform, his 277th career victory, and one of his finest efforts in years. Pitching with almost effortless rhythm, Tom allowed the hard-hitting Royals only five hits as he posted his 57th career shutout.

On May 19, Tom actually outpitched five Toronto hurlers in a game played at Toronto, but the Blue Jays managed to score one run to defeat Seaver and the White Sox in a 1–0 duel. Seaver allowed only six hits, struck out five, but the White Sox hitting during the past several days had dropped sharply and they were held to three base hits, all singles off of the combined pitching of Jim Gott, Roy Lee Jackson, Bryan Clark, and Dennis Lamp, who finished the game for the Jays.

Sporting a 5–4 record at this stage of the pennant race, Seaver said, "There isn't much difference in the batters between the National and American leagues. The only difference I see," said Tom with a wry smile, "is guys in this league hit longer home runs. I've given up some beauties that haven't come down yet."

Catcher Carlton Fisk liked the way Seaver had performed. "Before a game, we'll talk things over," said Pudge, "about how he is going to pitch to hitters, and Tom will say, 'If I get into this kind of a situation, I won't let this guy beat me.' He'll bypass him if he has confidence in getting the next guy out.

I'm not surprised to see him walk the bases full to get that batter he knows he can get out."

Fisk also admired the way Seaver sets up his fastball. "He lulls batters to sleep. They forget that he can still rear back and throw that ball about 92 mph and when it isn't expected, he just zips it by them."

On June 5, Seaver went the entire nine innings against the California Angels and, in allowing the Reggie Jackson–led Angels only four singles, Tom brought the White Sox to within a game and a half of the division-leading Angels. The win by a 4–0 score was Tom's 278th career win and his 58th shutout. Seaver hurled one of his finest games in enabling the struggling White Sox to put together a five-game winning streak.

The White Sox gained a measure of revenge by beating the league-leading Tigers on July 3 by a 9–5 score. Seaver, with a 6–6 record, achieved the win over pitcher Jack Morris, ace of the Tigers pitching staff, who had beaten the White Sox at the beginning of the season in a no-hit no-run contest.

Tom Seaver, with eight victories, was now the leading White Sox hurler, and on July 14 in a spine-tingling victory over the first-place Orioles, Seaver struck out the Orioles' leading slugger, Eddie Murray, on three different occasions in a thrilling 3–2 win.

Then, in a valiant effort to personally halt the slide of the White Sox—they had slumped to sixth place in the Western Division, some four games behind the leading Minnesota Twins—Seaver won three more games in rapid succession, defeating the Cleveland Indians by a 3–0 score on July 30, then drubbing the Red Sox via another shutout, 7–0, and trouncing Milwaukee by a 7–3 score on August 4.

But as July faded into the August sun, the chances of the White Sox repeating as division champions faded with every game as the once unbeatable pitching staff of the White Sox continued to flounder. LaMarr Hoyt, with a 24–10 record in 1983, sported a 10–14 record. Richard Dotson, 22–7 in '83, was 13–10. Both pitchers had been knocked about in recent games and could not seem to come up with the answers for their poor showing. Anemic batting averages didn't help either: Carlton Fisk was hitting at a .239 pace, Kittle was hitting .216, Mike Squires at .193, Scott Fletcher at .257, Cruz at .215, Rudy Law hitting for a .251 average, and Vance Law down to .247. The Sox could not seem to bring their play together.

Manager Tony LaRussa, in a vain attempt to arouse the lethargic Sox, held a series of clubhouse meetings to discuss the players' attitudes, and Tom Seaver was asked to talk to the players. Tom pointed out that they were playing "like contented fat calves" and now had to start playing like they had in 1983.

"We've lost more games by not hitting," said LaRussa, "but the fact remains that our pitching has been spotty and quite inconsistent, especially the bullpen. We've lost any number of close games."

As the season neared its end, LaRussa said, "It may be possible that we thought we could pull away from the rest of the teams like we did last year when we won 99 games, but our hitters just didn't come through for us, and our pitching staff was hot and cold and mostly cold. You have to have good balance to win and this year we just haven't had that successful combination."

Tom Seaver, at age 39, had his finest full season since 1977 as he finished the year at 15–11 to lead all

White Sox pitchers. His record was remarkable, considering the fact that there were six games that he left with the White Sox leading, only to have the relief pitcher lose the game.

The White Sox, who finished 74–88, tumbled into a tie for fifth place in the Western Division, 10 games behind the Kansas City Royals who won the Western title.

White Sox fans can only wonder how much worse the Chicago White Sox' record would have been if Tom Seaver hadn't been with the ball club.

Seaver's 15 wins left him just 12 games short of 300. He had 10 complete games and pitched over 236 innings, the most for him since 1978. He struck out 131 batters and became the fifth pitcher in baseball to record more than 3,400 strikeouts.

"I said in spring training that if I won 15 games, I would be very happy," said Tom. "At this stage of my career, 15 wins and 225–230 innings should make me very happy.

"I threw somewhat the way I did in 1981 [when he was 14–2 for the Reds] and not really all that different from last year. There were just four or five starts I wasn't happy with.

"I'm going to keep going next year," said Seaver. "There is no doubt about that. There isn't much difference between 39 and 49 except they start with different numbers. So when I get to 300 wins, I'll decide just how much longer I want to go on. I have been told my mechanics are so fluid that my arm would be fine at 45," said Seaver.

27
GOING FOR THE RECORD

The White Sox had rested on their laurels in 1984 after romping to a division title by an unprecedented 20 games over their second-place rivals, the Kansas City Royals. That very inactivity, the sudden decline of the incredible five-man pitching staff, the half-season loss of the injured Carlton Fisk, and the inability of the team to sustain any regular momentum and drive led to a fifth-place finish in 1984. There were some minority stockholders calling for the head of the general manager Roland Hemond.

But to Hemond's credit, he never lost his calm. Undaunted, regardless of the consequences, he stalked into the annual baseball winter meetings in Houston on December 6, and the very next day traded LaMarr Hoyt, the White Sox 1983 Cy Young award winning pitcher, to the San Diego Padres in an eight-player deal.

The bombardment of rage against Hemond reverberated throughout baseball and drew sharp criticism from baseball men, as well as howls of anguish from vociferous White Sox fans at home, who were ready to tar and feather the general manager.

"We expected the initial reaction would be unpopular," said chairman Jerry Reinsdorf, "but in the final analysis what is important is winning."

"It might be unpopular," said Eddie Einhorn, "but only because our fans don't know how good the other players we got in return are."

"It never crossed our minds that we would trade Hoyt," said Hemond, "but Jack McKeon [general manager of the Padres] gave us Tim Lollar, a pitcher who won regularly; in 1982 he won 16 games and 11 in 1984. Then they gave us Ozzie Guillen, a classy shortstop who could be one of the great ones and could play for us for ten years. Then we got Salazar, a player with speed and a great arm and a solid line-drive hitter. And on top of that, San Diego threw in Bill Long, one of the most promising young minor-league pitchers; he won 14 games for Beaumont last year. That makes four quality players for one outstanding pitcher."

The following day Hemond sent Vance Law to Montreal in exchange for the right-hander Bob James, who appeared in 62 games for the Expos in 1983 and was considered their best short relief man. It was to prove one of the most vital deals of the year.

"Now," said manager Tony LaRussa, "we can once again win the division championship, IF:

"If Ozzie Guillen is ready to take over and be our regular shortstop.

"If rookie Daryl Boston can hit major league pitching.

"If Carlton Fisk can stay healthy all year.

"If Bob James can become the anchor in our bullpen.

"If Harold Baines and Greg Walker continue to improve.

"If Ron Kittle can hit about .270, instead of the .215 he hit in 1984.

"There are about 25 other teams who are saying the same thing," said LaRussa. "Even the Tigers are full of Ifs."

When the pitchers reported to Sarasota on February 19, a week or so before the rest of the players, it was readily apparent that Tom Seaver, who always was in excellent condition, was already in condition for the biggest year of his career, the year he would win his 300th game.

Six weeks later, after the White Sox had played some 25 Grapefruit League games, LaRussa announced that Tom Seaver would be his pitcher for the opening game of the season. His decision, said Tony, was based solely on merit, both for Tom's showing last season, and because of the way Seaver pitched in spring training. He was the team's winningest pitcher with a 4–1 record and a 1.57 ERA in his five spring starts.

As the White Sox prepared to open the 1985 season with high hopes of repeating their triumph of 1983, they were set to do so in record fashion.

Tom Seaver would be making his 15th opening day start, surpassing the immortal Walter Johnson.

But Tom wanted to look at the feat, for now, as just another day's work. "It's just great if you win that first day, lousy if you lose."

Tom already held the National League record for the most victories on opening day (six), but this would be his first opening day start with the White Sox and his first opening day start in the American League. But in typical Seaver fashion, he tried to downplay its importance.

At age 40, Tom Seaver was within reach of a number of personal milestones this season of 1985, most important, of course, being 300 victories. He had 288. He also needed 105 strikeouts to overtake Walter Johnson for fourth place on the all-time strikeout list.

"You reach a point in your career that you can't go back and reflect on the historical importance of such things because you lose perspective of what your everyday job is," said Tom. "After you've been playing a few years you can look back. But who knows.

"Maybe I'll have another opening day. I'm not finished yet."

The 1985 White Sox opened the season in Milwaukee on April 9 and a jam-packed crowd of 53,127 fans poured into County Stadium on a bright, clear, rather chilly day to see their favorite Brewers against Tom Seaver and the White Sox.

But the Brewer fans were unhappy with what they witnessed, for in the very first inning the White Sox, pumped up for the first game of the season, jumped on an old nemesis, pitcher Mule Haas, from the opening shout of "Play ball!"

Young White Sox shortstop Ozzie Guillen slapped Haas's first pitch to third baseman Paul Molitor, and Molitor's great throw nipped Ozzie by a flash at first base.

Rudy Law dropped a long fly along the first-base

line that went for a single. Harold Baines walked and big Greg Walker laced a single to center field to drive home Law with the first White Sox run of the season. Ron Kittle smashed a grounder to Cooper at first base, and Cooper threw to second, forcing Walter. But Baines scored on the play to give the White Sox another run. Daryl Boston popped out to end the inning. But the White Sox were off and running with two quick runs.

With a two-run lead, Seaver quickly got Paul Molitor, the Brewers first batter, to pop to Walker at first base for the first out. Robin Yount, startled by the speed of Seaver's pitches, just stood by and watched Tom zap three fastballs for three strikes and two outs. Cooper then slashed at a Seaver pitch and looped it into the hands of Harold Baines in center field for the third out.

In the second and third innings, Seaver set the Brewers down one, two, three, in order.

The White Sox added another run in the fourth inning, when Boston doubled, went to third on catcher Marc Hill's sacrifice fly, then raced home on a Julio Cruz sacrifice fly to left field.

Meanwhile, Seaver was pitching in mid-season form, setting the Brewers down in order in the fourth, fifth, and sixth innings, and allowing the hard-hitting Milwaukee team only three base hits.

In the seventh inning, Tom struck out the dangerous Cecil Cooper and forced Ben Oglivie to pop up for the second out. But DH Ted Simmons singled. Doug Loman, the center fielder, followed with a line-drive two-base hit, and the Brewers had their first run of the game.

But it was plainly discernible now that Seaver was tiring, laboring with every pitch, and manager

LaRussa and pitching coach Dave Duncan, plainly worried, were carefully watching Tom's reaction to each pitch.

Brewer catcher Bill Schroeder was the next batter, and after working the count to 3–2, Tom unleashed a wild pitch that allowed Loman to score. Now it was a 3–2 game.

LaRussa walked out to the mound, talked briefly to Seaver, took the ball from him, and signaled for relief pitcher Bob James.

Tom trudged off the mound, doffed his cap as the Milwaukee fans cheered him to the dugout. He had pitched magnificently, allowing the Brewers only five hits, striking out four batters, leaving the game with a 3–2 lead.

The White Sox scored another run in the eighth inning, and James held the Brewers in check for the save.

In the clubhouse after the game a happy Seaver said, "The big thing about being the starting pitcher in the opening game is to get the club off on the right foot. That's the way I've always felt, to keep the game close so our club can possibly win the game," said Tom, who recorded his 289th win in his 19th season.

But Seaver didn't overlook the record he shared with the legendary Walter Johnson.

"I'm very proud of it. It's terrific when you talk about doing something that no other pitcher in the history of the game has done. If we had been here now as a losing club, I wouldn't feel that way."

In his next assignment, against the Boston Red Sox on April 15, Tom held the slugging Bosox scoreless for four innings. In the fifth inning, Jim Rice hit a home run. They scored again in the sixth inning, but the White Sox had picked up three runs and had a 3–2 edge.

Tom tired suddenly in the seventh as the Red Sox tied the game at 3–3, and he was relieved by Bob James, who went on to pitch through the eleventh inning before the White Sox won by a 6–5 margin. But Seaver was not credited with the win.

The rampaging New York Yankees, fresh from five straight wins, stormed into Chicago on April 26, intent on clubbing Seaver in the opening game of a four-game series. And they started with a vengeance.

Seaver walked the speedy Rickey Henderson. Willie Randolph singled Henderson to third and Don Mattingly drove Rickey home with the first Yankee run off Seaver.

It looked like another Yankee avalanche.

Seaver tugged at his pants, set his jaw, and turned to face "Mr. Yankee," Dave Winfield, who had been a terror thus far in the five Yankee wins.

Seaver came in with his first pitch, a teasing floater that the overeager Winfield missed for strike one. Another half-speed pitch and another strike. Then Tom came in with a waist-high fastball that tore in at Winfield at about 92 mph, and just as Dave crashed his bat at the ball, the pitch darted down and away and Winfield missed it completely for strike three.

Don Baylor was next, and he popped up for out number two. As Baylor hit the ball, Willie Randolph started for third, could not get back to second, and was tagged out for the double play that ended the Yankee inning.

There was no further scoring in the contest as Seaver and Yankee pitcher Ed Whitson dueled each other through the second, third, fourth, and fifth innings.

Seaver was magnificent, holding the Yankees to four hits in six innings. In the seventh inning, Tom struck out Don Baylor and Ken Griffey on six of the fastest pitches he had thrown in the young season, and as he forced catcher Ron Hassey to fly out to end the seventh inning, LaRussa told Tom that Bob James would relieve him for the balance of the game. And a weary Seaver grinned, "I am tired."

James allowed the Yanks to score in the ninth, but the White Sox, behind Harold Baines's three-run homer, took the game 4–2 and Seaver had his 290th career victory.

In his next effort, Seaver once again faced the Red Sox. This time, however, it was a different tune. The Bosox jumped on Tom's best offerings for three runs in the very first inning, including a Tony Armas home run that cleared the fence in Comiskey Park.

But the White Sox came right back in the third inning with a couple of singles and a tremendous home run by Carlton Fisk that tied the score at 3–3. In the fifth inning, however, it was evident that Seaver was not up to par, for he was again hit hard as the Bosox came up with two additional runs on four solid base hits. With the score 6–3 in favor of the Red Sox, manager LaRussa relieved Tom, brought in Bob James, then Juan Agosto, and finally Gene Nelson in a vain effort to halt the rampaging Bosox. But the Red Sox pounded each relief hurler for solid base hits and six more runs for a 12–8 victory.

During the next several weeks, as the White Sox battled the California Angels and the Kansas City Royals for the lead in the Western Division—

sparked by the marvelous pitching of Tom Seaver and Britt Burns, the comeback play of Carlton Fisk, the defensive play of Harold Baines in center field, the hitting and stellar play at first base by Greg Walker, and the play of Ozzie Guillen at shortstop—the White Sox played the finest ball of the season and put together a winning streak of five straight games. They lost to Texas 7–3, then went on to win three more in a row.

During that period, Seaver outpitched three Oriole pitchers in a 5–2 victory. Then a week later, on May 30, Tom once again was the winning hurler in a 4–3 victory over the Kansas City Royals. The win was Tom's 293rd career victory.

Carlton Fisk, the team's sparkplug, regained the form that made him one of the game's greatest stars; Pudge went on an offensive tear and proceeded to terrorize every pitcher he faced. In one stretch of games near the end of May, Fisk drove out nine hits in 18 at-bats, including five home runs. Through the first 45 games, Fisk slammed out 13 home runs and drove in 36 runs.

Seaver's pitching combined with Fisk's incredible turnaround evidently inspired others on the club. Ozzie Guillen, the agile shortstop, began to display the kind of acrobatics that White Sox fans had not seen since the incredible All-Star play of Luis Aparicio back in the late 1950s and 1960s.

Harold Baines in center field played like an antelope as he ran down drives labeled "base hit." And he began to hit the ball with power and with men on base. Greg Walker's ability at first base and at the plate was a revelation as the team caught fire and went on to win five straight games. On June 17, the White Sox were perched on top of the Western

Division, a game and a half ahead of the California Angels, two and a half in front of the Kansas City Royals.

And White Sox fans began to hope and pray for another 1983.

It was during this stretch that Tom Seaver proved almost invincible as he won three straight games, starting with a 5–2 defeat of the slugging Orioles. Tom held the tough Oriole batters without a hit for four innings, struck out five batters, and allowed a total of five hits for his 294th career victory. On May 30, at Comiskey Park, Seaver scattered eight hits and struck out five batters as he led the White Sox to a 4–3 win over the Kansas City Royals.

A week later Seaver allowed the Angels two base hits over the seven innings he pitched, as the White Sox pounded four Angel hurlers for 11 hits and a 4–2 victory. In this game, Seaver struck out Reggie Jackson twice with men in scoring position. It was Tom's 295th career win.

The week of July 15, the 75th anniversary of Comiskey Park, was supposed to be a marvelous week of celebration, starting with band music, fireworks, and prizes, but it was spoiled by the present and the future.

The White Sox stars of 1959, American League pennant winners, were on hand for the festivities— Earl Torgeson, the all-time great Luis Aparicio, Sherm Lollar, Early Wynn, Bob Shaw, Billy Pierce, Dick Donovan. But the festivities were dampened as the White Sox lost game after game, a total of eight straight at home, to slowly fade from first place in the division; down, down, down to third place, seven full games behind Kansas City—and there they remained.

The losing streak all but ruined the gala.

"We're not dead yet," said Jerry Reinsdorf, "we're just not hitting the ball. But I do think we may come up with some trades and I want to say that the only player on this team who is untouchable is Tom Seaver."

"We're so bad," said LaRussa, "that Seaver lost his bid for his 296th win three times because our offense produced one, three, and three runs when Tom was pitching."

On July 5, Tom Seaver outpitched four Cleveland hurlers to gain his 296th career win as the White Sox slugged out an 8–3 win over the Indians. Greg Walker and Tim Hulett drilled home runs to power the offense.

On the 14th at Baltimore, Tom pitched one of his better games of the year as he struck out 11 Oriole batters, including the powerful Eddie Murray, on three separate occasions, each with a man on base, to beat the Orioles by a 5–3 score.

Five days later at Comiskey Park, Tom displayed his finest form of the year as he shut out the Indians to win a squeaker 1–0 victory. Tom allowed only four base hits for his 61st shutout victory and his 298th career win. Once again Fisk showed the way with a home run for the only run of the game.

In victory number 299 against the Red Sox on July 30, Tom had been guilty of sloppy pitching, giving away a 4–0 lead before the White Sox rallied in the tenth inning on a driving home run by Pudge Fisk to gift-wrap a 7–5 victory. Seaver had been lucky and he knew it.

But five days later on August 4, when the fly ball plopped into the glove of his left-fielder Reid Nichols for win 300, there was no luck involved. It was

335

sheer pitching genius, and Tom Seaver doubled over in relief. Then he did a little dance for joy. Teammates were surging forward and 54,000 people at Yankee Stadium were cheering him, but for just a fleeting moment he was alone on the mound, not quite knowing what to do. He was back in New York where it all started but the scene was strange—his uniform said SOX across the chest, and he had just beaten the Yankees on a six-hitter to win his 300th major league game.

It was another masterpiece of pitching in the Seaver gallery, and the artist had only a brief instant to savor his work before his teammates smothered him with affection as they rushed him off the mound to the locker room.

Eighteen years before this game, Tom Seaver beat the Chicago Cubs, 6-1, for his first major league victory. Now he had number 300. And for those who believe in omens, the final score, 4-1, matched his uniform number, 41.

And where is Tom Seaver going?

That question is easy to answer.

As of the end of the 1985 season, Tom Seaver led all active pitchers in the major leagues with a 2.80 ERA. He was second among active pitchers in victories with 304 career wins.

How many more victories would Tom have scored playing for the top teams in the majors?

He ranks first among active pitchers in the number of shutouts, with a total of 61, and eighth on the all-time list.

He was third among all active pitchers and sixth all-time with 3,537 strikeouts.

He was third in career winning percentage of active pitchers with a mark of .614.

The records roll on and on and on.

There will be new ones in 1986 for Tom Seaver. For the Chicago White Sox. There will be changes: new faces, a new spirit under a new general manager, Ken Harrelson, and perhaps another championship in 1986.

And where is Tom Seaver going? Well, for sure, no matter this season or the next with the White Sox, Tom Terrific is headed for a niche in the justly honored and celebrated Baseball Hall of Fame.

And no one—past, present—has better earned that singular recognition and honor than George Thomas Seaver, number 41 of the Chicago White Sox.

28
APPENDIX: CAREER HIGHLIGHTS AND STATISTICS

CAREER HIGHLIGHTS

1956
- Pitched a no-hit–no-run game, Little League ball.

1958-62
- Fresno High School baseball and basketball

1962
- Awarded All-City honors, both sports.
- U.S. Marine Corps Reserve

1963
- Fresno Junior College baseball record, 11–2
- Voted Most Valuable Player.
- Won last eight games of season in succession.
- Pitched Fresno to conference title.

1964-65
- University Southern California (scholarship)
- College All-Stars, Alaska League
- Named to Alaska All-Star team both years.
- Drafted by L.A. Dodgers, but when Tom Lasorda

offered him only $2,000 bonus, turned it down and remained in school.

1966

- Drafted by the Atlanta Braves and signed a contract for a $51,500 bonus.
- Atlanta contract void because the signing violated college rule.
- Seaver appealed to Baseball Commissioner Eckert and the commissioner drafted a new plan stating that "Any team in the league who wished to match the original Atlanta bonus offer could attempt to draft Seaver."
- Three clubs matched the offer: the Cleveland Indians, the Philadelphia Phillies, and the New York Mets.
- The Mets won lottery and drafted Seaver.
- Seaver assigned to the Mets' farm team, Jacksonville.
- Pitched first game in professional baseball, defeating Rochester Red Wings, 4–2.
- Defeated Buffalo Bisons, 2–0 in a two-hitter.
- Finished year with a 12–12 record.
- Led International League in strikeouts with 188.
- Led International League in starts with 32.

1967

- Compiled a 16–13 record and a 2.76 ERA for Mets.
- Won Rookie of the Year award.

1969

- Won first of three Cy Young awards.
- Had record of 25–7.
- Mets win the pennant, defeat Baltimore Orioles in World Series.
- First pennant, first World Series for the Mets.

1970
- Won National League strikeout and ERA titles with 283 strikeouts, 2.81 ERA.
- Tied major-league record striking out 19 San Diego batters at Shea Stadium; struck out 10 straight batters in same game to set new mark.

1971
- Won National League strikeout and ERA titles with 289 strikeouts, 1.76 ERA.
- Had record of 20–10.

1972
- Had record of 21–12.

1973
- Won National League strikeout and ERA titles with 251 strikeouts, 2.08 ERA.
- Established major-league all-time record by striking out 200 or more batters in nine straight seasons.
- Won second Cy Young award, record of 19–10.
- Mets win second pennant, but lose to Oakland in the World Series, 4 games to 3.

1975
- Won third Cy Young award, record of 22–9, 2.38 ERA.

1977
- Had record of 21–6 to win 20 or more games in a season five times.
- Traded to Cincinnati Reds.

1978
- Pitched a no-hit–no-run game for Cincinnati against St. Louis.

1981
- Named UPI Comeback Player of the Year with a 14–2 record and a 2.55 ERA.

- Winning percentage of .875 was best in National League since 1959.
- Became the fifth pitcher in history to reach the 3,000 strikeout mark after striking out Keith Hernandez.
- Named National League Player of the Month for September when he posted a 5–0 record and a 2.72 ERA.

1982

- Traded to the Mets for pitcher Charlie Puleo, catcher Lloyd McClendon, and outfielder Jason Felice.

1984

- Selected by the Chicago White Sox as player not protected by the New York Mets.

1985

- Won 300th game, defeating New York Yankees in Yankee Stadium by a 4–1 score.
- Joins most select group of baseball immortals who have won 300 or more games including:

Cy Young—511	Eddie Plank—327
Walter Johnson—416	Gaylord Perry—314
Christy Mathewson—373	Steve Carlton—314
Grover Alexander—373	Mickey Welch—311
Warren Spahn—363	Hoss Radburn—310
Pud Galvin—361	**TOM SEAVER**—304
Kid Nichols—360	Lefty Grove—300
Tim Keefe—344	Early Wynn—300
John Clarkson—327	Phil Niekro—300

TOM SEAVER'S PITCHING STATISTICS

YEAR	CLUB	W	L	ERA	G	GS	CG	SHO	SV	IP	H	R	ER	BB	SO
1966	JACKSONVILLE	12	12	3.13	34	32	10	4	0	210	184	87	73	66	188
1967	METS	16	13	2.76	35	34	18	2	0	251	224	85	77	78	170
1968	METS	16	12	2.20	36	35	14	5	0	278	224	73	68	48	205
1969	METS	25	7	2.21	36	35	18	5	0	273	202	75	67	82	208
1970	METS	18	12	2.81	37	36	19	2	0	291	230	103	91	83	283
1971	METS	20	10	1.76	36	35	21	4	0	286	210	61	56	61	289
1972	METS	21	12	2.92	35	35	13	3	0	262	215	92	85	77	249
1973	METS	19	10	2.08	36	36	18	3	0	290	219	74	67	64	251
1974	METS	11	11	3.20	32	32	12	5	0	236	199	89	84	75	201
1975	METS	22	9	2.38	36	36	15	5	0	280	217	81	74	88	243
1976	METS	14	11	2.59	35	34	13	5	0	271	211	83	78	77	235
1977	METS-CINN	21	6	2.58	33	33	19	7	0	261	199	78	75	66	196
1978	CINCINNATI	16	14	2.87	36	36	8	1	0	260	218	97	83	89	226
1979	CINCINNATI	16	6	3.14	32	32	9	5	0	215	187	85	75	61	131
1980	CINCINNATI	10	8	3.64	26	26	5	1	0	168	140	74	68	59	101
1981	CINCINNATI	14	2	2.55	23	23	6	1	0	166	120	51	47	66	87
1982	CINCINNATI	5	13	5.50	21	21	0	0	0	111	136	75	68	44	62
1983	METS	9	14	3.55	34	34	5	2	0	231	201	104	91	86	135
1984	WHITE SOX	15	11	3.95	34	33	10	4	0	237	216	108	104	61	131
1985	WHITE SOX	16	11	3.17	35	30	6	1	0	238	223	105	101	69	134

TOM SEAVER PITCHING RECORD

CHAMPIONSHIP SERIES

YEAR	CLUB	W-L	ERA	G	GS	CG	IP	H	R	RB	SO
1969	METS	1-0	6.43	1	1	0	7	8	5	3	2
1973	METS	1-1	1.62	2	2	1	17	13	4	5	17
1979	CINCINNATI	0-0	2.25	1	1	0	8	5	2	2	5
	TOTALS	2-1	2.81	4	4	1	32	26	11	10	24

WORLD SERIES

YEAR	CLUB	W-L	ERA	G	GS	CG	IP	H	R	RB	SO
1969	METS	1-1	3.00	2	2	1	15	12	5	3	9
1973	METS	0-1	2.40	2	2	0	15	13	4	3	18
	TOTALS	1-2	2.70	4	4	1	30	25	9	6	27